Date Due

MARGI CLARKE'S
Better Than Sex™ *Cookbook*

Better Than

ALSO BY PETER COX:

Linda McCartney's Home Cooking (with Linda McCartney)

LifePoints™ (with Peggy Brusseau)

MARGI CLARKE'S

Sex Cookbook™

Margi Clarke and Peter Cox

Hodder & Stoughton

First published in Great Britain in 1996 by Hodder and Stoughton.
A division of Hodder Headline PLC.

10 9 8 7 6 5 4 3 2 1

ISBN 0 340 65380 9

PROPRIETARY NAMES
This book may include words, brand names and other descriptions of
products which are or are asserted to be proprietary names or trademarks.
No judgement concerning the legal status of such words is made or implied
thereby. Their inclusion does not imply that they have acquired for legal
purposes a non-proprietary or general significance nor any other
judgement concerning their legal status.

Book design by Peter Ward
Styling by Gerrit Buntrock
Home economy by Nicole Szabazon
Margi Clarke's make-up by Julie Fellows
Grateful acknowledgement is made to Phase Eight of Richmond, London
Recipe development by Peggy Brusseau, Margi Clarke, Peter Cox,
Ursula Ferrigno, Janet Hunt and Colin Spencer.

Printed and bound in Great Britain by
Butler & Tanner Ltd, Frome and London

HODDER AND STOUGHTON
A Division of Hodder Headline plc
338 Euston Road
London NW1 3BH

CONTENTS

In loving memory of my mother, Frances Clarke.

For the food inspiration down on Hooley's Farm.
Thanks to Frank Clarke, first family veggie; Jamie Reid;
Theresa Hickey; Rowena Webb and all the great team at Hodder;
Linda McCartney; the Cox family for making all this possible and
to all vegetarians past, present and to come.

Love Margi

INTRODUCTION:
Why Food Is Better Than Sex

You know, orgies aren't what they used to be. In the third century BC, the Greek writer Athenaeus tells us about a modest little wedding celebration – no more than twenty people – which went something like this. First of all came the *hors d'oeuvres*, consisting of chickens, ducks, ring-doves, geese, hares, young goats, 'curiously moulded cakes', pigeons, turtle-doves, partridges and 'other fowl a plenty'. 'When we had taken leave of all sobriety,' remarked one sozzled guest, 'there entered flute-girls and singers. To me these girls looked quite naked, but some said they had on tunics.' These entertainers were followed by a large pig, which 'entered on a silver platter gilded all over to no little thickness . . . roasted inside it were thrushes, ducks, and warblers in unlimited quantities, pease purée poured over eggs, oysters and scallops . . .'

Then it was time for the entertainment. 'Dancers, clowns, and some naked female jugglers who performed tumbling acts among swords, and blew fire from their mouth.' After a break for some serious drinking (three kinds of wine, served in very large gold cups, which the guests took home – along with anything or anyone else they fancied), it was time for the fish course and, just for a change, some dancing girls, this time dressed as nymphs. 'The wonderful thing about it was,' recalled one guest, 'although we were relaxed and heavy with wine, as soon as we saw any of these new things introduced we all became sober enough to stand on our feet.'[1]

Unless you're royalty, you don't get invited to many weddings like that nowadays. Actually, I'm not sure I'd want to be – there wasn't so much as a stuffed vine leaf for a vegetarian like me, was there? And yet today, the pendulum seems to have swung too far the other way. Food is supposed to be low fat, low calorie, low cholesterol, low sodium, low sugar, low additive, low enjoyment. If it's not, we feel guilty about it.

Well, this book gives old Althenaeus a run for his money. And by the way did you know that the world's first cookbook was written by another ancient Greek in the fourth century BC? Archestratus was his name and he called the book *Hedypathia*, which means 'pleasant living' – and it's title was bang on! The pleasure of preparing and sharing good, honest food is far greater than almost anything else you care to mention. Of course, if you ask a hundred modern people what the greatest human pleasure is, they'd probably say 'sex', without thinking much about it. But when you *do* think about it, it doesn't seem such a great deal. After all, for the first sixteen years of our lives it's prohibited, for the last sixteen it's impossible, and for the time in between it's mostly impractical!

The ancient Greeks and Romans – and almost every society except our own – always realised that the pleasures of eating and the pleasures of lovemaking were very close bedfellows. Orgies, in the days when they knew how to do them properly, were as much about consuming as they were about coupling. The Romans even officially

1 *A History of Orgies*, Burgo Partridge, Spring Books 1958

scheduled a regular yearly orgy for everyone – Bacchanalia – which went on for three days and nights, in honour of Bacchus, the god of wine. Makes the befuddled antics of today's lager louts seem a bit pathetic, doesn't it?

I believe – and I bet you do too, otherwise you wouldn't be reading this – that a little of what you fancy does you good. So in this book, we've put together a cracking collection – over two hundred and fifty – of the very, very best recipes you'll ever find – with the emphasis on pleasure, pleasure, pleasure! Whether you're looking for food on the move or a romantic dinner on an impulse, you'll find the answers right here. Some people may be startled that all these recipes are vegetarian – after all, vegetarians aren't supposed to enjoy their food, are they? Rubbish! In fact, I can tell you that I enjoy my food far more now that I'm vegetarian, because it's 100 per cent pleasure and no guilt!

All these recipes are easy to make, most of them are very quick, and none of them use hard-to-find ingredients (check out The Ingredient Finder on page 280 for some instant meal suggestions using food that's already in your larder). They are all, I hope, stylish, romantic and sensual without being snobbish. Actually, nothing irritates me more than food snobs . . . but that's another story. I hope you have as much fun with them as we've had, and I wish you pleasures of all kinds in great abundance!

Margi

XXX

QUIZ:
How Do You Rate as a Sensual Chef?

Preparing and consuming good food is meant to be all about *pleasure!* After all, if eating wasn't first and foremost a sensual experience, then we'd all have been reduced to pill-popping automatons by now. So next time you're preparing food, take a moment to ask yourself 'How can I make this meal more enjoyable?' You'll quickly find that the pleasure of eating even the humblest of snacks can be hugely increased, often in very simple ways. Here's a quiz to get you thinking about the sensual aspects of food. Be honest! Then check your answers with the scores that follow.

1. You're on your own at home and feeling peckish. The larder's low – just a tin of beans, breakfast cereal and a lettuce in the fridge. Do you:
   a) Make the best of it: beans to start with, and cereal if you're still hungry.
   b) Send out for a takeaway.
   c) Go shopping at the late-night supermarket.

2. Your new boyfriend has come round, and you're making a fresh salad (e.g. Salade Niçoise page 101, Tabbouleh page 105, Tzatziki page 107). He wants to watch you in the kitchen, but you're nervous. Do you:
   a) Put him in front of the TV with a can of beer until you've finished.
   b) Just roll your sleeves up and let him watch.
   c) Ask him to do something useful round the house while he's waiting.

3. It's a special anniversary, and you're dining out. Your partner would settle for the local Chinese (he hates dressing up), but you want to put on the style at a more elegant restaurant. Do you:

    a) Settle for a cosy time at the Chinese.
    b) Do something romantic at home.
    c) Insist on the up-market restaurant.

4. You're throwing together a few vegetables for a quick side-salad. So far you have kidney beans and chopped tomato. Do you add:

    a) Baby sweet corn and crisp lettuce leaves.
    b) Tin of sweet corn and chopped onions.
    c) Grated carrots and thinly sliced green pepper.

5. You've just made some late-night sandwiches for a few friends who've popped over. Do you serve them:

    a) On individual plates with a garnish of parsley.
    b) In the kitchen, with the crowd choosing what they want.
    c) All together on one big plate.

6. Name the three most important ingredients for a romantic *dîner-à-deux*:

    a) Wine, candlelight and flowers on the table.
    b) Fine food, elegant setting, pretty tablecloth.
    c) Anything unusual, surprising or enticing.

7. What type of wine would best go with a light pasta meal?

    a) Red.
    b) White.
    c) Champagne.

8. You've spent hours (poor dear) slaving over a hot stove, and he's late for the meal. Typical! As he comes through the door, do you:

    a) Listen to his explanation, but warn him it's the last time.
    b) Playfully tweak his credit card and book a restaurant table.
    c) Tell him his dinner is in the dog as you pass him on your way to your mother's.

9. Which of the following are aphrodisiacs?

    a) Alcohol.
    b) Carrots, bananas, and cucumbers.
    c) Spanish fly.

10. Your boyfriend has invited you over to his place for a meal. Only problem is, he can't cook. As you survey the burnt offering placed in front of you, do you:

    a) Open the bottle of wine you've brought and cheerily wash down the charred remains.

    b) Go into his kitchen and whip up something decent.

    c) Claim you're allergic to charcoal and leave.

Scoring

1.
    a) Sorry, beans (not even toast?) and cereal *isn't* a sensual meal!
                Score 0

    b) The slob's choice. Takeaways rarely look attractive, are usually high in fat and don't solve your fundamental problem – there's no food in the house!
                Score -5

    c) The only sensible option – you obviously need to stock up, with the bonus that a trip to the supermarket will yield a treat of one or two really fresh food ingredients for immediate use.
                Score +5

2.
    a) No! You're training him for a lifetime of male slobbery!   Score -5

    b) Yes, plunge your arms in right up to the elbows . . . The sheer physical pleasure of touching food is missing in our society. Try it and find out what a turn-on it can be – both to do, and to watch!
                Score +5

    c) Yes, men should be useful, but why miss the fun? That leaky drain-pipe can wait!   Score 0

3.
    a) You know it *won't* be cosy, it'll just be dull.   Score 0

    b) Doing the dishes is *not* a good way to celebrate your anniversary!
                Score -5

    c) Don't fight about it – just book the table, book a taxi, and get him into those glad rags (judicious flattery will help)! If the restaurant's stylish, but not snobbish, he can go without a tie – and that's what most men really object to. Remember to kick off with a Champagne Cocktail!   Score +5

4. This question is all about the texture of food.

    a) Even baby sweet corn are unmanageably large for a salad, and the lettuce leaves need to be torn apart if they're to be eaten gracefully.
                Score 0

5.

b) This combination is unimaginative, and the raw onions could well overwhelm the whole thing. **Score 0**

c) An interesting and colourful mixture with a good texture, easy to eat. **Score +5**

5. a) The usual way of presenting sandwiches is also the most uninteresting (just what *do* you do with that parsley?). **Score 0**

b) Well, if you feel that way about it, why not let them make their own sandwiches? **Score -5**

c) This can be very impressive and hearty looking. Slice them into quarters and arrange them horizontally, edge to edge . . . and watch those eyes pop! If you add a garnish, make sure it's edible – spring onions are good, or tomato slices, olives, radishes . . . **Score +5**

6. a) It's worked for millions, but it's a cliché. **Score 0**

b) Sorry, but the quality of the food (even less the *tablecloth*, for heaven's sake!) is the last thing that lovers think about. **Score -5**

c) The essence of romance is instinctive, impulsive, surprising! Even chips can be romantic served with champagne on a dewy midsummer morning . . . Go ahead and break the rules! **Score +5**

7.   The choice of wine is an area where snobbery too often triumphs over good taste. When choosing wine, the golden rule is to enhance, not obliterate, the flavour of the food – and *don't* be intimidated!

a) This is the 'classic' choice for pasta. **Score +5**

b) A dry, even roughish, well-chilled white wine can work brilliantly with many of the lighter pasta dishes (pesto, for example). **Score +5**

c) Dry champagne (*brut*) nicely chilled goes with all kinds of food and can be served throughout any meal. **Score +5**

You can't lose with this one!

8. a) The worst choice – you know it won't be the last time, and *now* what do you eat tonight? **Score -5**

b) If he's the man you hope(d) he is, he'll grin and bear this opportunity to make up to you. And don't play too easy to get . . . **Score +5**

c) Depending on your circumstances, this *could* be the right choice, but it isn't the most romantic! **Score 0**

9. a) Moderate amounts may loosen inhibitions, but too much is a passion-killer. **Score 0**

b) The erotic potential of salaciously shaped fruit and vegetables is enormous – if you have the nerve! **Score +5**

c) Made from crushed beetles, Spanish fly is a vicious irritant which has caused many fatal poisonings. **Score -10**

10. a) If you like the guy, this is the most tactful choice. **Score +5**

b) This is what his mother would do. **Score -5**

c) Well, if you're looking for a way to end the relationship, this would do it. **Score 0**

Your Rating

35 or more

You obviously have little left to learn about sensual cooking, or about men, for that matter! If it's true that the way to a man's heart is through his stomach, then you've probably caused more broken hearts than most of us have had hot dinners . . .

15 – 35 points

You're a budding sensualist and no mistake . . . but you'll have to learn a few more tricks before you qualify as a Mistress of Pleasure! Keep reading!

less than 15 points

Well, at least you can take comfort in the Bible, which says: 'Better is a dinner of herbs where love is, than a stalled ox and hatred therewith.' In other words, it's love, not food, that makes the world go round. Which in your case is just as well . . .

Stack o'Jacks (page 25)

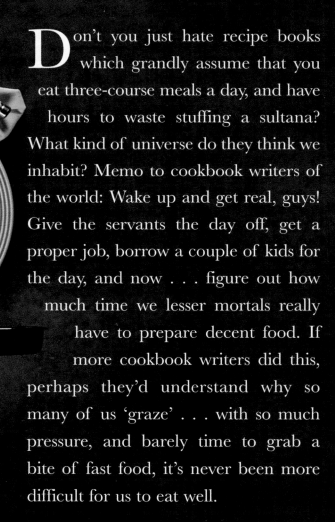

PART ONE
Short-order Cooking

Don't you just hate recipe books which grandly assume that you eat three-course meals a day, and have hours to waste stuffing a sultana? What kind of universe do they think we inhabit? Memo to cookbook writers of the world: Wake up and get real, guys! Give the servants the day off, get a proper job, borrow a couple of kids for the day, and now . . . figure out how much time we lesser mortals really have to prepare decent food. If more cookbook writers did this, perhaps they'd understand why so many of us 'graze' . . . with so much pressure, and barely time to grab a bite of fast food, it's never been more difficult for us to eat well.

Waffles (page 26)

In this section, I wanted to compile a superb selection of fast food – nothing takes longer than 30 minutes to prepare – which satisfies your sensual instincts, as well as your appetite. After all, fast food doesn't have to be crude food! Also, if the truth be told, I wanted to kick off the recipe book with something which would really irritate the food snobs. Care for some toast?

TOAST TEMPTATIONS

French Toast

1 LOAF DAY-OLD BREAD, THICKLY SLICED
570ML (1 PINT) SKIMMED MILK
½ VANILLA POD OR ½ TEASPOON VANILLA
EXTRACT

55G (2OZ) CASTOR SUGAR
2 EGGS
1 TABLESPOON ICING SUGAR, SIFTED

1. Prepare the bread.
2. Heat the milk and vanilla pod to simmering point, then stir in the castor sugar until it is dissolved. Leave to cool to blood heat. Beat the eggs and whisk them into the warm milk.
3. Dip each slice of bread into the milk mixture, holding the slice on the end of a fork, for instance. Let the excess liquid drip from the bread then place immediately on a hot, lightly oiled griddle.
4. Leave to cook for 3-5 minutes, until the toast is brown and crusty, then turn and cook the other side.
5. Serve on to a warmed plate and sprinkle some of the icing sugar over the toast; serve hot. Some people prefer these with jam, still others prefer them sugar-free with simply a dab of melting butter on top.

Serves 4

⏱ 30 mins

Pepper Mushroom Grillers

450G (1LB) LARGE MUSHROOMS

1 TABLESPOON OLIVE OIL

3 CLOVES GARLIC, FINELY CHOPPED

1 TEASPOON FRESHLY GROUND BLACK PEPPER

2 FL OZ (60ML) WATER

1 TABLESPOON WINE VINEGAR

4 MEDIUM TOMATOES, CUT INTO WEDGES
(OPTIONAL)

8 SLICES WHOLEWHEAT BREAD

Serves 4

🕐 30 mins

Funky veggie fillers

1.   Prepare the mushrooms by cleaning or peeling them and removing the stalks.

2.   Heat the oil in a large frying pan over a medium heat and sauté the garlic for 2-3 minutes. Add the pepper and stir for 1 minute.

3.   Place the mushrooms in the pan bottom side down and cover the pan. Reduce the heat and leave to cook for 5-7 minutes. Peek once during this time to make sure the mushrooms are releasing their juices and not sticking. If necessary, add a little of the water. Turn the mushrooms bottom side up and replace the cover, again adding a little water if necessary to prevent sticking. Let the mushrooms cook a further 5 minutes.

4.   Add the vinegar to the mushrooms and arrange the tomato wedges over the mushrooms (these are optional: they are delicious and colourful but you may wish to try this with just the mushrooms). Cover the pan and leave over a very low heat while you prepare the toast.

5.   Trim the bread of its crust and toast under the grill until brown and crisp. Place two slices on each plate and immediately spoon the mushroom mixture and some of the liquor over each piece of toast and serve hot. Try a dash of Tabasco sauce for a real kick!

Scouse Rarebit

2 TABLESPOONS BUTTER
PINCH OF SALT
½ TEASPOON FRESHLY GROUND
BLACK PEPPER

¼ TEASPOON GROUND CINNAMON
140ML (¼ PINT) BEER
100G (4OZ) STRONG CHEESE, GRATED
2 SLICES THICK, BUTTERED TOAST

1. Melt the butter in a saucepan and gently sauté the pepper and cinnamon in it, about 1 minute. Add the beer, stir well and bring close to a simmer. Do not let the mixture boil. Add the grated cheese and stir for 1 minute, until the cheese is just melted.
2. Place one piece of toast on each plate and pour the mixture over the toast. Push under a grill for 1-2 minutes to give a light crust to the cheese sauce.
3. Serve immediately – with more beer, but in a glass this time!

Serves 2

🕐 15 mins

Raisin Bread Toast with Cinnamon Butter

2 TABLESPOONS BUTTER
1 TABLESPOON GRANULATED SUGAR

½ TEASPOON GROUND CINNAMON
4 SLICES RAISIN BREAD

1. Blend the butter, sugar and cinnamon together in a small bowl.
2. Toast the raisin bread and immediately spread the cinnamon butter over it.
3. Serve hot.

Serves 2

🕐 10 mins

Toasty Tips

BEANS ON TOAST Spread a little yeast extract on to the toast before adding the beans. This is delicious and the yeast extract adds a lot of useful B vitamins to your life.

CROÛTONS A fancy French word for bits of toast!
1. Mix some garlic salt and a few dried herbs into a bowlful of butter and spread day-old bread with this mixture.

For a lovely sweet breakfast or tea

2.   Cut the bread into cubes or pretty biscuit shapes and arrange on a baking tray. Bake in a moderate oven, at 180°C/350°F/Gas Mark 4 until golden and crisp.

3.   Serve that day – on soup or stews – or store in an airtight container for a day or two longer.

HOT BREAKFASTS

Sweetly Spiced Breakfast Rice

This is a gorgeously divine way to start the day . . . If you're fed up with picking bits of muesli out of your teeth in the morning, try this!

100G (4OZ) BASMATI RICE
570ML (1 PINT) APPLE JUICE
1 x 7.5CM (3-INCH) CINNAMON STICK

3 WHOLE CLOVES
55G (2OZ) RAISINS OR CURRANTS
1 ORANGE, PEELED AND SEGMENTED

Serves 2-4

⏲ 30 mins

1.   Rinse and drain the rice and place in a saucepan with the apple juice, spices and raisins. Bring to a simmer, cover the pan and reduce the heat. Leave to cook for about 15 minutes, until all the liquid has been absorbed, then remove from the heat and leave covered for a further 5-10 minutes.

2.   Prepare the orange and chop the segments into small chunks; turn these gently into the rice and serve at once in a colourful bowl.

3.   Other fruits may be added, to taste, such as chopped dried apricots, prunes, chopped apple or bits of mango.

Stack o' Jacks

'Jacks' is short for flapjacks, which are thick, American-style pancakes. These are always served in a stack – hence the name of this dish. Try these on a wintry Sunday morning to add a little warmth to your life.

340G (12OZ) PLAIN FLOUR
2 TEASPOONS BAKING POWDER
PINCH OF SALT
2 EGGS, BEATEN

285ML (½ PINT) PLAIN YOGURT, BUTTERMILK
  OR DAY-OLD MILK
1 TABLESPOON OIL

1. Mix the dry ingredients together in a large mixing bowl. Whisk the remaining ingredients together in a separate bowl then add these to the dry ingredients. Stir briefly and leave to stand for 10 minutes.

2. Heat a griddle or frying pan and brush with a tiny bit of oil.

3. When very hot, pour a ladleful of batter on to the griddle and leave for 3-5 minutes. The top of the pancake should bubble and this is an indication that the pancake may be turned: just lift one edge to make sure it is browned underneath. Turn the jack and leave to cook a further 2-3 minutes then lift on to a hot plate.

4. Serve two to four jacks in a stack with butter, jam, syrup, fruit paste or yeast extract between the layers.

Serves 4

⏱ 20 mins

Variations

1. 450g (1lb) fresh, frozen or tinned berries may be added to the batter at the point of combining dry and moist ingredients.

2. 55g (2oz) ground almonds, walnuts or hazelnuts may be added to the dry mix. A further amount may be sprinkled over the top of the stack just before serving.

3. Replace half the flour (180g/6oz) with buckwheat flour for a more earthy flavour and texture.

4. Add 55g (2oz) wheatgerm to the dry mix (do not reduce the flour) for a flakier and more fibre-rich jack.

5. Replace the eggs with an additional 1 tablespoon oil or tahini and an extra 120ml (4 fl oz) yogurt, buttermilk or milk. For a vegan jack, the yogurt or milk may be soya based.

6.   For a sourdough jack, prepare the vegan version and leave your batter covered with a paper towel and a plate overnight in a draught-free place. In the morning, stir well, add an extra 1-3 tablespoons liquid and continue as above.

Waffles

450G (1LB) PLAIN FLOUR

1 TABLESPOON BAKING POWDER

PINCH OF SALT

2 EGGS, SEPARATED

285ML (½ PINT) MILK

2 TABLESPOONS OIL

Serves 4

⏱ 25 mins

1.   Mix the dry ingredients together in a large mixing bowl.
2.   Whisk the egg yolks, milk and oil together in a separate bowl then add these to the dry ingredients.
3.   Stir briefly and leave to stand while you beat the egg whites to a soft peak. Fold these into the batter and drop spoonfuls of the batter on to a hot waffle iron.
4.   Cook until brown and crisp and serve hot with your favourite topping.

Variations

1.   Add 25g (1oz) shredded coconut to the dry mix.
2.   Add 55g (2oz) cooking chocolate powder to the dry mix.
3.   Add 55g (2oz) grated cheese to the batter before folding in the egg whites. Try a strong cheese such as Parmesan or Cheddar.

Glamorgan Sausages

180G (6OZ) DRIED BREADCRUMBS

100G (4OZ) CHEESE (I.E. CHEDDAR, CHESHIRE), GRATED

2 TEASPOONS PREPARED MUSTARD

2 SPRING ONIONS, VERY FINELY CHOPPED

½ TEASPOON EACH CHOPPED FRESH OR DRIED BASIL, SAGE, OREGANO AND PARSLEY

FRESHLY GROUND BLACK PEPPER, TO TASTE

1 EGG, BEATEN

A LITTLE MILK OR WATER

A LITTLE PLAIN FLOUR

OIL OR BUTTER FOR FRYING

1. Blend the first six ingredients together and add the beaten egg to bind the mixture. Add liquid if necessary, but only a very little.
2. Shape the mixture into sausages, keeping your hands moist with water as you do so. Roll the sausages in a little flour for a very thin coating and then shallow-fry these in a little oil or butter.
3. Serve hot with grilled tomatoes, baked beans on toast and plenty of brown sauce.

Serves 4

30 mins

Variations

1. For a vegan (i.e. dairy-free) sausage, replace the cheese with soya cheese and the egg with 1 tablespoon tahini beaten with 2 tablespoons water.
2. For a more spicy sausage, add ½ teaspoon chilli powder to the mixture and ½ teaspoon ground pepper to the flour in which the sausages are rolled before cooking.

Spanish Omelette

4 TABLESPOONS OIL

1 LARGE POTATO, PEELED AND CUBED

1 MEDIUM CARROT, GRATED

225G (8OZ) BROCCOLI, CUT INTO SMALL
  FLORETS

2 SPRING ONIONS, FINELY CHOPPED

285G (10OZ) SILKEN TOFU

140ML (¼ PINT) SOYA MILK

1 TABLESPOON CHOPPED FRESH PARSLEY

½ TEASPOON DRIED SAGE OR THYME

Serves 2-4

⏱ 30 mins

1.   Heat half the oil in a frying pan and sauté the potato until golden and just tender. Add the carrot and broccoli and cook a further 2-3 minutes with the pan covered. Now stir in the onion and leave to cook, covered, while you whisk together the remaining ingredients, including the remaining oil, to make a thick cream.

2.   Pour this cream over the sauté mixture. Leave to cook, uncovered, for 5 minutes over a medium heat.

3.   Lift one edge of the omelette with a spatula: the underside should be golden. Turn the omelette in sections, as it may break easily. Cook a further 3-5 minutes then lift out in sections.

4.   Serve hot with fresh toast or alongside the Glamorgan Sausages (page 27) and plenty of grilled tomatoes and mushrooms.

Tip

Silken tofu is very soft and creamy. Most supermarkets sell it now – look in the Chinese and Indian meals section.

SANDWICHES

Hot TLT

225G (8OZ OR 1 BLOCK) TEMPEH, DEFROSTED

2 TEASPOONS PREPARED MUSTARD

3 TABLESPOONS OIL

SOY SAUCE

4 TABLESPOONS MAYONNAISE

4 SLICES BREAD OR 2 BAGUETTES, PLAIN OR TOASTED

4-6 LETTUCE LEAVES

2 LARGE TOMATOES, THICKLY SLICED

1.   Slice the block of tempeh (want to know what it is – then see page 266) in half diagonally, stand the triangles on their longest sides and slice in half again.

2.   Sauté the tempeh in the oil and, when golden brown, remove from the heat and sprinkle with a little soy sauce.

3.   Spread the mustard and mayonnaise on the bread, place the hot tempeh over and arrange the lettuce and tomato over that. Close and eat!

Makes 2 sandwiches

20 mins

Named after the BLT

California Protein Crunch

2 TABLESPOONS MISO (FERMENTED SOYA BEAN PASTE)

4 TABLESPOONS TAHINI (SESAME SEED PASTE)

JUICE OF 1 LEMON

4 SLICES BREAD OR 2 BAGUETTES

HANDFUL OF ALFALFA OR MUNG BEAN SPROUTS, RINSED AND DRAINED

1.   Blend the miso (see page 264), tahini and lemon juice together in a bowl to make a thick paste and spread this on the slices of bread.

2.   Sprinkle the sprouts over the spread, close the sandwich, and crunch.

Makes 2 sandwiches

5 mins

Cuba Tubes

2 THICK SLICES BREAD, BUTTERED

1 TEASPOON PREPARED MUSTARD

1 TABLESPOON MAYONNAISE

¼ PORTION (APPROXIMATELY 55G/2OZ) CHIPS

SALT AND FRESHLY GROUND BLACK PEPPER, TO TASTE

1 EGG (OPTIONAL)

Serves 1

⏱ 15 mins

1. Lay out the buttered bread and spread one side with mustard, the other with mayonnaise and arrange the chips over. Season to taste, close the sandwich and eat in private!

2. If you really want to die and go to heaven, fry the egg and pop it immediately over the chips before you close the sandwich.

Grand Slam Slayers

4 SLICES BREAD, BUTTERED

2 TABLESPOONS MAYONNAISE

1 TEASPOON PREPARED MUSTARD

100G (4OZ) CHEESE, GRATED

1 LARGE CARROT, GRATED

2 SPRING ONIONS, VERY FINELY CHOPPED

½ BUNCH WATERCRESS, WASHED AND FINELY CHOPPED

Makes 2 sandwiches

⏱ 15 mins

1. Lay out the bread and spread two slices with the mayo and two slices with the mustard.

2. Mix the remaining ingredients together in a mixing bowl and arrange over two slices. Season if you wish, though I find the onions do it for me, then close and go.

Hickory Stickory

4 SLICES BREAD

1 TABLESPOON YEAST EXTRACT

100G (4OZ) SMOKED TOFU OR
SMOKED CHEESE (SUCH AS HALOUMI),
THINLY SLICED

3 TABLESPOONS BUTTER

1 SMALL ONION, THINLY SLICED

1 TABLESPOON FINELY CHOPPED FRESH SAGE
OR THYME (OR YOUR FAVOURITE HERB)

2 TEASPOONS SESAME SEEDS

1 TEASPOON OIL (OPTIONAL)

1. Lay out the bread and spread with the yeast extract. Place the slices of tofu over.

2. Melt 1 tablespoon of the butter in a frying pan and sauté the onion until slightly browned. Place immediately over the tofu and close the sandwich.

3. Now blend the remaining ingredients together, adding the oil if necessary to make a whipped butter. Spread half of this mixture over the outside, top sides of both sandwiches.

4. Place them under a hot grill for 5-7 minutes, until they are browned and crusty. Turn the sandwiches with a spatula, spread the remaining butter mixture over the other sides and grill for a final 5-7 minutes.

5. Slice each in half and serve immediately with lots of pickled cucumbers.

Makes 2 sandwiches

🕐 25 mins

Tip

Smoked tofu is much firmer than silken tofu, with a dense more-ish flavour.

DIPS AND SPREADS

St Malo Herb Cheese and Olive Roll

225G (8OZ) CREAM CHEESE

½ TEASPOON EACH DRIED PARSLEY,
    SAGE, ROSEMARY AND THYME

½ TEASPOON FRESHLY GROUND BLACK PEPPER

55G (2OZ) CHOPPED WALNUTS

55G (2OZ) STONED GREEN OLIVES, FINELY
    CHOPPED

Serves 4

🕐 15 mins, plus
chilling time

1. Blend the cream cheese with the dried herbs in a mixing bowl. Mix the pepper, walnuts and olives together in a separate bowl and then turn out on to a large plate.

2. Shape the cheese, with a pair of damp wooden spoons, into a cylinder and place on the walnut mixture. Carefully roll the cheese in the nut mixture so that the outer surface is well covered. Press any excess into the cheese so that it forms a sort of crust.

3. Roll the cheese on to a piece of greaseproof paper and wrap well. Refrigerate for at least 1 hour.

4. Slice with a damp knife and serve with crackers.

Simple Almond Butter

225G (8OZ) BUTTER

100G (4OZ) ALMONDS, BLANCHED

ZEST OF 1 LEMON

1 TABLESPOON LEMON JUICE

PINCH OF FRESHLY GROUND BLACK PEPPER
    (OPTIONAL)

Makes approximately
340g (12oz)

🕐 15 mins, plus
chilling time

Exquisite!

1. Ensure the butter is at room temperature and that the almonds are blanched (skins removed). Beat the butter in a small bowl so that it is soft and creamy. Grind the almonds to a fine paste and add to the butter along with the remaining ingredients.

2. Cream them together, chill and serve in a pretty serving dish.

3. This is an excellent and delicious surprise on morning toast, between two crackers or plain biscuits or melted over steamed broccoli or spring greens.

Variations

1.   Other nuts, such as hazelnuts, walnuts or cashews, may be used instead of the almonds.

2.   You may also experiment with spices and additional flavours, such as orange instead of lemon, nutmeg instead of pepper. Over to you.

Baja Bacchanal

2-3 CLOVES GARLIC, CRUSHED
¼-½ TEASPOON CHILLI POWDER
¼ TEASPOON SALT
2 VERY RIPE TOMATOES, FINELY CHOPPED, OR
  2 TINNED TOMATOES, MASHED

225G (8OZ) PLAIN YOGURT
2 RIPE AVOCADOS
JUICE OF 1 LEMON

1.   Blend the garlic, chilli and salt together in a mixing bowl. Add the tomatoes and yogurt and stir well.

2.   Slice the avocados in half and remove the stones. Scoop the flesh into a mixing bowl and mash to a smooth, even consistency.

3.   Add the lemon juice and blend well, though I prefer to blend with a fork and not an electric mixer. Now fold in the yogurt and spice mixture and whisk with the fork for 1 minute.

4.   Serve immediately with hot pitta, toast or crudités.

Serves 4 polite people or 2 greedy ones

15 mins

Skinny Dip

285G (10OZ) SILKEN TOFU,
MASHED
1 TABLESPOON OIL
A LITTLE SOYA MILK

1 LARGE BUNCH CHIVES, WASHED AND FINELY
CHOPPED
FRESHLY GROUND BLACK PEPPER, TO TASTE
PINCH OF SALT

Makes approximately
285ml (½ pint)

🕐 10 mins, plus
chilling time

1.   Blend the tofu and oil to a very smooth consistency, adding a tablespoon or two of soya milk if necessary to give a soured cream texture.

2.   Stir in the chives and seasoning and leave covered in the fridge to let the flavours blend, about 1 hour.

3.   Serve chilled with crudités, baked potatoes or crisps.

All the delights of sour cream with chives... but without the coating of fat on your tongue afterwards!

LUSCIOUS LOVEBITES

Squabble 'n Beak

2 TABLESPOONS BUTTER OR MARGARINE

1 SMALL ONION, FINELY CHOPPED

FRESHLY GROUND BLACK PEPPER, TO TASTE

450G (1LB) LEFTOVER COOKED VEGETABLES,
   ANY SORT, CHOPPED

UP TO 100G (4OZ) FRESH VEGETABLES,
   FINELY CHOPPED

1 TABLESPOON CHOPPED FRESH HERB, OR
   1 TEASPOON DRIED HERB

2 EGGS, BEATEN

140ML (¼ PINT) MILK

1. Melt the butter in a frying pan and sauté the onion until clear and tender. Add the pepper and stir for 1 minute before adding the vegetables, both pre-cooked and fresh, and the herbs. Stir well then spread the mixture out.

2. Cover the pan and leave to cook over a medium heat for 5-7 minutes. Turn the sauté with a spatula and cook, covered, for a further 3 minutes.

3. Whisk the eggs and milk together and pour over the Squabble, cover the pan and cook for about 5 minutes longer, until the egg mixture sets.

4. Lift out with a spatula and serve on a warmed plate with plenty of tomato ketchup or brown sauce.

Serves 2

🕐 15 mins

Variations

1. Leave out the eggs and milk altogether but make a marinating sauce as follows: 1 teaspoon arrowroot dissolved in 1 tablespoon soy sauce, juice of ½ orange, and 90ml (3 fl oz) water. Mix together in a jug and pour over the vegetables. Leave to cook a further 5 minutes, uncovered, then serve.

2. Replace the eggs and milk with 140g (5oz) silken tofu blended with 140ml (¼ pint) soya milk and 1 tablespoon oil. Pour over the vegetables at the same point as you would have added the egg, cook to setting point and serve.

Hero Pancakes

900G (2LB) PRE-COOKED
    VEGETABLES, ANY SORT, FINELY
    CHOPPED
100G (4OZ) CHEESE, GRATED
SALT AND FRESHLY GROUND BLACK PEPPER,
    TO TASTE
2 TABLESPOONS BUTTER OR MARGARINE

For the pancakes:
180G (6OZ) PLAIN FLOUR
1 TEASPOON BAKING POWDER
1 EGG
285ML (½ PINT) MILK
A LITTLE OIL

Serves 2-4

⏱ 30 mins, plus
    standing time

1.   For the pancakes, mix the flour and baking powder together in a bowl.

2.   Whisk the egg and milk together in a jug and stir swiftly into the flour mixture. If possible, let this batter stand for up to 2 hours.

3.   When you are ready to use it, first place the vegetables in a saucepan over a low heat to warm them. Brush a little oil over a large frying pan or griddle and place over a medium heat.

4.   Ladle in some of the batter and tilt the pan to spread the batter into a thin film. Let the pancake cook for about 3 minutes, until it lifts easily at one edge, then turn it with a spatula and cook the other side for 2-3 minutes.

5.   Spread some of the vegetable mixture in the centre of the pancake and top with grated cheese. Sprinkle a little seasoning over the cheese then roll the pancake and place in an oven dish or tray. Continue until all the pancakes are made. Spread a little butter on each pancake top and brown under a grill for 3-5 minutes.

6.   Serve hot.

Variations

1.   For a richer pancake, make a cheese sauce. Melt 1 tablespoon butter in a saucepan and stir in 1 tablespoon plain flour. Add 425ml (¾ pint) milk, a little at a time, stirring after each addition to make a sauce. Finally, stir in 85g/3oz grated cheese and immediately remove the sauce from the heat. Pour it over the vegetables and roll the pancake as stated.

2.   Cheddar or mozzarella are obvious choices for the cheese, but you might try Stilton or another of the blue cheeses, especially if your vegetable mix has a fair proportion of greens in it.

3.   Add 3-5 chopped spring onions to the grated cheese or cheese sauce.

Fruity Hero Pancakes

1 x recipe HERO PANCAKES (OPPOSITE)
4 LARGE APPLES, PEELED AND CORED,
OR ABOUT 450G (1LB) OF ANY FRESH
FRUIT OR MIXTURE (I.E. BERRIES, PEACHES,
PEARS, CURRANTS)
2 TABLESPOONS DARK BROWN SUGAR
1 TEASPOON GROUND CINNAMON

100G (4OZ) CHEDDAR CHEESE, GRATED
55G (2OZ) CHOPPED NUTS SUCH AS
WALNUTS, HAZELNUTS, ALMONDS, BRAZILS
OR CASHEWS
¼ TEASPOON GROUND NUTMEG
¼ TEASPOON FRESHLY GROUND BLACK PEPPER
2 TABLESPOONS BUTTER OR MARGARINE

1. Prepare the batter as instructed opposite and leave to stand.
2. Prepare the apples, slice them into thin wedges and cook in a saucepan over a medium heat along with the sugar and cinnamon. You may need to add a teaspoon or two of water to prevent sticking, but no more. Let the apples cook until just tender, though still holding their form, then remove from the heat.
3. Cook the pancakes as instructed and spread some of the apple mixture over. Mix the cheese, nuts and spices and sprinkle over the apple, then roll the pancake and place in an oven dish.
4. Spread the top of the prepared pancakes with butter and grill for 3-5 minutes, until nicely browned.
5. Serve hot.

Serves 2-4

30 mins, plus standing time

Tips

1. Citrus fruits are best used mixed with cooking fruits such as apples, pears or peaches. Pineapple is an excellent addition.
2. Dried fruits may be used but are best soaked in fruit juice for at least an hour before you start cooking them.
3. All spices may be altered to suit the precise fruit mixture you are using, or to make use of what you have lurking in your cupboards.

BURGERS AND LUNCHEON PLATTERS

Ultraburger with Pick of Pickles and Watercress Salad

550G (1¼ LB) SILKEN TOFU, MASHED

55G (2OZ) RICE FLAKES OR ROLLED OATS

1 TEASPOON FRESHLY GROUND BLACK PEPPER

1 TEASPOON DRIED MARJORAM OR OREGANO

½ TEASPOON DRIED THYME

2 TABLESPOONS TAHINI

140ML (¼ PINT) WATER

2 TABLESPOONS SOY SAUCE

1 TABLESPOON WINE VINEGAR

1 TABLESPOON PREPARED MUSTARD

55G (2OZ) DRIED BREADCRUMBS

VEGETABLE OIL FOR SHALLOW-FRYING

Serves 2-6
(makes 4-6 burgers)

 30 mins

1.   Mash the tofu, rice flakes, pepper and herbs together in a mixing bowl.

2.   Blend the remaining ingredients, except the breadcrumbs and oil, together and add to the tofu mixture. Add a little more water if necessary to make a slightly firm but wet mixture.

3.   Leave to stand for 15 minutes, stirring once during that time and adding a little more water if the mixture seems to be getting too thick. (Note: sorry to be so inexact, but the precise amount of liquid needed depends on the exact type of tofu you use as well as whether you use rice or oat flakes.)

4.   Shape the mixture into patties or cutlets, coat with breadcrumbs and shallow-fry for 5-7 minutes each side, until hot and crusty.

5.   Serve on its own or in a toasted bap on a platter with the Pick of Pickles and Watercress Salad (pages 39 and 40).

Pick of Pickles

1. PICKLED SKEWERS can be quickly constructed by skewering baby gherkins, pickled onions, whole black olives, coarsely chopped red pepper or pimento and chunks of marinated tofu on to bamboo skewers. One or two of these per serving will be adequate.

2. PICKLED LACE makes a magnificent pickle from unlikely beginnings. Simply peel and grate 2 medium carrots, 1 medium turnip and 1 small or ½ medium raw beetroot into a mixing bowl. Add 1 medium onion, thinly sliced. Sprinkle 1 tablespoon salt and 1 teaspoon freshly ground black pepper over the vegetables and mix well. Pour over 1 glass of red wine (120-180ml/4-6fl oz) and 140ml (¼ pint) wine vinegar, stir again and press the mixture down with a wooden spoon. Cover the pickle and keep in the fridge all day or overnight if possible. Drain most of the liquid away from the pickle just before ready to use. For a hotter pickle substitute all or part of the black pepper with chilli powder. This is a pretty pickle, so make the most of displaying it creatively on your plate.

3. PICKLED BALLS (that made you look twice, didn't it?) is simply a mixture of pickled capers, pickled walnuts and, if you like them, pickled eggs. I prefer these placed in a cluster on the plate, perhaps halving the eggs and walnuts. You may wish to keep them whole or finely chop them.

All of the above need to be arranged on a simple watercress salad (next page).

Watercress Salad

1 SMALL RED PEPPER, VERY
THINLY SLICED

2 TABLESPOONS OLIVE OR
WALNUT OIL

JUICE OF ½ LEMON

PINCH OF SALT AND FRESHLY GROUND BLACK
PEPPER

1 TEASPOON FINELY CHOPPED FRESH BASIL

1 BUNCH WATERCRESS, WASHED AND DRAINED

1 BUNCH CHIVES, WASHED AND DRAINED

Serves 2-6

🕐 20 mins, plus
standing time for
the peppers

1. Prepare the red pepper and dress with the well-mixed oil, lemon, seasonings and basil. Leave to one side until the burgers and everything else is quite ready.

2. Chop the watercress and chives together and toss into the dressed red pepper just before serving with the burgers and pickles.

Bean and Buckwheat Burger on a Bed of Roses Salad

450G (1LB) COOKED KIDNEY BEANS, DRAINED

450G (1LB) COOKED BUCKWHEAT

1 TABLESPOON DRIED PARSLEY

1 TEASPOON DRIED SAGE

¼-½ TEASPOON CHILLI POWDER

55G (2OZ) DRIED BREADCRUMBS

2 TEASPOONS YEAST EXTRACT

140ML (¼ PINT) WATER

2 TABLESPOONS TAHINI

140ML (¼ PINT) MILK

55G (2OZ) PLAIN FLOUR

VEGETABLE OIL FOR SHALLOW-FRYING

1. Mix the beans, buckwheat, herbs, chilli and breadcrumbs together in a bowl, mashing the beans a little as you mix.

2. Dissolve the yeast extract in the water then stir in the tahini and add this liquid to the bean mixture. Stir well, adding a little more water if necessary to make a firm mixture. Leave to stand for 10 minutes then shape the mixture into patties or cutlets.

3. Brush both sides of each patty with a little milk and then sprinkle with a little flour.

4. Shallow-fry for 5-7 minutes each side until hot and crispy.

5. Serve in baps with your favourite garnishes, and on a plate with the following salad.

Serves 2-6
(makes 4-6 burgers)

🕐 30 mins

Tips

1. If you don't have buckwheat, cooked rice or barley will do, although the flavour and texture will change a bit.

2. The flour used to coat the prepared burgers may be spiced to give these burgers extra zap. Try freshly ground pepper, chilli powder or dried mustard.

Bed of Roses Salad

16-20 FIRM RED RADISHES

1 CUCUMBER

¼ HEAD OF LETTUCE

RADICCHIO LEAVES

55G (2OZ) ALMOND SLIVERS

140G (5OZ) PLAIN YOGURT

1 TEASPOON ROSE WATER

1 TABLESPOON CHOPPED CHIVES

Serves 2-6

 20 mins

1.   Trim the radishes and slice them vertically four times to three-quarters of their length. Place them in icy water while you prepare the other vegetables: they will open out into flower shapes.

2.   Score the outside of a whole cucumber to remove half of the peel, then cut the cucumber into four chunks and quarter each of these.

3.   Cut the lettuce into thin strands and break the radicchio into small pieces. Arrange the lettuce and radicchio along the bottom or around the edge of a platter and lay cucumber strips so that they appear as stalks growing out of the lawn of lettuce.

4.   Place the radish roses on top of the stalks and garnish the garden with almond sliver thorns.

5.   Finally, blend the yogurt, rose water and chives and dress the salad in a lattice-shaped drizzle. Place your burgers on the rose bed and serve.

BEAUTY AND THE FEAST:
The Secrets of Sensual Cooking

Beauty, so they say, is in the eye of the beholder . . . and nowhere is this more true than when you're preparing and serving highly sensual food. The world's most expensive restaurants know very well that it's the ambiance, rather than the quality of food alone, that keeps the customers paying those high prices. Although there is something fascinating about watching an overweight, sweaty chef with a hairy tummy slap a well-fried egg on to a once-used plate, it doesn't bring up the goose pimples quite like a romantic meal with candles, soft music and low-cut ideas. Good restaurants know that a little extra theatre in the way they present your food will stimulate your senses to full enjoyment of the food, the place and, of course, the company. And make no mistake, food, like sex, is all about senses. To enjoy a sensual meal you must engage all of your senses. To provide a sensual meal you must engage all of his senses, too!

My advice is: go the extra mile. Do what you can to create a little theatre, a little over-the-topness (you can always tone it down a notch or two next time), a little headiness. In this atmosphere, the full sensual beauty of your food will be savoured and appreciated.

Sense of Hearing

How can you hear your food? Please don't go on about carrots screaming. Think back to your childhood and recall the sounds of breakfast . . . Was there the scraping sound of knife against toast? Was there sizzling? Bubbling kettles? Slurping of tea? You see, it is important. So when you turn the Rösti (page 165), use a wooden spatula to prevent the sound of metal against metal. When you offer coffee, make sure it's the shoosh of espresso or the blub blub of percolated rather than the chink clink of instant being stirred into boiling water. When you offer more bread, let it be preceded by the sound of knife slicing through to wood rather than the crackle of a plastic bag being opened.

Sense of Touch

Isn't just about everyone raised to 'don't play with your food'? Well, I never was one for food fights or wasting food but I have always enjoyed the feel of food. I like touching food and I believe it is a very important aspect of how we select and enjoy food. Let me remind you of some of the ways you already enjoy touching food. At the greengrocers, you might find yourself *squeezing* melons, avocados and bulbs of garlic; *rubbing* the leaves of fresh mint and coriander; *tapping* pumpkins, marrows and water-melons; *holding* oranges to test for juiciness. If you can do that in a public place then you can more fully enjoy touching your food in the privacy of your dining-room or kitchen. When is the last time you ate with your hands, for instance? Why not boil up an artichoke or two, tear the leaves off, dunk them in a bowlful of sauce and scrape the flesh off against your bottom teeth. Why not prepare the Mango Mantrap (page 96) so that you can practise stroking a mango? And how about making your own fresh bread so that you can know the unique sensations of kneading sticky dough into a firm ball? Over to you.

Senses of Smell and Taste

These senses are inextricably linked and rightly so. Like so many pleasures, one precedes the other, giving hints and clues and arousing interest long before the full pleasure is experienced. Just so, the aromas of food and cooking are often described as tantalising, irresistible, even bewitching; and a whole language of scent has matured over the centuries to describe aroma in its fullness, its impact on first the nose then the palate, its overtones and its ability to linger. In fact, a recognised, appealing aroma has the power to trigger salivation: your body gets so excited at the prospect of tasting the source of the aroma that it jumps the gun!

Obviously, these two senses have to be made the most of. Like I said, though, they are linked and so must be treated as a long-married couple: you can't have one without the other.

How Do You Smell?

To smell a cooking food, lift the lid and use your hand to waft some of the steam towards your nose. Be ready for it and breath in gently and slowly. Smell the cooking food several times during its progress and, after one or two practice meals, you will be able to detect imbalances in the aroma which would come out in the flavour of the finished dish. You can adjust your seasonings and balance of ingredients accordingly to guarantee a top-class blend of aroma with flavour.

To smell a herb or spice, rub or crush a little in your hand to release its oils; smell your fingers, not the herb or spice, to catch the strength of aroma most likely to emanate from food with this ingredient added. To smell raw vegetables and fruits, get basic and hold them up to your nose. Root vegetables should smell earthy and slightly wood-like; tomatoes should smell of cat's piss; greens should smell . . . well, green! Remember that the aroma of most foods comes from the oils they contain. If the food is old, if it has been poorly stored or if you have cooked it to death, you can expect it to give only the most meagre of aromas.

After smell comes taste. The best flavour is usually the natural, unadorned flavour of a good quality-food. However, some foods, dishes and cooking techniques need a little help.

SECRET INGREDIENTS

TEN TOP TASTES THAT TANTALISE AND TRANSFORM ANY MEAL

1 GINGER Grate fresh ginger root into a dish of carrots or pumpkin to transform these simple vegetables into food of the gods. Ginger is sold in 'hands' and must be peeled before being grated. Use the fine grade on your grater or buy a special grater from an Asian grocer.

2 ZEST The grated rind of oranges, limes or lemons. Use the very finest grade on your grater and don't waste any of it. Zest is really the essential oils of the fruit concentrated in the outer, brightly coloured skin. It is an intense flavour and a little goes a long way. It's best added towards the end of preparation; also best to use organic fruits.

3 FRESHLY GROUND BLACK PEPPER This spice is everywhere but sadly underestimated. If you add it to the sauté stage of cooking, its effect is a stronger 'bite' but a more subtle after-taste. Pepper is so often added as an after-thought and its effect can then be harsh and overpowering.

4 CORIANDER Whether seed or leaf, this ingredient perfectly creates a bridge between sweet and savoury. So, a little in a curry will round the edges of the sharper, more fiery spices as well as enhance the natural sweetness of the vegetables it contains. The seeds should be ground with a pestle in a mortar when you need them; they may be added to biscuits, fruit dishes and savoury ragoûts. The leaves are very aromatic and should be 'revived' before you use them. Buy the leaves a few hours or a day before you need them and immerse the whole bunch, not just the roots, in cold water. Leave them there until the leaves perk up and stand up in the water, then drain and use as soon as possible. They are excellent chopped into soups, salsas and salads.

5 BASIL Another aromatic herb that is wonderful dried but exquisite when fresh. Grow some in a small pot on your windowsill, all the year round, and add a few chopped leaves to the top of your pasta sauce, pizza, salad or soup just a moment before serving.

6 GARLIC This grows like an onion but gets treated like an oyster – smelly and objectionable. Well, it's all in the way you treat them! I rarely use garlic raw; when I do it is embraced by other strong flavours which complement its own powerful nature. So, for instance, raw garlic crushed into Baja Bacchanal (page 33) is wrapped around by avocado, lemon and chilli. In Tahini Lemon Sauce (page 109) the earthy flavour of tahini and the fresh flavour of the coriander neatly subvert the intensity of garlic flavour. In cooking, garlic should be sautéed *in a particular order* with other ingredients. First, heat the oil in a pan, add the finely chopped garlic all by itself and stir it for 2-3 minutes over a medium flame. The garlic must seem to slightly puff and float and it must only begin to change colour. At this precise stage, you should add the onions (it usually is onions) and stir until they are clear and tender, or slightly golden if that is called for. This way of sautéing the garlic will bring out its finer flavours and cut out the reputation it has of making everyone who goes near it smelly.

7 PARSLEY A strong, slightly bitter herb that is packed full of goodness but sorely deprived of a chance to give it to you. Truly, how many people do you know who actually eat that little green apology on their plate? Use fresh parsley whenever you can get it, revive it as you would coriander (see 4, above), chop it finely and add it by the handful to soups, sauces and salads. Like basil, it is best added last of all. Other herbs in this spectrum of flavour are tarragon, thyme and savory, though these must be used sparingly compared to the lavish use you can make of parsley.

8 SESAME SEEDS One of the world's most overlooked foods, sesame is the mother of tahini and in the West is most famous for being sprinkled over bread rolls. Buy raw, rough sesame seeds and roast them as and when you need them. Heat a large frying pan (dry and unoiled) over a medium flame and turn a couple of ounces of seeds into it. Hold the pan over the flame and shake it gently but constantly while the seeds roast. They will turn a deep golden colour (don't let them darken too much or they will become bitter), some will pop (a lovely sound) and, most importantly, they will release the most appealing, nutty aroma! This will take about 3 minutes. Tip them from the pan on to a plate to cool, and sprinkle generously over stir-fries, salads or just a bowlful of steamed brown rice.

9 FENNEL A herb which is a vegetable, or is it a vegetable which is a herb? Sweet fennel grows a fleshy, celery-like bulb and this is braised, sautéed or chopped raw into salads to give a flavour of anise to the dish.

Fennel herb and seed are stronger in flavour and more aromatic; they are excellent in soups which include beans or potatoes and in egg dishes. They may be added early in the cooking process. Both fennels lend a fresh, exotic flavour to a meal.

10 SOY SAUCE A product of fermented soy beans. Commercial brands are strong and produced quickly by speeding up the fermentation process using chemical additives. Shoyu is a natural, lengthy ferment of soy beans and wheat. Tamari is also a natural, lengthy ferment of soy beans, but without wheat. It is stronger in flavour than shoyu. Soy sauce is rich and salty but has a mellowing effect on the flavour of a finished dish. Use it sparingly and serve it in a pretty cruet or tiny bowl or jug.

Sense of Sight

Much may be done to tease, tantalise and entice without ever letting your man lay eyes on the meal. Appealing to his other four senses will create a (sixth?) sense of anticipation which you can fulfil by stimulating his sense of vision and providing a meal that is colourful, textured and beautifully presented.

Colouring your mood

Colour is visible light and, as such, occupies just one small part of the spectrum of electro-magnetic waves. Colours are produced by light waves of varying lengths. These light waves are interpreted as colour by an interplay between your eyes and your brain, and a person with good colour-sight (i.e. not colour blind) can enjoy hundreds of subtle shades of colour in their life. Although there are theories under study which purport that light and therefore colour can actually penetrate bone and muscle tissue, the use of colour to manipulate mood and general well-being is generally based on the effect of light striking the retina. As light, and therefore colour, strikes the retina, an immediate change in brain function and hormone production occurs. In broad terms, these changes range from stimulating to relaxing. It is no wonder then that colour in food, clothing and environment is considered so important to most people.

Colour is often divided into categories of bright, cool and warm.

♡ Bright colours are commonly associated with children or with people and places that appear cheerful and energetic. They are stimulating and tend to arouse autonomic functions such as heart and respiratory rates.

♡ Cool colours are linked with quiet concentration, repose and mental calm. They are non-stimulating and can subdue.

♡ Warm colours are uplifting both physically and mentally but do not provoke or over-stimulate, as would bright colours.

These are only broad guidelines, however, as there are hundreds of hues and shades of colour. So let us look at ten colours in more detail so that you may begin using colour to create the ambiance and presentation that will celebrate all that is sensual in your food.

WHITE A fresh colour which creates an atmosphere of simplicity. Too much of it can give the appearance of a cold, antiseptic environment, so be certain to warm it with natural wood, bright or pastel colours and plenty of pattern and texture. Used with care, white allows you to feel the innocence and *joie de vivre* that lingers in even the most jaded of us.

IN YOUR FOOD: White or cream coloured foods should dominate. Think of pasta, rice and potatoes and you will see that they can easily and pleasantly take up a large portion of the serving plate. To use white as a highlight for your food, think of fresh cream being poured over brightly coloured strawberries and you will understand how this colour can lift a food and make it seem pure.

IN YOUR SETTING: A white linen tablecloth is an excellent background to almost any meal. Although it can be a huge expanse of white, it rarely dominates but provides that feeling of simplicity and clarity that is so compatible with good feasting. White china has a similar effect – it is an excellent background for most foods – yet it can be placed against a coloured tablecloth and be transformed, suddenly, into a point of contrast or highlight for your table setting. White is classic and classy at once. Whether it is paint, paper, cloth or china; whether it is pure white, creamy white,

starched, embroidered, embossed or otherwise patterned, somehow you can't really overdo it.

RED A stimulating colour which can therefore counter depression, sloth and reticence. However, it is not recommended for those who are anxious or aggressive as it would only exaggerate these characteristics. A red room will help you to feel outgoing, vigorous and ambitious so it may be a perfect antidote to the shy and self-effacing. If you really like red, be certain to use it with a light hand as it can also promote crudeness, ruthlessness and impulsiveness. Red is strong, optimistic and uncomplicated – a definite stimulant.

IN YOUR FOOD: Red is a highlight or point of contrast. Think of radish flowers, diced red pepper, chillies or fresh tomato wedges and you will understand that just a little of this colour goes a long way. The one exception is probably tomato sauce over pasta, but then, you do have all that lovely creamy white pasta dominating things . . .

IN YOUR SETTING: Dining rooms of the rich and famous are, or were, sometimes red. I guess if you often entertain large groups of people, some of whom might not know each other, the red will bring out the gregarious side of them and conversation will flourish. Just between you and your man, however, it might be a bit heavy-handed. Red, or a more subtle shade of it, might be best kept as a point of contrast or a highlight here, too. Think of a single red serving bowl, a red rose or two on the table, a red pattern on the napkin and you will begin to get the idea of how to use this colour.

BLUE A very soothing, calming colour, good for times and places where you wish to create a retreat from the world. It promotes deliberation, introspection and duty and is also restful to the eyes. It helps promote sleep, reduces blood pressure and creates a mood of serenity, emotional control and compassion.

IN YOUR FOOD: There aren't that many blue foods, but when you find them you should treat them as points of contrast or highlights in your dish. The Roman Cup (see Cold Drinks, page 278) has the only blue ingredient in this book: a borage flower. And it looks absolutely beautiful floating in the light golden wine!

IN YOUR SETTING: Let's keep blue a highlight colour here, too. A blue stripe around the china, blue candles or a little blue embroidery on the linen will do nicely.

PINK has a calming, even soporific, effect which has been used to good result in the treatment of violent people (you're not dating one of those, are you?). In Britain and the United States, pink cells are used to calm aggressive people being held in detention centres. After just ten to thirty minutes in a pink cell, the detainees are reported to become peaceful and sometimes fall asleep. For non-violent people, this warm colour creates a mood of love, affection and gentleness (that's more like it).

IN YOUR FOOD: I always think of watermelon when I need a pink food. I know it's not a pure pink, but it is in that general area of colour, along with blood oranges, guava,

pink grapefruit, papaya and pomegranate. These foods are often served as starters, not surprising considering the loving mood this colour creates. If the loving mood lasts longer than one week, try pink champagne.

IN YOUR SETTING: A deep rosy pink dining-room would be just wonderful, I think. However, pink is generally kept as a good background colour for your meal. A soft pink linen tablecloth, pink carnations in a vase or a pink motif on the china will be enough to add the air of softness this colour provides.

ORANGE creates a mood of flamboyance and camaraderie. It promotes curiosity, fearlessness, and restless inquiry. This invigorating colour should therefore be used with considered restraint to ensure that its benefits are not overdone. You could soften it by choosing a more apricot shade of orange.

IN YOUR FOOD: Orange is a very dominant food colour. Think of carrots, mangoes, oranges, pumpkins, sweet potatoes and squashes, and you will realise how strong this colour is against the white of your rice, potato or pasta. In fact, every meal you eat should have a serving of orange food to provide you with nutrients essential to good heath. So, although it should be a very common colour on your plate, it should also act to highlight and contrast. For this reason, take special care to arrange orange food thoughtfully on the plate so that it appears an artistic enhancement of your meal. Try Iced Chocolate-lined Orange Bowl (page 255) for an orange dessert.

IN YOUR SETTING: Orange candles, flowers or napkins are about my limit as non-food orange can be a little garish.

YELLOW is the colour of happiness. It inspires wisdom, imagination, mental acuity and adventurousness. Yellow is often liked by clear and precise thinkers. A golden shade of yellow has a more soothing effect.

IN YOUR FOOD: Yellow food ranges from the bright yellow of sweetcorn and polenta to the soft yellow-oranges of swede and apricot. It should be considered in the same breath and in the same way as orange foods: dominant, important to health, yet serving to highlight and contrast with other foods.

IN YOUR SETTING: The best yellow is either sunlight or the flame of your candles.

GREEN The colour of harmony, hope and peace. It creates a mood of renewal, gentleness and a sense of 'everything's all right'. Make sure there is a lot of this colour around if your meal is a setting for reconciliation.

IN YOUR FOOD: Green means greens and these are as important to the look of your plate, and to your health, as are the orange-yellow foods. They must be present at virtually every meal yet must be arranged as a sort of highlight and point of contrast to the other colours on your plate or they will look, and probably taste, just awful. Apart from good old greens (lots of recipes for *very* good old greens on pages 171-175), avocados, peas, grapes, some plums and apples,

green peppers and cucumbers are easy-to-find green foods. Green garnishes such as parsley and mint are much adored but sadly under-appreciated. If it's on the plate, eat it!

IN YOUR SETTING: Keep green as a soft background such as a lawn or orchard while you picnic, or else limit it to the green leaves of your spider plants and aspidistras.

PURPLE creates a very grand and flamboyant atmosphere, just perfect for the extrovert in you. It has its solemn and fastidious effect as well, as implied in the decor and garments of church and monarch. But purple is really a colour of extremes: either exhilaration or depression and it should therefore be wielded with a light hand. Its softer shades, such as lavender and mauve, create a mood of aloofness and aspiration.

IN YOUR FOOD: Yes, there are purple foods! Aubergine, some plums, grapes and many berries such as raspberry, blackberry and blueberry. I even happen to think that beetroot should be considered a purple, rather than red, food. All of these are strong foods, in colour as well as flavour and texture; a little of these foods goes a long way. I keep them in the side dishes, desserts and sauces which accompany my main presentation.

IN YOUR SETTING: I can imagine one or two dark plum coloured bits of china or glass being attractive, but otherwise I keep this colour very much in the occasional category. As for mauves and lavenders, maybe in the bouquet on the corner table or maybe if it's tea with an elderly aunt . . .

BROWN is a perfect companion to white. Its mood of solidity, stamina and patience combines extremely well with the innocence and purity of white. As in so many simple settings where wood floors and exposed beams soften the all-white glare of walls and ceiling, brown gently introduces the ideas of work, duty and dependability. Too much brown in your environment may induce you to reject change and to tend towards inertia and paranoia, never good features of a loving relationship, so use a light hand.

IN YOUR FOOD: Whole bread, wholegrain rice and, of course, chocolate and coffee are my favourite brown foods. I like all of them served in their purest, most unadorned form and, usually, against a simple white background. Brown foods which are not appreciated are often served in a heap on dull coloured plates with faded, peculiar-looking substances draped or poured over them. Yuk! Celebrate your brown food without restraint.

IN YOUR SETTING: Brown can be as much or as little of your setting as you like without causing a problem. If you have wooden floors or a scrub-top table then you have brown as a significant part of your setting and you can augment or reduce its impact as you please – by covering the table, for instance, or polishing the floor to highlight its grain. On the other hand, if you have only wooden salad bowls then make the most of them by filling them with a really colourful salad and leave it at that.

GREY creates an attitude of caution, composure and a measured expenditure of energy.

IN YOUR FOOD: It shouldn't be there! I really can't think of a grey food except some very unhappy meals I have seen in canteens and cafés round the country. My motto: if it's grey, throw it away.

IN YOUR SETTING: It could only be his suit and you can invite him to take that off!

INSPIRING DESIRE:

TEN TIPS TO CREATE A CULINARY CLIMAX

1 PLAN YOUR MENU Choose recipes that are within your skill and budget constraints, yet have a lot of pzazz.

2 BUY QUALITY INGREDIENTS IF YOU WANT A QUALITY MEAL Remember, some foods go out of season so refer back to your menu plan if you need to change. Foods are best if they are fresh; after that (in descending order of quality) buy frozen, bottled or tinned.

3 TREAT YOUR PLATE LIKE A PALETTE Every meal should have a variety of colours and textures that complement one another.

4 MAKE SURE YOU'VE INCLUDED THE NUTRIENTS A quick visual guide for a nutritious meal is to allow:

½ the plate for cereal or starch (rice, pasta, potato);

¼ the plate for greens;

¼ the plate for yellow/orange vegetables;

a topping or side dish of beans or nuts;

a dessert of fruit.

5 LEARN THE ART OF CREATIVE CUTTING

If all the ingredients are chopped your dish will look and cook dull. If they are diced, sliced, cubed, chopped, grated and shredded then you have instantly increased your meal appeal.

6 GET KNOWN FOR YOUR TIMING

If the soup isn't ready until after you've eaten the dessert then you're not really on track for a culinary climax. Timing isn't everything, but it's close! Schedule your meal preparation so that it lands on the table when it's meant to.

7 IN COOKING, LESS IS MORE

Do not overcook. All the cost and effort of purchasing quality ingredients will be wasted, as will the possibility of producing a delicious, visually appealing meal. Unless, of course, you *want* to make a school dinner.

8 WHEN YOU PUT ON MAKE-UP YOU AIM TO ENHANCE WHAT YOU'VE ALREADY GOT

The same applies to cooking really good food. Get to know and appreciate the real flavours, textures, characteristics and qualities of the unprepared food before you start doing things with it. Then it is simply a case of combining and adding to enhance that naturally wonderful starting point.

9 LAY THE TABLE FOR A MEAL, NOT A FUNERAL

It is important to make him feel there is an abundance of food – that is sensual and enticing – but not a glut of it. Some people, men especially, feel they have to finish everything put in front of them. The trouble is, that will, at best, lead to a very bloated tummy and a much reduced interest in anything but sleeping it off. Who said 'enough is as good as a feast'? We want to feel the spirit of the feast without the damage done by overeating.

10 RELAX

You've done what you can, now forget the petty hiccoughs and complications; enjoy it all as it is and let the rest take care of itself.

Spanish Omelette (page 28)

PART TWO

Snacks and Starters

Many of these recipes would make succulent short-order foods (see previous section), but in addition, all of them would also make wonderfully teasing starters for larger meals.

Falafel (page 59)

SAVOURY SNACKS

*S*ushi

This classic dish is really a special way of preparing rice, which is then topped by a vegetable mixture and the whole thing rolled in a sheet of nori. Sushi is a very portable food, useful as a snack, lunch or appetiser, which keeps for several days if left unsliced. Experiment with different fillings and use left over rice on occasion, if that is more convenient.

570ML (1 PINT) WATER

1 STRIP KOMBU SEAWEED

400G (14OZ) BROWN RICE, PREFERABLY
    SHORT-GRAIN

120ML (4 FL OZ) RICE OR WINE VINEGAR

2 TABLESPOONS BARLEY MALT SYRUP

1 TEASPOON SALT

2 TABLESPOONS SOY SAUCE

5 PEPPERCORNS, CRUSHED

100-180G (4-6OZ) MUSHROOMS, CLEANED,
    TRIMMED AND CHOPPED

8 SPRING ONIONS, THINLY SLICED LENGTHWISE

100G (4OZ) FRESH PARSLEY OR CORIANDER,
    FINELY CHOPPED

8 SHEETS NORI

---

1.   Heat the water and kombu (if you want to know what it is, see page 263) in a saucepan over a medium heat. Bring to the boil and boil for 5 minutes. Remove the kombu and add the rice to the boiling water. Cover the pan, bring to the boil again and immediately reduce the heat.

2.   Leave the rice covered and simmering gently for about 45 minutes, until the rice is tender and the water absorbed. Remove from the heat and leave 5-10 minutes in the pan.

3.   Heat the vinegar, half the syrup and the salt in a small saucepan until well mixed and hot. Do not boil this mixture. Remove from the heat and cool until you can comfortably touch the liquid.

4.   Turn the rice out on to a large platter and spread it out to cool. Sprinkle the vinegar and syrup mixture over it, stirring the rice as you do so with a fork or table knife.

5.   Ideally, you should cool the rice quickly and some cooks even recommend using an electric fan, blowing over the rice, to speed this process. The quick cooling, combined with the coating of vinegar and syrup mixture that each grain of rice acquires, helps the rice

Serves 4-8
(makes 8 sushi rolls)

🕐 1 hr 30 mins

stay sweet and moist for several days – perfect for the sushi process.

6.   In a small saucepan, mix the soy sauce, remaining syrup and the peppercorns. Place over a medium heat, stir well and add the mushrooms just before the sauce begins to boil. Simmer for 5-10 minutes over a low heat, stirring often.

7.   Prepare the spring onions and parsley and have ready on separate plates. If the nori is untoasted, you must toast each sheet over a flame until it alters colour and becomes slightly brittle. Put to one side.

8.   It is time to make the sushi roll and for this you must keep the nori dry *but* it helps to keep your hands wet so the rice does not stick to them.

9.   Place a sheet of toasted nori on a dry board or bamboo mat (*su*). Spoon some rice on to the nori, spreading to the side edges but leaving 3-4cm (1¼-1¾ inches) clear at the front and back edges. Arrange the strips of spring onion on the rice, sprinkle with the parsley and spoon some of the mushroom mixture over all.

10. Begin to roll the nori, keeping one hand dry for the nori (or using the *su*) and the other wet so that you can keep tucking the rice and vegetables into place. When the roll is finished, dry both hands and roll the sushi backwards and forwards to make a firm, tight roll.

11. Rest the sushi on a platter with the end of the nori pressing on to the platter. Do the same with the remaining sheets of nori. Chill for 2-4 hours then slice into thin (1cm/½ inch) rounds with a cold, wet knife.

12. Arrange on individual serving plates and serve with freshly ground ginger blended with a little vinegar or with a tiny bowl of soy sauce for dipping.

13. Sushi may be kept, wrapped in cling film, in the refrigerator for 3-4 days provided you keep the roll intact. This is a very portable food, perfect for picnics, parties and packed lunches.

Tip

Nori is a seaweed. It is sold in nice square sheets and the best sort is a kind of purple-green colour.

Falafel

180G (6OZ) CHICK PEAS, SOAKED
    OVERNIGHT
55G (2OZ) BREADCRUMBS
2 CLOVES GARLIC, CRUSHED
1 TEASPOON GROUND CORIANDER
1/2 TEASPOON DRIED THYME

1/2 TEASPOON DRIED SAGE
1/4 TEASPOON FRESHLY GROUND BLACK PEPPER
1 LARGE EGG, LIGHTLY BEATEN
A LITTLE PLAIN FLOUR
VEGETABLE OIL FOR DEEP-FRYING

1. Drain and rinse the chick peas and put them into a saucepan with fresh water; bring to the boil and continue boiling for 10 minutes. Cover the pan, lower the heat, and simmer for 20-30 minutes, until they are partially cooked.

2. Drain the chick peas, then grind them as finely as possible in a blender, mouli or mortar. Turn the ground chick peas into a mixing bowl and stir in the breadcrumbs, garlic, coriander, herbs and seasoning.

3. Stir in the beaten egg, and leave the mixture to stand for 30 minutes.

4. Flour your hands, then roll the mixture into walnut-sized balls. Heat the oil to a high temperature. Drop the balls in a few at a time and cook for about 5 minutes, until browned. Drain, and pat with kitchen paper to remove excess oil.

5. Serve hot or cold with Tahini Lemon Sauce (see page 109).

Serves 4

🕐 1 hr 30 mins

Dolmades of Lettuce

6-12 LETTUCE LEAVES
285ML (1/2 PINT) COOKED RICE
140G (5OZ) CURD CHEESE OR TOFU
1/2 BUNCH SPRING ONIONS, FINELY CHOPPED
25G (1OZ) BUTTER OR MARGARINE, SOFTENED

1 TABLESPOON GREEN PEPPERCORNS
2 TABLESPOONS FINELY CHOPPED FRESH
    PARSLEY
PINCH OF SALT
1/4 TEASPOON FRESHLY GROUND BLACK PEPPER

1. Blanch the lettuce leaves by pouring boiling water over them; drain them in a colander.

2. Mix all the other ingredients together. Place a heaped table-

Serves 4

🕐 35 mins, plus
chilling time

spoon of the filling at one end of the lettuce leaf and carefully roll up, folding in the sides, so that you have a neat package.

3.   Continue with all the leaves and refrigerate for half a day.

Tip

Greek dolmades are actually stuffed vine leaves, which you can find in super-markets or speciality shops – try this and the following recipe using them. I find, however, that vine leaves can sometimes be very tough, which is why I suggest these two alternatives. For a buffet party they are best served as they are, but at other times you could try them with a rich tomato sauce.

Choux Dolmades

12 LARGE CABBAGE LEAVES

25G (1OZ) BUTTER OR MARGARINE

3 SPRING ONIONS, FINELY CHOPPED

55G (2OZ) MUSHROOMS, CHOPPED

55G (2OZ) CURRANTS

55G (2OZ) PINE NUTS

140G (5OZ) BROWN RICE, COOKED
   (APPROXIMATELY 450G/1LB WHEN COOKED)

1 TEASPOON ALLSPICE OR MIXED SPICE

¼ TEASPOON FRESHLY GROUND BLACK PEPPER

1 TABLESPOON EACH OF FINELY CHOPPED
   FRESH MINT AND PARSLEY

285ML (½ PINT) VEGETABLE STOCK
   (SEE PAGE 87)

Makes 12 dolmades

 30-45 mins

1.   Preheat the oven to 180°C/350°F/Gas Mark 4.

2.   Trim the cabbage leaves then lower into a large pan of boiling water and cook for 2-3 minutes, or until soft. Run the blanched leaves under cold water and pat dry. Lay the leaves out on a board or towel.

3.   Melt the butter in a frying pan and lightly sauté the onions and mushrooms. Stir in the currants, pine nuts, cooked rice, spices and herbs. Taste and adjust the flavour if necessary.

4.   Divide the mixture between the leaves: place a spoonful at one end, fold the sides and then roll up to make a small parcel. Arrange the stuffed leaves close together in an ovenproof dish. Pour on the stock, cover the dish and bake for about 20 minutes, until the leaves are tender.

5.   Lift out the dolmades one by one, drain them, and serve hot or cold.

Roasted Sunflower and Pumpkin Seed Mix

55G (2OZ) SUNFLOWER SEEDS
55G (2OZ) PUMPKIN SEEDS
2 TABLESPOONS SOY SAUCE

¼ TEASPOON CHILLI POWDER OR A FEW DROPS
OF TABASCO SAUCE

1. Place a large, dry, unoiled frying pan over a medium heat. Measure the seeds into it and stir with a wooden spoon while they roast. You may also shake the pan gently so that the seeds roast evenly. The seeds will brown slightly and some may swell and pop – sometimes right out of the pan.

2. When most of the seeds seem roasted, remove the pan from the heat.

3. Mix the soy sauce and chilli or Tabasco, and drizzle this over the hot seeds, stirring briskly all the while. Keep stirring for another minute or two then turn the seeds into a serving dish and stir them gently over the next 5-10 minutes to help them cool (they hold their heat well and can be *very* hot).

4. Serve warm or cool.

Serves 2-4

🕐 20 mins

Don't miss these!

Dressed-up Brochettes

285G (10OZ) PLAIN, FIRM TOFU, CUBED
100G (4OZ) BUTTON MUSHROOMS, CLEANED
3 TABLESPOONS TOMATO PURÉE
JUICE OF 1 LEMON
3 TABLESPOONS WINE VINEGAR

1 TABLESPOON SOY SAUCE
1 TEASPOON DRIED MARJORAM
2 CLOVES GARLIC, CRUSHED
½ TEASPOON FRESHLY GROUND BLACK PEPPER
100G (4OZ) BLACK OLIVES, STONED
1 LARGE RED PEPPER, COARSELY CHOPPED

1. Arrange the tofu and mushrooms in a shallow bowl or oven dish.

2. Blend the tomato, lemon juice, vinegar, soy sauce, herb, garlic and black pepper in a bowl and pour over the tofu and mushrooms. Gently stir the mixture to ensure all the pieces are covered in the dressing.

3. Cover and leave in the fridge all day or for at least 2 hours.

Serves 2-4

🕐 10 mins, plus 2 hrs marinating time

4. Lift the tofu chunks and mushrooms out of the dressing and push them on to a skewer (steel) along with the olives and chunks of red pepper. Place the brochette under the grill for 2-3 minutes, turn and grill a final 2 minutes.

5. Roll the hot brochette in the dressing once more and serve immediately.

SWEET SNACKS

Figgy Fudge

225G (8OZ) DRIED FIGS, FINELY CHOPPED

JUICE OF 1 LEMON

200ML (7 FL OZ) WATER

55G (2OZ) BUTTER OR MARGARINE

55G (2OZ) PLAIN FLOUR

½ TEASPOON VANILLA EXTRACT

55G (2OZ) WALNUTS, FINELY CHOPPED

Serves 4-8

🕐 30 mins

Don't ask — just bite!

1. Turn the chopped figs into a saucepan with the lemon juice and water and place over a medium flame. Bring to the boil and simmer for 5-7 minutes, until the figs have softened and become sticky.

2. Turn the figs through a mouli or food processor to bring them to a fine, even consistency.

3. In a separate pan, melt the butter and sprinkle the flour over it. Cook over a medium heat, stirring constantly, to make a thick paste, or roux.

4. Stir the fig mixture into the flour mixture and blend well. Stir in the vanilla and the walnuts and spread the mixture into a lightly buttered 23cm (9 inch) tin. Allow to cool, then slice into 2.5cm (1 inch) pieces and serve.

5. This candy may be chilled if you prefer.

Variation

Add desiccated coconut or chopped crystallised ginger to the warm mixture then spread in the pan.

*D*ate and Almond Nougat

450G (1LB) DATES, FINELY
CHOPPED
100G (4OZ) ALMONDS, BLANCHED
AND FLAKED
100G (4OZ) SUGAR

60ML (2 FL OZ) WATER
100G (4OZ) BARLEY MALT SYRUP (ABOUT 4
OVER-FULL TABLESPOONS)
1 TABLESPOON ROSE WATER
½ TEASPOON GROUND CLOVES

1.   Roughly crush the chopped dates and flaked almonds together in a mortar with a pestle.

2.   Cook the sugar and water together in a saucepan over a medium heat to make a syrup: the sugar must dissolve completely to make a slightly thickened, glossy liquid.

3.   Stir the barley malt syrup and the dates and almonds into the sugar syrup and blend well. Add the rose water and cloves after the mixture has cooled slightly.

4.   When the mixture is cool enough to handle, wet or lightly butter your hands and roll the mixture into a 2.5cm (1 inch) diameter sausage. Slice 7.5cm (3 inch) lengths from the sausage; stretch and twist each into a circle. Leave to cool completely.

5.   These may be stored in an airtight container for a few days.

Makes approximately
450g (1lb) nougat

1 hr, plus
additional
cooling time

Tips

1.   Keeping your hands wet or lightly buttered simply prevents the mixture from sticking to you and also gives the nougat a slight sheen and outer seal, making it easier to handle.

2.   You may, of course, shape the nougat any way you like: roll it into a sheet and cut it into shapes; cut the sausage into tiny nuggets; even make three strands and braid them into a nougat display for your table!

Fruit Jelly

285ML (½ PINT) WATER   285ML (½ PINT) GRAPE JUICE

1 X 3G (¹⁄₁₀ OZ) SACHET AGAR

Serves 4-8

 2 hrs

1. Bring the water to a boil in a saucepan and dissolve the agar in it. Stir for 2-3 minutes, then remove from the heat and leave to cool for 10 minutes. Stir in the grape juice and pour the liquid into a jelly mould.

2. Cover and leave to cool completely at room temperature, or chill it in the fridge until ready to serve.

3. Turn out of the mould by dipping the outside of the mould briefly in hot water, cover the mould with a plate and turn it over.

4. Serve with cream, Soya Creem (a non-dairy dessert cream widely available in supermarkets) or ice cream.

Variations

1. The grape juice may be replaced by apple juice or cranberry juice, both of which will make a clear jelly.

2. Any fruits or fruit pieces may be added to the mould, including halved grapes of both colours, sliced bananas, chopped pear, apple, pineapple or orange and thin slices of kiwi. Place fruits in the mould and pour the jelly over them to make a 'top-heavy' mould. Or, if you have the patience, place in a layer of fruit with some jelly poured over, then chill the mould in a bowl of ice for about 10 minutes. Repeat this process of layering the fruit, pouring in the jelly and chilling it, until the mould is full. Cover and chill thoroughly.

Tip

Agar is a seaweed, though you will never taste it in this dish; it sets the jelly instead of gelatine.

Lick Me Lollies

JUICE OF 1 LEMON

1 TABLESPOON GRATED FRESH GINGER

450G (1LB) FRESH OR FROZEN RASPBERRIES

1 LITRE (2 PINTS) APPLE JUICE

1. Blend the lemon juice and grated ginger together in a jug and leave to stand – up to 4 hours is ideal. Strain the juice and discard the ginger.
2. Purée the lemon juice, raspberries and apple juice together with a blender or mouli and pour the mixture into lolly moulds.
3. Pop them in the freezer and wait.

Makes 8-12 lollies

⏱ approximately 12 hrs

Candied Chestnuts

400G (14OZ) SWEET CHESTNUTS

225G (8OZ) SUGAR

8 TABLESPOONS WATER

FEW DROPS OF VANILLA ESSENCE

25G (1OZ) ICING OR CASTOR SUGAR

1. Peel the chestnuts and carefully remove the inner skins.
2. Put the first measure of sugar in a heavy-based saucepan, add the water and bring to a boil over a medium flame. Stir continually so that the sugar dissolves completely.
3. Add the chestnuts to the syrup, stir well and bring back to a boil. Now add the vanilla. Lower the heat and simmer until the chestnuts are tender, about 20 minutes.
4. Lift them from the syrup and drain well on kitchen towels. Roll the chestnuts in the second measure of sugar, place on greaseproof paper and leave to dry.
5. Candied chestnuts can be served as a sweet or with coffee at the end of the meal.

Serves 4-8

⏱ 45 mins

Ripe and delectable

Variation

For a quick, delightful and very unusual dessert, put four or five chestnuts in each serving dish and top with Nut Cream (see page 95).

PÂTÉS

Rich and Famous Pâté

225G (8OZ) COOKED CHICK PEAS
ZEST AND JUICE OF 1 ORANGE
55G (2OZ) BUTTER OR
MARGARINE
55G (2OZ) CHEDDAR CHEESE, GRATED

1 TEASPOON FINELY CRUSHED BLACK PEPPER OR
PIMENTO SEEDS (SWEET OR CHILLI PEPPER
SEEDS)
PINCH OF GROUND NUTMEG
60ML (2 FL OZ) PORT

Makes approximately
425ml (¾ pint)

⏱ 20 mins, plus
chilling time

1.   Mash the chick peas in a bowl or mortar and work in the orange zest and juice.

2.   Melt the butter in a small saucepan, remove from the heat and stir in the cheese, chick-pea mixture, pepper and nutmeg. When roughly mixed, add the port and stir well.

3.   Press into a serving dish and leave to cool. Chill if desired. Serve with crackers or dry toast.

Rosy Lentil Pâté

225G (8OZ) RED LENTILS, WASHED
AND DRAINED
570ML (1 PINT) WATER
1 TABLESPOON SOY SAUCE
2 TABLESPOONS OIL

3 CLOVES GARLIC, FINELY CHOPPED
2 TABLESPOONS GRATED FRESH GINGER
½ TEASPOON CHILLI POWDER
1 LARGE RED PEPPER, FINELY CHOPPED
100G (4OZ) ROLLED OATS OR RICE FLAKES

Makes approximately
1 litre (2 pints)

⏱ 45 mins, plus
cooling time

Tasty and easy

1.   Turn the lentils into a large saucepan with the water and place over a medium heat. Bring to the boil then reduce the heat and cover the pan, but stir frequently for the next 5 minutes to avoid boiling over. Leave the lentils to simmer for about 20 minutes, stirring occasionally, until they lose their form.

2.   Remove from the heat and stir in the soy sauce.

3.   Heat the oil in a small pan and sauté the garlic, ginger and chilli powder for about 3 minutes over a low to medium heat. Add the

finely chopped red pepper and continue to sauté a further 3-5 minutes, stirring often.

4. Now add the sauté and the rolled oats to the lentils and stir well. Turn into a lightly oiled soufflé dish, press firmly into place and leave to cool.

5. Chill the pâté in the refrigerator and garnish with pickled pimentos before serving with crackers or dry toast.

Curried Hazelnut Pâté

4 TABLESPOONS OIL	100G (4OZ) MUSHROOMS, FINELY CHOPPED
1 SMALL ONION, FINELY CHOPPED	100G (4OZ) GROUND HAZELNUTS
2 TEASPOONS CURRY POWDER	LEMON TWISTS TO GARNISH

1. Heat the oil in a saucepan and sauté the onion until it begins to colour. Stir in the curry powder and cook a minute longer. Add the finely chopped mushrooms and sauté for about 5 minutes, until they begin to release their juices.

2. Remove the pan from the heat and stir in the hazelnuts, mixing thoroughly.

3. Transfer to a small dish, smooth the top and set aside to cool.

4. Cover and chill before serving with a garnish of lemon twists.

Serves 4

15 mins, plus chilling time

Sunflower and Pepper Pâté

140G (5OZ) SUNFLOWER SEEDS	3 CLOVES GARLIC, FINELY CHOPPED
55G (2OZ) BUTTER OR MARGARINE	½ TEASPOON FRESHLY GROUND BLACK PEPPER
1 RED PEPPER, FINELY CHOPPED	½ TEASPOON DRIED OREGANO

1. Roast the sunflower seeds in a dry frying pan over a low heat, stirring frequently. When they begin to pop and turn a golden colour, set them aside to cool. Grind the sunflower seeds to a powder once cooled.

2. Melt the butter in a saucepan and sauté the chopped red

Serves 4

20 mins, plus chilling time

pepper and garlic, about 5 minutes over a medium heat. Add the black pepper and stir a further 1 minute.

3. Remove from the heat and stir in the ground seeds and oregano until all the ingredients are well blended.

4. Spoon the mixture into a small serving dish, smooth the top, cover with greaseproof paper and chill until needed. Serve with a garnish of paprika or whole sunflower seeds.

Mushroom and Cashew Pâté

450G (1LB) MUSHROOMS, CLEANED

100G (4OZ) CASHEW NUTS

2 TABLESPOONS OIL

1 SMALL ONION, VERY FINELY CHOPPED

1 TEASPOON FRESHLY GROUND BLACK PEPPER

1 TABLESPOON FINELY CHOPPED FRESH SAGE OR 1 TEASPOON DRIED SAGE

1 TABLESPOON TOMATO PURÉE

1 TABLESPOON SOY SAUCE

25-55G (1-2OZ) DRIED BREADCRUMBS

1 TABLESPOON CASHEW-NUT BUTTER OR BUTTER

Makes approximately 570ml (1 pint)

25 mins, plus chilling time

1. Pick over and chop the mushrooms and cashew nuts – the mushrooms coarsely chopped, the nuts more finely so.

2. Heat the oil in a large frying pan and sauté the onion until clear and tender. Add the pepper and stir for 1 minute then add the mushrooms and cashews. Stir over a low to medium heat for about 7 minutes, until the mushrooms release their juices and become quite tender.

3. Add the sage and stir for a further 2 minutes then add the tomato purée, soy sauce and some of the breadcrumbs.

4. Remove from the heat and continue stirring until all the juices are absorbed. Adjust by adding more breadcrumbs or a little water or lemon juice if necessary.

5. After 5 minutes, ensure the mixture is quite firm, then press it into a lightly oiled soufflé dish. Cover the surface of the pâté with a thin coating of cashew-nut butter or butter and leave in the fridge to chill.

6. Garnish with fresh sage leaves and green or black peppercorns before serving with crackers or dry toast.

Flageolet Dip

225G (8OZ) FLAGEOLETS, SOAKED
    OVERNIGHT
100G (4OZ) DAIRY OR TOFU MAYONNAISE
JUICE OF ½ LEMON

½ TEASPOON FRESHLY GROUND BLACK PEPPER
¼ TEASPOON SALT
1 TABLESPOON EACH OF FINELY CHOPPED
    FRESH MINT AND CHIVES

1. Drain and rinse the soaked beans and turn into a pan with fresh water. Bring to the boil over a high flame, boil for 10 minutes, then lower the heat, cover the pan, and simmer for 45 minutes, until the beans are soft.

2. Drain well. Mash or purée the beans, then gradually stir in the other ingredients.

3. Chill briefly – about 30 minutes – and serve with crudités, crackers or pitta.

Tip

Quark, soured cream or plain yogurt may be used instead of mayonnaise in this recipe.

Serves 4

1 hr 30 mins, plus soaking and chilling time

Eat it, don't whip it

SAVOURY PASTRIES

Quorn and Beansprout Parcels

2 TABLESPOONS OIL

2 SPRING ONIONS, FINELY CHOPPED

1 LARGE CARROT, GRATED

1 TEASPOON GROUND GINGER

100G (4OZ) QUORN, COARSELY
CHOPPED

25G (1OZ) SUNFLOWER SEEDS

FRESHLY GROUND BLACK PEPPER, TO TASTE

SOY SAUCE, TO TASTE

85G (3OZ) BEANSPROUTS

8 SHEETS FILO PASTRY

55G (2OZ) BUTTER OR OIL

Serves 4

45 mins

1. Preheat the oven to 200°C/400°F/Gas Mark 6.
2. Heat the oil in a pan over a medium flame and sauté the onion and carrot for 5 minutes. Add the ginger and stir for 1 minute longer. Mix in the Quorn and sunflower seeds and stir frequently until the carrots are tender and the Quorn is lightly coloured.
3. Add the pepper and soy sauce to taste then cover the sauté with the beansprouts and leave over a low flame.
4. Cut each sheet of pastry in half to make squares. Brush one with butter or oil, top with a second sheet and brush that also. Continue in this way until you have four piles of four sheets.
5. Drop a spoonful or two of the Quorn mixture into the centre of each square, and fold in the sides of the pastry to make a packet. Cut off any excess pastry. Dampen the edges with water and press gently to seal.
6. Transfer the packets to a lightly oiled baking sheet, join-side down, and brush again with butter or oil. Bake for 20 minutes or until lightly browned.
7. Serve hot or cold as a snack or starter or as part of a rice and stir-fry meal.

Variation

Replace the Quorn with cubes of tofu or whole cashew nuts. To add extra colour and texture to the packets, brush them lightly with the oil and then sprinkle with sesame seeds.

Walnut, Pepper and Celery Samosas

OIL

1 SMALL ONION, THINLY SLICED

1 SMALL RED PEPPER, FINELY CHOPPED

1 LARGE STICK CELERY, FINELY CHOPPED

1 TEASPOON CURRY POWDER, OR TO TASTE

55G (2OZ) SHELLED PEAS

55G (2OZ) WALNUTS, BROKEN OR CHOPPED

8 SHEETS FILO PASTRY

55G (2OZ) MELTED BUTTER OR OIL

1. Heat 2 tablespoons oil in a large pan over a medium flame and sauté the onion, pepper and celery for 5-7 minutes, stirring frequently. Add the curry powder and sauté for a further 3 minutes.

2. Add the peas and the walnuts to the pan and stir well. Cover the pan and remove from the heat.

3. Cut each sheet of pastry in half along its length. Lay one strip on a board and brush with butter or oil. Drop a spoonful of the mixture close to one end, then fold the pastry over it, forming a triangle. Carefully lift the parcel and fold it over on to the strip of pastry, keeping the triangle shape.

4. Continue in this way until you reach the end of the strip of pastry. Dampen the edge with water and gently press to seal. Use the remaining ingredients in the same way to make sixteen small samosas.

5. Place the samosas into a pan of hot oil, one by one, and deep-fry for a few minutes until crisp and brown. Drain well on kitchen towel before serving.

6. Serve as a light snack with a salad or as an accompaniment to curry.

Serves 4-8

40 mins

Apple and Cheese Bundles

8 SHEETS FILO PASTRY

450G (1LB) SWEET APPLES, PEELED, CORED AND GRATED

JUICE OF 1/2 LEMON

180G (6OZ) EDAM CHEESE, GRATED

85G (3OZ) SULTANAS

1 TEASPOON GROUND CINNAMON

1/2 TEASPOON GROUND NUTMEG

55G (2OZ) MELTED BUTTER OR OIL

Serves 4

⏱ 45 mins

I love these! Fun, fancy and filling

1. Preheat the oven to 180°C/350°F/Gas Mark 4. Unfold the pastry and carefully peel off the top sheet. Cover the remainder with a very lightly dampened cloth.

2. Put the apple into a bowl, and stir in the lemon juice. Mix in the cheese, sultanas and spices.

3. Lay a sheet of pastry on a lightly floured board or worktop. Brush the surface with melted butter or oil, making sure you go right to the edges. Lay a second sheet on top of the first, brush this with the butter or oil, then fold in half to make a square. Brush the top with more butter or oil. Drop a quarter of the apple mix into the centre.

4. Gather the corners up to make a bundle and pinch the pastry together to form a neck. For a firmer shape, tie a piece of string around the top of each bundle and fold back the corners to make a flounce; trim off any excess. Make three more bundles in this way.

5. Transfer to a lightly oiled baking sheet and bake for 20 minutes, until golden and crisp. Cut and remove the string before serving.

6. Garnish the bundles with a pinch of lemon zest.

Garlic Mushroom Strudel

25G (1OZ) BUTTER OR MARGARINE

2 CLOVES GARLIC, CRUSHED

340G (12OZ) MUSHROOMS, CHOPPED

2 TABLESPOONS CHOPPED FRESH CHIVES

FRESHLY GROUND BLACK PEPPER, TO TASTE

100G (4OZ) FROMAGE FRAIS

6 SHEETS FILO PASTRY

60G (2 FL OZ) MELTED BUTTER OR OIL

2 MEDIUM TOMATOES, SLICED

CHIVES TO GARNISH

1. Preheat the oven to 190°C/375°F/Gas Mark 5.
2. Melt the butter over a medium flame and stir in the garlic and mushrooms. Sauté gently for 5 minutes, stirring often. Lift the garlic and mushrooms from the pan. Stir the chives, pepper and fromage frais together with the mushrooms in a bowl.
3. Lay one sheet of the pastry on a board and brush lightly with the melted butter or oil. Repeat with the remaining five sheets, piling them on top of each other. Spread the mushroom mixture evenly across the top sheet, leaving a space along the edges.
4. Fold in the sides to hold the filling in place, then carefully roll up the pastry so that it resembles a Swiss roll. Place join-side down on a lightly oiled baking sheet, brush with melted butter or oil and bake for 20-30 minutes, until golden.
5. Serve cut into thick slices with a garnish of sliced tomato and strands of chive.

Serves 4

55 mins

Also great with puff pastry – and don't skimp on the garlic or chives.

Simple Eggless Pancakes

100G (4OZ) PLAIN FLOUR

55G (2OZ) SOYA FLOUR

1 TEASPOON BAKING POWDER

285ML (½ PINT) WATER

1-3 TABLESPOONS OIL

1. Sieve the flours and baking powder together in a mixing bowl, then gradually stir in the water. Beat for a few minutes, cover and leave in the fridge for at least 30 minutes.
2. Whisk the batter again before using: it should be the consistency of single cream, so add a drop more water if it is too thick.
3. Brush a little oil on to a small heavy-based pan or griddle and

Serves 4-8

45 mins

place over a medium heat. Ladle in a little batter, tilting the pan to spread it into a paper-thin pancake.

4.   Cook for a minute or two, shaking the pan occasionally to prevent sticking. Use a spatula to turn the pancake, then cook the other side, another 1-2 minutes.

5.   Repeat until the batter is used up, placing cooked pancakes on a covered plate over a pan of hot water to keep them warm.

Variations

1.   Sprinkle each pancake lightly with castor or icing sugar, roll up, and serve at once with a drizzle of lemon juice.

2.   Also ideal with savoury fillings such as ratatouille, scrambled tofu, stir-fried beansprouts or lightly steamed spinach.

Asparagus Filo Pie

675G (1½ LB) ASPARAGUS SPEARS
140G (5OZ) CURD OR RICOTTA CHEESE
3 TABLESPOONS GREEK YOGURT OR FROMAGE FRAIS
1 EGG, BEATEN
PINCH OF SALT

¼ TEASPOON FRESHLY GROUND BLACK PEPPER
OLIVE OIL
20 SHEETS FILO PASTRY
A LITTLE MILK, FOR GLAZING
1 TABLESPOON SESAME SEEDS

Serves 4-6

55 mins

1.   Preheat the oven to 200°C/400°F/Gas Mark 6.

2.   Steam the asparagus spears, about 15 minutes. Cut them into chunks, discarding any fibrous ends, and place in a mixing bowl with the cheese, yogurt, beaten egg and seasoning.

3.   Pour a little oil on to a baking tray. Lay out the first two filo sheets in a shallow oven dish, oil the top surface and lay out two more, continuing for ten sheets.

4.   Spread the asparagus mixture over the filo to within 1cm (½ inch) of the edges. Place two sheets of filo over the mixture, oil them, then continue with two more until you have used ten sheets. Brush the top of the pastry with a little milk and scatter with sesame seeds.

5. Bake for 25-30 minutes, until golden brown and crunchy. Leave to rest in the tray for 5 minutes before slicing and serving.

Crêpes Provençal

1 x recipe Eggless Pancakes (see page 73)
VEGETABLE OIL
25G (1OZ) BUTTER OR MARGARINE, MELTED
25G (1OZ) BREADCRUMBS
FRESH PARSLEY TO GARNISH

For the filling:
1 SMALL AUBERGINE
SALT
3 TABLESPOONS OIL
1 ONION, THINLY SLICED

2 COURGETTES, SLICED
225G (8OZ) TOMATOES, CHOPPED
2 TABLESPOONS TOMATO PURÉE
3-5 CLOVES GARLIC, CRUSHED
3 TABLESPOONS FINELY CHOPPED FRESH PARSLEY
1 TEASPOON DRIED MARJORAM
1 TEASPOON FRESHLY GROUND BLACK PEPPER
VEGETABLE OIL
25G (1OZ) BUTTER OR MARGARINE, MELTED
25G (1OZ) BREADCRUMBS
FRESH PARSLEY TO GARNISH

1. Prepare the pancake recipe and refrigerate the batter for at least 30 minutes.
2. Cut the aubergine into thick slices and sprinkle with salt. Set aside for 15 minutes, then rinse with cold water and pat dry. Dice the aubergine.
3. Heat the oil in a large saucepan and sauté the onion, aubergine and courgette until tender, about 7 minutes. Add the remaining filling ingredients to the sauté and stir well. Cover and simmer 5 minutes then remove from the heat.
4. To make the crêpes whisk the batter again and, if it has thickened, add a drop more water to make it the consistency of single cream. Heat a little oil in a heavy-based pan then pour in a small ladleful of batter. Tip the pan to spread it evenly and cook until the crêpe begins to colour underneath. Turn with a spatula and quickly cook the other side – about 3 minutes in total. Keep cooked crêpes on a warm plate.
5. Fill each crêpe with some of the vegetable mixture, roll up the crêpes and place them side by side in a shallow, ovenproof dish.
6. Brush the surface of the crêpes with a little butter, sprinkle with

Serves 4

55 mins, plus standing time for the batter

the breadcrumbs and set under a medium-hot grill for 3 minutes to crisp the crumbs. Garnish generously with fresh parsley.

Variation

Add 55g (2oz) pine nuts to the filling after removing it from the heat.

Spiced Wellingtons

340G (12OZ) PUFF PASTRY

1 TABLESPOON OIL

3-5 CLOVES GARLIC, FINELY CHOPPED

1 MEDIUM ONION, FINELY CHOPPED

1 TEASPOON CUMIN SEEDS

1 TEASPOON GROUND CORIANDER

1/2 TEASPOON FRESHLY GROUND BLACK PEPPER

225G (8OZ) QUORN OR TVP MINCE

180ML (6 FL OZ) VEGETABLE STOCK
(SEE PAGE 87) OR WATER

450G (1LB) POTATOES, PEELED, QUARTERED
AND STEAMED

3 MEDIUM CARROTS, PEELED AND STEAMED

2 TABLESPOONS FINELY CHOPPED FRESH
PARSLEY

Makes 8-12
wellingtons

🕐 1 hr

TVP is texturised vegetable protein – an unimaginative name for a great product!

1. Preheat the oven to 180°C/350°F/Gas Mark 4.

2. Roll the pastry to a thickness of 5mm (¼ inch) and cut into eight to twelve 15cm (6 inch) squares. Heat the oil in a saucepan over a medium flame and sauté the garlic and onion until clear and tender, about 3 minutes. Add the spices and stir a further 1 minute. Add the Quorn or TVP and stir well. Pour in the stock and simmer for about 5 minutes, stirring occasionally.

4. Meanwhile, steam the potatoes and carrots and, when they have cooked, roughly mash them into the sauté. Remove the pan from the heat and stir in the parsley.

5. Place large spoonfuls of this mixture in the centre of each pastry square. Fold the tips of the squares up over the filling and pinch the edges together to form a package.

6. Place the wellingtons on a baking tray and bake for 30 minutes, until crisp and golden. Serve hot or cold.

Spiced Pumpkin Bastella

225G (8OZ) PUFF PASTRY

2 TABLESPOONS OIL

4 MEDIUM ONIONS, FINELY CHOPPED

½ TEASPOON FRESHLY GROUND BLACK PEPPER

1 TEASPOON GROUND CINNAMON

675G (1½ LB) PUMPKIN, PEELED AND CUBED

4 TABLESPOONS CRANBERRY SAUCE OR JAM

1. Preheat the oven to 180°C/350°F/Gas Mark 4.

2. Roll the pastry to 5mm (¼ inch) thickness and cut into eight rounds.

3. Heat the oil in a large frying pan and sauté the onions over a low flame until they begin to caramelise (they will become slightly sticky and a rich golden colour; allow about 20 minutes for this stage). Add the spices and stir a further 2 minutes.

4. Meanwhile, steam the pumpkin cubes until they are just tender, slightly undercooked. Turn them into the finished sauté and roughly mash the mixture together.

5. Place a dollop of the mixture in the centre of each round of pastry, dampen the edges and fold the pastry up or over to make an envelope. Seal the edges and place the bastella on a baking tray.

6. Bake for 30 minutes, until crisp and golden. Serve hot or cold with a spoonful of the cranberry sauce to dip into.

Makes 8 bastella

 1 hr 15 mins

Roulade of Spinach

675G (1½ LB) SPINACH LEAVES,
    WASHED AND STALKS REMOVED
1 MEDIUM ONION, FINELY CHOPPED
25G (1OZ) BUTTER OR MARGARINE
25G (1OZ) PLAIN FLOUR
200ML (7 FL OZ) MILK
½ TEASPOON GROUND NUTMEG

¼ TEASPOON FRESHLY GROUND BLACK PEPPER
100G (4OZ) BLUE CHEESE (GORGONZOLA OR
    ROQUEFORT)
340G (12OZ) PUFF PASTRY
1 EGG, BEATEN
SESAME SEEDS FOR GARNISH

Serves 4-6

🕐 1 hr 15 mins

Superb results without much effort

1. Preheat the oven to 200°C/400°F/Gas Mark 6.
2. Layer the spinach and chopped onion in a large saucepan and cook over a gentle heat, with no added water, until the spinach is one-third of its original bulk, about 5 minutes. Drain away the liquid, roughly chop the leaves with the edges of a wooden spoon and place the spinach and onion in a mixing bowl.
3. Melt the butter in a small saucepan and sprinkle the flour over it. Stir over a medium flame for 2 minutes while it thickens to a paste, or roux. Add the milk a little at a time, stirring after each addition, then stir in the nutmeg and black pepper. Crumble in the cheese and stir until the sauce is fairly smooth.
4. Fold the cheese sauce into the spinach to make a thick, chunky, green paste.
5. Roll out the pastry to form a 30 x 20cm (12 x 8 inch) rectangle. Spread the paste over the pastry, leaving 1cm (½ inch) clear around the edges. Roll up as you would a Swiss roll and place on a lightly buttered baking tray with the join underneath. Dampen the edges and fold them inwards.
6. Brush the top of the roulade with beaten egg and sprinkle with sesame seeds. Bake for about 40 minutes, until puffed up and golden brown.
7. Leave to stand for 5 minutes before slicing.

SOUPS

*H*aricot Bean Soup

2 TABLESPOONS OLIVE OIL

3 CLOVES GARLIC, FINELY CHOPPED

1 ONION, THINLY SLICED

1 TEASPOON EACH DRIED SAGE, ROSEMARY
AND CELERY SALT

3 CARROTS, DICED

3 SMALL TURNIPS, DICED

3 STICKS CELERY, FINELY CHOPPED

2 MEDIUM POTATOES, PEELED AND CHOPPED

100G (4OZ) HARICOT BEANS, SOAKED
OVERNIGHT

2 LITRES (4 PINTS) VEGETABLE STOCK
(SEE PAGE 87) OR WATER

PINCH OF SALT

1/2 TEASPOON FRESHLY GROUND BLACK PEPPER

1.   Heat the oil in a large saucepan. Add the garlic and onion and sauté over a medium flame until clear and tender, about 5 minutes. Add the herbs, stir for 1 minute longer, then add all the chopped vegetables.

2.   Cover the pan and cook for 7-10 minutes, stirring two or three times in that period. The vegetables will begin to release their juices.

3.   Drain and rinse the soaked beans and add them to the vegetables along with the vegetable stock and seasoning. Bring to the boil, boil hard for 10 minutes, then reduce the heat and simmer, covered, for 1 hour.

4.   Test the beans are very tender and serve hot with lots of fresh bread.

Serves 4-8

🕐 1 hr 30 mins,
plus soaking
time

Mulligatawny Soup

2 MEDIUM CARROTS, PEELED
AND DICED

1 LARGE POTATO, PEELED AND
DICED

1 LARGE ONION, FINELY CHOPPED

1 GREEN PEPPER, DICED

1 COOKING APPLE, DICED

2 TABLESPOONS OIL

15G (½ OZ) PLAIN FLOUR

2 TEASPOONS CURRY POWDER

55G (2OZ) SULTANAS

850ML (1½ PINTS) VEGETABLE STOCK
(SEE PAGE 87) OR WATER

55G (2OZ) RED LENTILS

SALT AND FRESHLY GROUND BLACK PEPPER,
TO TASTE

Serves 4

 45 mins

1.   Prepare the vegetables and apple, putting a little pepper and apple to one side.

2.   Heat the oil in a large frying pan and sauté the vegetables for 7-9 minutes over a medium heat, stirring often.

3.   Mix together the flour and curry powder and sprinkle over the sauté. Stir well and cook a minute or two more. Add the sultanas, stock and lentils.

4.   Bring to a boil, cover the pan and reduce the heat; simmer about 20 minutes, until the vegetables are just tender and the lentils have lost their form.

5.   Season to taste and serve hot with a garnish of the reserved diced pepper and apple.

Variation

Liquidise in a blender, return the soup to the saucepan and reheat gently. Garnish with croûtons.

Pumpkin Soup

2 TABLESPOONS OIL

1 SMALL ONION, FINELY CHOPPED

675G (1½ LB) FRESH PUMPKIN, PEELED AND CUBED

850ML (1½ PINTS) VEGETABLE STOCK (SEE PAGE 87)

½ TEASPOON RAW CANE SUGAR

¼ TEASPOON GROUND CLOVES

285ML (½ PINT) MILK

½ TEASPOON FRESHLY GROUND BLACK PEPPER

1.   Heat the oil in a large saucepan over a medium flame and sauté the onion until just golden. Add the pumpkin and continue to sauté a further 5 minutes. Add the stock, sugar, cloves and milk.

2.   Bring to a low boil, cover the pan and reduce the heat. Simmer 12-15 minutes, until the pumpkin is cooked.

3.   Turn the mixture through a sieve or hand mouli and return the purée to the pan. Reheat gently and season with pepper.

4.   Serve at once in warmed bowls, with a garnish of croûtons or twist of orange peel.

Serves 4

45 mins

Make this as spicy as you like

Variation

Add 1 tablespoon dry sherry to each bowlful of soup just before serving. A dollop of cream or plain yogurt on each serving sets off the flavour and texture of this soup wonderfully.

Celery and Stilton Soup

2 TABLESPOONS OIL

1 MEDIUM HEAD CELERY, THINLY
SLICED

1 MEDIUM ONION, THINLY SLICED

25G (1OZ) PLAIN FLOUR

850ML (1½ PINTS) VEGETABLE STOCK
(SEE PAGE 87)

55G (2OZ) STILTON (OR OTHER BLUE CHEESE),
CRUMBLED

½ TEASPOON FRESHLY GROUND BLACK PEPPER

1 TABLESPOON FINELY CHOPPED FRESH PARSLEY

CROÛTONS TO GARNISH

Serves 4

45 mins

1. Heat the oil in a saucepan over a medium flame and sauté the celery and onion until tender, about 7 minutes. Sprinkle the flour over the sauté and stir for 1 minute longer.

2. Add the vegetable stock, a little at a time, stirring after each addition. Bring the soup to the boil, reduce the heat, cover the pan and simmer for about 20 minutes.

3. If you like a smooth soup, liquidise it at this stage.

4. Remove the soup from the heat and whisk in the cheese. Add the pepper and parsley and serve hot with a garnish of croûtons.

Spiced Lentil Soup

180G (6OZ) BROWN (CONTINENTAL)
LENTILS, SOAKED OVERNIGHT

2 TABLESPOONS OIL

1 LARGE ONION, THINLY SLICED

1 RED PEPPER, THINLY SLICED

1-2 TABLESPOONS MILD OR HOT CURRY PASTE
(TO TASTE)

JUICE OF 1 LEMON

850ML (1½ PINTS) VEGETABLE STOCK
(SEE PAGE 87) OR WATER

100G (4OZ) CREAMED COCONUT, GRATED

Serves 4-8

45 mins, plus
soaking
overnight

1. Drain and rinse the lentils, turn into a large saucepan and just cover with fresh water. Bring the liquid to a boil over a medium flame then reduce the heat and simmer the lentils until they begin to soften.

2. In a separate pan, heat the oil over a medium flame and sauté the onion and pepper for 5 minutes, stirring often.

3. Add the curry paste and juice of the lemon and stir a further 2

minutes. Add the stock and stir as it comes to a simmer. When the stock is hot, stir in the coconut and continue heating gently until it has dissolved.

4. Add the drained lentils and cook in the soup until they are tender.

5. Adjust the seasoning if necessary and serve hot.

*B*orscht

3 MEDIUM RAW BEETROOTS, FINELY
   GRATED
1 ONION, THINLY SLICED
¼ SMALL RED CABBAGE, FINELY GRATED
850ML (1½ PINTS) VEGETABLE STOCK
   (SEE PAGE 87)
1 TABLESPOON LEMON JUICE

1 TEASPOON RAW CANE SUGER
¼ TEASPOON FRESHLY GROUND BLACK PEPPER
1 TABLESPOON EACH FINELY CHOPPED FRESH
   PARSLEY AND CHIVES
140ML (¼ PINT) SOURED CREAM OR PLAIN
   YOGURT

1. Turn the beetroot, onion, cabbage and vegetable stock into a saucepan. Bring to the boil over a medium flame, then lower the heat and simmer, uncovered, for 20 minutes.

2. Add the lemon juice, sugar and seasoning as necessary.

3. Borscht can be blended to make a smooth soup, or served as it is. It can also be served either chilled or piping hot. Sprinkle with parsley and chives for extra flavour.

4. Traditionally a swirl of soured cream or yogurt is added to each bowl just before serving.

Serves 4-6

⏱ 45 mins

To reach the peak of pleasure eat this with Yogurt Soda Bread

Red Pepper Soup

2 TABLESPOONS OIL

3 CLOVES GARLIC, FINELY CHOPPED

1 ONION, THINLY SLICED

2 SMALL RED PEPPERS, VERY THINLY SLICED

1 SMALL CAULIFLOWER, COARSELY CHOPPED

1 x 400G (14OZ) TIN TOMATOES

½ CUCUMBER, PEELED AND CHOPPED

850ML (1½ PINTS) VEGETABLE STOCK
 (SEE PAGE 87)

½ TEASPOON DRY MUSTARD

½ TEASPOON DRIED BASIL

½ TEASPOON FRESHLY GROUND BLACK PEPPER

FRESH BASIL LEAVES TO GARNISH

Serves 4-6

40 mins

1. Heat the oil in a deep saucepan over a medium flame, and sauté the garlic and onion until clear and tender, about 5 minutes. Add the red pepper and continue to sauté a further 3 minutes.

2. Stir in the cauliflower, broken tomatoes and cucumber pieces and leave to cook for 5 minutes, stirring once or twice in that time.

3. Add the stock, mustard, basil and black pepper and bring to a low boil. Cover the pan, reduce the heat and simmer for 12-15 minutes, until the vegetables are tender.

4. Serve hot with a garnish of basil leaves.

Variation

You can liquidise this soup if you prefer a smooth texture, in which case you will need to reheat it before serving.

Green Vichyssoise

2 BUNCHES WATERCRESS

25G (1OZ) BUTTER OR MARGARINE

1 SMALL ONION, FINELY CHOPPED

710ML (1¼ PINTS) VEGETABLE STOCK
 (SEE PAGE 87)

¼ TEASPOON FRESHLY GROUND BLACK PEPPER

340G (12OZ) POTATOES, PEELED AND DICED

285ML (½ PINT) MILK

60ML (2 FL OZ) DOUBLE CREAM

Serves 4-6

30 mins, plus
chilling time

1. Wash and trim the watercress; put a few of the leaves to one side.

2. Melt the butter in a saucepan and sauté the onion until clear and tender, about 5 minutes.

3.   Add the stock, pepper and potatoes to the pan. Stir well and bring to a low boil. Cover and simmer 10 minutes, until the potatoes are tender.

4.   Add the chopped watercress and remove the pan from the heat. Stir in the milk and leave the soup to cool in the pan.

5.   Turn the soup into a tureen and chill in the refrigerator. Serve cold with a spoonful of cream and a garnish of reserved watercress leaves.

Variation

As with many soups, you may prefer to turn this through a sieve or hand mouli for a smooth-textured soup.

Chilled Peanut Soup

2 TABLESPOONS VEGETABLE OIL
1 SMALL ONION, FINELY CHOPPED
1 CARROT, FINELY CHOPPED
1 STICK CELERY, FINELY CHOPPED
1 TEASPOON CURRY POWDER
55G (2OZ) PEANUT BUTTER

570ML (1 PINT) VEGETABLE STOCK
  (SEE PAGE 87)
285ML (½ PINT) MILK
½ TEASPOON FRESHLY GROUND BLACK PEPPER
CELERY LEAVES TO GARNISH

1.   Heat the oil in a large pan over a medium heat and sauté the onion, carrot and celery for 5-7 minutes, stirring often. Add the curry powder and peanut butter and cook 2-3 minutes more.

2.   Stir in the vegetable stock and milk and bring to a low boil. Cover the pan, reduce the heat and simmer the vegetables for 10 minutes.

3.   Stir in the black pepper and remove the soup from the heat.

4.   Leave to cool in the pan, then pour into a tureen and chill the soup in the refrigerator.

5.   Pour into bowls and garnish with a sprinkling of chopped celery leaves.

Serves 4-6

30 mins, plus chilling time

Autumn Soup in Baked Pumpkin Tureen

1 WHOLE PUMPKIN, ABOUT 23CM (9 INCHES) IN DIAMETER

1 TABLESPOON GRATED FRESH GINGER

5 CLOVES GARLIC, CRUSHED

2 TABLESPOONS BUTTER OR MARGARINE

2 TABLESPOONS CHOPPED FRESH PARSLEY

1 TEASPOON DRIED THYME

2 TABLESPOONS OIL

2 MEDIUM ONIONS, THINLY SLICED

1 TEASPOON FRESHLY GROUND BLACK PEPPER

1 MEDIUM SWEDE, PEELED AND CHOPPED

2 PARSNIPS, PEELED AND CHOPPED

¼ WHITE CABBAGE, SHREDDED

450G (1LB) GREEN BEANS, TRIMMED AND SLICED

1 LITRE (2 PINTS) VEGETABLE STOCK (SEE PAGE 87) OR WATER

4 MEDIUM TOMATOES, COARSELY CHOPPED

Serves 4-8

🕐 1 hr 15 mins

A great one for the kids at Halloween

1. Slice a lid, at least 5cm (2 inches) deep, off the pumpkin. Scoop out the seed pulp and discard (or dry the seeds for planting next year). Carefully cut and scrape the stringy pumpkin flesh out of the shell. Check the shell to make certain it is still intact – without any holes except the top opening. Prick the inside of the pumpkin many times with a fork.

2. Mix the ginger, garlic, butter, parsley and thyme and spread the mixture around the inside of the pumpkin: it will adhere especially well where the pumpkin has been pricked.

3. Heat the oil in a saucepan and sauté the onion slices until clear and tender, about 7 minutes. Add the black pepper and stir a further 1 minute. Add the evenly chopped swede and parsnip and stir occasionally over a medium heat while the vegetables sauté.

4. When they begin to stick, add the cabbage, green beans and 140ml (¼ pint) of the stock. Stir well and cook for 5 minutes. Add the remaining stock.

5. Bring the soup to a simmer, cover the pan and simmer gently for 15 minutes.

6. Meanwhile, preheat the oven to 180°C/350°F/Gas Mark 4. Place the prepared pumpkin shell – with its lid in place – on a lightly oiled flan dish and bake for 20 minutes.

7. Pour the prepared soup into the pumpkin shell and continue baking for 15 minutes. Remove from the oven and serve the pumpkin on the flan dish as soon as possible, although the pumpkin and soup will keep their heat quite well. When serving the soup, gently scrape the lining of the pumpkin to include some of the herb and ginger mixture.

Vegetable Stock

2 TABLESPOONS BUTTER OR MARGARINE

1 MEDIUM ONION, SLICED

1 TEASPOON FRESHLY GROUND BLACK PEPPER

1 x 7.5CM (3 INCH) CINNAMON STICK

450-1350G (1-3LB) VEGETABLE SCRAPS
(SUCH AS ONION AND GARLIC SKINS, ENDS
OF CARROT, PARSNIP OR BROCCOLI, OUTER
LEAVES OF LETTUCE OR CABBAGE), CLEANED
AND COARSELY CHOPPED

100-225G (4-8OZ) WHOLE GRAIN (SUCH AS
RICE, BARLEY OR MIXTURE), WASHED AND
DRAINED

1-3 LITRES (2-6 PINTS) WATER

A HANDFUL OF FRESH HERB IF AVAILABLE OR
1 TABLESPOON DRIED HERB

1. Melt the butter in a very large saucepan and sauté the onion until clear and tender. Add the pepper and cinnamon and stir a further 1 minute then add all the cleaned and chopped vegetable pieces and the grain.

2. Pour over the water (the vegetables should be well covered) and bring to the boil. Cover the pan, reduce the heat and simmer for 20 minutes. Add the herb and simmer a further 20 minutes, topping up the water if necessary.

3. Remove from the heat and allow to cool, covered, then strain the vegetables and grain from the broth. Discard the vegetables and use the broth as a stock for other dishes.

4. You may freeze measured portions of stock for easy use another day.

5. Although you can make vegetable stock using 'whole' ingredients, this is just as colourful and tasty and is, to me, the essence of creative and economical use of scraps, leftovers and less-than-perfect food items.

Makes 1-3 litres
(2-6 pints)

 1 hr

TEN REASONS WHY FOOD IS BETTER THAN SEX

1   You can try a new recipe every day without worrying about being unfaithful to your present cookbook.

2   Vegetables, unlike males, never complain about washing.

3   You sometimes get a 'thank-you' after cooking a meal.

4   Letting the milk boil over won't get you pregnant.

5   Men are used to giving microwave ovens a few seconds to warm up.

6   A cucumber never feels inadequate when it sees a man.

7   Most men can manage to eat three times a day or more.

8   After a good meal you can make love; but after making love all you get is a cigarette.

9   A good meal can sometimes last longer than 12 minutes (and you never have to fake a culinary climax).

10 Food is fattening: sex isn't. OK, there had to be *some* reason why sex is still popular . . .

Spiced Pumpkin Bastella (page 77)

Salade Niçoise (page 101)

There's something unashamedly sensual about the naked allure of raw food – it puts us back in touch with our animal instincts, and provides a huge boost of lifeforce. Of course, there's nothing worse than a limp lettuce or a flaccid fruit, so the freshness of your ingredients is absolutely crucial (for some tips, see 'Getting Fresh With Your Food' on page 219). Many of these recipes depend for their effect upon one strong idea – the first one, for example, is a striking combination of fruit and vegetable which is unique and highly creative. Once you've found that central idea, go with it as far as you can – the result will be simply stunning and highly memorable.

FRUITY SALADS

Carrot and Fruit Salad

3 MEDIUM CARROTS, PEELED AND
    GRATED
100G (4OZ) DATES, FINELY CHOPPED
100G (4OZ) SEEDLESS GRAPES
1 LARGE DESSERT APPLE, CHOPPED

JUICE OF 1 LEMON
1 TABLESPOON OLIVE OIL
1 BUNCH WATERCRESS, WASHED AND CHOPPED
55G (2OZ) ROASTED SUNFLOWER SEEDS

1. Toss all the ingredients together in a large salad bowl and serve at once.

Serves 4

⏱ 20 mins

Variations

1. Add 100g (4oz) finely cubed tofu or mozzarella for a more substantial salad.

For a coleslaw effect, serve this with a creamy dressing instead of the lemon juice and olive oil. Try mayonnaise on its own or diluted slightly with juice of ½ lemon. See also page 108 for some delicious dressings.

ruit Salad Mould

570ML (1 PINT) APPLE JUICE

1 x 3G (¹/₁₀ OZ) SACHET AGAR

3-4 RIPE KIWI FRUIT, PEELED AND SLICED

180G (6OZ) BLACK GRAPES, HALVED

2 MEDIUM BANANAS, SLICED

1 SMALL GRAPEFRUIT OR ORANGE, SEGMENTED AND CHOPPED

55G (2OZ) WALNUTS, CHOPPED

Serves 4-6

🕐 1 hr 30 mins, plus chilling time

1. Measure the juice into a saucepan and bring to a low boil. Whisk in the agar and set aside to cool briefly.

2. Rinse a medium ring mould with cold water. Arrange some of the kiwi slices across the base of the mould. Top with grapes then banana slices, some of the grapefruit segments and a light sprinkling of nuts. Pour in just enough fruit juice to cover the fruits, then stand the mould in ice water and leave to set, about 15 minutes.

3. Arrange more layers of kiwi, grapes, bananas, grapefruit and nuts and add more of the apple juice until all the ingredients are used up, finishing with liquid.

4. Chill in between each layer so that the ingredients stay in place, then place the mould in the fridge and leave at least 2 hours to set firm.

5. To serve, dip the outside of the mould quickly into hot water then invert it so that it slides on to the serving plate. This is delicious as a dessert but is most refreshing when served with a selection of salads such as coleslaw, watercress salad and potato salad.

Tropical Fruit Salad

1 RIPE MANGO, PEELED, STONED AND
  CUBED
1 STARFRUIT, TRIMMED AND SLICED
6 LYCHEES, PEELED, STONED AND SLICED
2 BANANAS, SLICED
2 SLICES PINEAPPLE, CUBED

225G (8OZ) RASPBERRIES OR REDCURRANTS
140ML (¼ PINT) ORANGE JUICE
2 TABLESPOONS KIRSCH (OPTIONAL)
¼ TEASPOON MIXED SWEET SPICE OR ALLSPICE
15G (¼ OZ) COCONUT FLAKES, ROASTED

1. Combine all the prepared fruit, mixing them gently so as not to damage them.
2. Stir together the orange juice, Kirsch and spice and pour over the mixed fruit. Cover and chill for an hour or two for the flavours to mingle.
3. Serve sprinkled with coconut flakes.

Serves 4

🕐 30 mins, plus chilling time

Melon Fruit Salad with Nut Cream

2 SMALL OGEN OR CANTALOUPE
  MELONS
  JUICE OF ½ LEMON
100G (4OZ) CHERRIES, STONED
100G (4OZ) WHITE GRAPES
1 LARGE NECTARINE, CHOPPED
100G (4OZ) FRESH DATES, QUARTERED

60ML (2 FL OZ) ORANGE JUICE OR KIRSCH

For the nut cream:
85G (3OZ) FINELY GROUND ALMONDS
¼ TEASPOON ALMOND ESSENCE
1 TABLESPOON CREAM OR SOYA CREEM

1. Halve the melons and scoop out the seeds. Brush the cut surfaces with lemon juice.
2. Stir the cherries, grapes, nectarine and date pieces together with the orange juice or Kirsch in a bowl. Spoon the fruit into the melon halves and chill in the fridge for 30 minutes.
3. Meanwhile, make the Nut Cream by mixing the almonds and essence with the cream. Adjust the flavour and consistency to taste.
4. Serve the melon halves topped with a little more Kirsch and a dollop of nut cream.

Serves 4

🕐 55 mins

serve as a breakfast in bed special!

Mango Mantrap

2 RIPE MANGOES

1 RIPE POMEGRANATE

25G (1OZ) FLAKED ALMONDS

1 SPRIG FRESH MINT

2 PLAIN BREADSTICKS

Serves 2

⏱ 20 mins

1.   Peel the mangoes and slice away the flesh in narrow strips. Do this over a bowl so that you reserve all the juices.

2.   Open a pomegranate and scoop out all the seeds, again reserving the juice. Mix the pomegranate seeds, their juice and the flaked almonds in a small bowl: this may be done some time before you wish to serve the salad, and well before you prepare the mango, if you like.

3.   Arrange the mango slices on two plates and spoon the almond mixture over. Drizzle the mango juice over that and garnish the plate with mint and a single breadstick. Both the mint and the breadstick are intended to be eaten, though best eaten after the salad is finished.

4.   This is a very pretty salad, so do try to arrange it thoughtfully on the plate.

Tip

Mangoes are like some people I know: they prefer to be stroked rather than squeezed. Squeezing is a good thing to do to some fruits but to tell if a mango is ripe, stroke the skin quite firmly. It should feel supple and deep and soft underneath. If you bought the mango before it was fully ripe, you will also notice that the skin changes colour and you may detect a fuller scent as it ripens.

BEANY SALADS

Bean and Nut Salad

100G (4OZ) COOKED RED KIDNEY
BEANS

55G (2OZ) GROUND WALNUTS

1 SMALL CELERIAC, PEELED AND GRATED

2 CARROTS, GRATED

2 POTATOES, PEELED, STEAMED AND DICED

2 TABLESPOONS PLAIN YOGURT

1 TABLESPOON LEMON JUICE

PINCH OF SALT

1/4 TEASPOON FRESHLY GROUND BLACK PEPPER

1. Combine all the ingredients together and toss thoroughly.
2. Serve on a bed of crisp lettuce and garnish with fresh watercress or croûtons – or both!

Serves 2-4

 10 mins

Tip

This salad is so quick because the potatoes are already cooked. Next time you are cooking, use the extra ring on your cooker to steam some potatoes and then pop them in the fridge. They can always be added to salads, stir-fries or scrambles or simply dressed and eaten all by themselves.

Mixed Bean Salad

55G (2OZ) RED KIDNEY BEANS,
SOAKED OVERNIGHT

55G (2OZ) BLACK-EYED BEANS,
SOAKED OVERNIGHT

55G (2OZ) CHICK PEAS, SOAKED OVERNIGHT

1 TABLESPOON WALNUT OIL

2 TABLESPOONS OLIVE OIL

1 TABLESPOON LEMON JUICE

PINCH OF SALT

1/4 TEASPOON FRESHLY GROUND BLACK PEPPER

1 ONION, THINLY SLICED

2 CLOVES GARLIC, CRUSHED

1 GREEN PEPPER, SLICED

1 RED PEPPER, SLICED

1. Drain and rinse the beans and put in a pressure cooker with just enough fresh water to cover them. Cook at pressure for about 25 minutes then immediately rinse under cold water. Drain and leave to cool.

Serves 4

55 mins, plus soaking time

2. Whisk the oils, lemon juice and seasoning together in a jug. Toss all the vegetables, beans and the vinaigrette together in a large salad bowl.

3. Serve with lots of watercress and rocket or radicchio.

Kidney Bean Salad

225G (8OZ) COOKED KIDNEY BEANS, DRAINED AND COOLED

½ SMALL CAULIFLOWER, CUT INTO FLORETS

1 SMALL LEEK, TRIMMED AND FINELY CHOPPED

2 TOMATOES, CHOPPED

½ ICEBERG LETTUCE, SLICED

3 TABLESPOONS FINELY CHOPPED FRESH PARSLEY

For the dressing:

4 TABLESPOONS OLIVE OIL

2 TABLESPOONS RASPBERRY OR WINE VINEGAR

1 CLOVE GARLIC, FINELY CHOPPED

¼ TEASPOON CHILLI POWDER

¼ TEASPOON FRESHLY GROUND BLACK PEPPER

PINCH OF SALT

Serves 4

🕐 30 mins, plus marinating time

Throw on some croutons for an added crunch!

1. Stir the beans, cauliflower and leek together in a large salad bowl.

2. Combine the dressing ingredients, stir well and pour over this salad mixture. Put aside, or in the fridge, to marinate – all day is ideal.

3. Stir the tomatoes, lettuce and parsley together in a large salad bowl and turn the bean salad over it.

4. Serve at once, with a garnish of croûtons if desired.

Five-bean Salad

450G (1LB) COOKED CHICK PEAS
450G (1LB) COOKED KIDNEY BEANS
450G (1LB) COOKED HARICOT BEANS
450G (1LB) COOKED BUTTER BEANS
450G (1LB) COOKED GREEN BEANS
450G (1LB) FRESH OR FROZEN BROCCOLI,
    FINELY CHOPPED
1 SMALL ONION, FINELY CHOPPED
3-5 CLOVES GARLIC, FINELY CHOPPED

1 EATING APPLE, PEELED AND FINELY CHOPPED
1 TABLESPOON GRATED FRESH GINGER
2 TEASPOONS FRESHLY GROUND BLACK PEPPER
1 TEASPOON BROWN SUGAR
1 PIECE CINNAMON STICK
5-10 WHOLE CLOVES
285ML (½ PINT) WINE VINEGAR
140ML (¼ PINT) APPLE JUICE
JUICE OF 4-6 LEMONS

1.   Turn all the ingredients, except the lemon juice, into a large enamel saucepan and stir well. Place over a medium heat, cover the pan and bring to a soft boil.
2.   Reduce the heat and simmer for 7-10 minutes then stir the salad, cover it again and remove the pan from the heat. Leave it to cool then stir in the lemon juice, tasting the sauce as you add juice.
3.   Leave to stand or chill in the refrigerator.
4.   Serve cool in a good-sized helping with a slice of fresh, whole-wheat bread.

Serves 4-8

30 mins, plus cooling time

French Bean Salad with Tofu Dressing

100G (4OZ) BUTTON MUSHROOMS,
    SLICED
1 RED PEPPER, THINLY SLICED
1 SMALL ONION, THINLY SLICED
JUICE OF 1 LEMON
½ TEASPOON FRESHLY GROUND BLACK PEPPER
340G (12OZ) FRENCH BEANS, TRIMMED AND
    SLICED

55G (2OZ) FLAKED ALMONDS

For the dressing:
100G (4OZ) SILKEN TOFU
2 TABLESPOONS OLIVE OIL
½ TEASPOON CURRY POWDER

1.   Place the sliced mushrooms, red pepper and onion slices in a large salad bowl with the lemon juice and black pepper, and leave to marinate while the beans cook.

Serves 4

25 mins

2. Cook the beans in a pan of boiling, salted water for 5-10 minutes; drain well and plunge them at once into very cold water. Drain and dry them.

3. Toss the beans in with the mushroom marinade.

4. Blend the ingredients for the dressing with a hand-held blender, adjusting the taste to suit.

5. Serve the salad in bowls with a dollop of the dressing on top and a garnish of flaked almonds.

Beansprout Salad

100G (4OZ) MIXED BEANSPROUTS
(I.E. MUNG, ALFALFA, FENUGREEK)
1 BUNCH WATERCRESS, WASHED AND
CHOPPED
1 STICK CELERY, FINELY SLICED
1 RED PEPPER, FINELY SLICED
1 SPRING ONION, FINELY CHOPPED
55G (2OZ) COOKED PEAS

55G (2OZ) FLAKED ALMONDS

For the dressing:
3 TABLESPOONS OLIVE OIL
2 TABLESPOONS RASPBERRY OR WINE VINEGAR
¼ TEASPOON FRESHLY GROUND BLACK PEPPER
PINCH OF SALT

Serves 4

 15 mins

1. Toss all the salad ingredients together in a large salad bowl.

2. Measure the ingredients for the dressing into a screw-top jar and shake until well mixed. Pour the dressing over the salad, toss and serve.

Variation

Add 100g (4oz) smoked tofu, cut into thin strips, to the salad. A smoked cheese, such as haloumi, is a similar variation.

VEGETABLE SALADS

Salade Niçoise

Like many 'classic' recipes in this book, this one takes a classical theme and gives it a new and exciting twist!

1 LARGE COS LETTUCE

1 x 285G (10OZ) TIN BRAISED TOFU, DRAINED

2 ONIONS, FINELY CHOPPED

55G (2OZ) BLACK OLIVES, STONED

2 TABLESPOONS CAPERS

675G (1½ LB) TOMATOES, CHOPPED OR QUARTERED

1 GREEN PEPPER, COARSELY CHOPPED

2-4 ARTICHOKE HEARTS, SLICED OR CHOPPED

1 TABLESPOON FINELY CHOPPED FRESH BASIL

JUICE AND ZEST OF 1 LEMON

3 TABLESPOONS OLIVE OIL

1.   Separate the leaves of the lettuce and arrange them round the edges of a very large bowl.

2.   Flake the braised tofu and mix with the onions, olives, capers, tomatoes, peppers and artichoke hearts in a large bowl. Stir the basil, lemon and oil together in a jug and pour over the salad. Toss and turn it into the bowl with the cos lettuce.

3.   Serve immediately, with a garnish of croûtons if desired.

Serves 4-6

⏱ 20 mins

Tip

You can find braised tofu in most health-food shops. Make croûtons by crushing 2-3 cloves of garlic into 2 tablespoons of olive oil in a frying pan. Heat over a medium flame then add 3-4 slices of wholemeal bread which has been cubed. Sauté briskly, stirring the cubes constantly, until golden brown. Serve immediately.

Simple Beetroot Salad

4 SMALL BEETROOT, SCRUBBED AND
    STEAMED
  1-2 SMALL ONIONS, THINLY SLICED
450G (1LB) ROCKET OR BABY SPINACH,
    WASHED AND DRAINED
2 TEASPOONS FRESH DILLWEED, FINELY
    CHOPPED
1 TABLESPOON FINELY CHOPPED FRESH CHIVES

For the dressing:

3 TABLESPOONS OLIVE OIL
1 TABLESPOON WINE VINEGAR
1 SCANT TEASPOON PREPARED MUSTARD
PINCH OF SALT
¼ TEASPOON FRESHLY GROUND BLACK PEPPER

Serves 4-6

 1 hr 30 mins

1.   Steam the beetroot without cutting any part of their skin. When they have steamed for approximately 30 minutes, they may be removed from the heat and left to cool. When cool enough to handle, peel them and grate the tender flesh into a bowl.

2.   Prepare the onion and leave to one side.

3.   Arrange some of the rocket in a large salad bowl, place some onion slices over and some grated beetroot over that. Sprinkle a mixture of dillweed and chives over the beetroot. Repeat the layers in this way – rocket, onion, beetroot, herbs – until all the ingredients are used.

4.   Make the dressing by stirring all the ingredients together in a jug or jar; pour the dressing over the salad and leave to stand, covered, for at least 10 minutes. This salad may be left for up to 1 hour.

5.   Toss the ingredients together just before serving with plenty of freshly baked bread.

Chinese Leaf Salad

8 CHINESE LEAVES
8 KUMQUATS
1 TABLESPOON THIN HONEY

PINCH OF SALT
¼ TEASPOON FRESHLY GROUND BLACK PEPPER
25G (1OZ) FLAKED ALMONDS

Serves 4

20 mins

1.   Slice the Chinese leaves into narrow strips and blanch in boiling water for 2 minutes. Drain the leaves and place in a serving dish.

2. Slice the kumquats very thinly, saving the juice. Mix the juice with the honey, salt and pepper.
3. Toss the leaves in this mixture then garnish with the sliced kumquats and almonds.
4. Serve immediately as a starter or side dish.

Tip

If the kumquats don't provide enough juice for your taste, add 2 teaspoons orange juice or fruit vinegar to the honey and continue as above.

Steamed Celeriac Salad

3 SMALL CELERIAC, PEELED AND
    QUARTERED

For the sauce:
JUICE AND ZEST OF 2 LIMES
1 TABLESPOON WALNUT OIL

90ML (3 FL OZ) SOURED CREAM OR PLAIN
    YOGURT
PINCH OF SALT
1/4-1/2 TEASPOON FRESHLY GROUND BLACK
    PEPPER

1. Slice each celeriac quarter downwards into several strips. Steam for 15 minutes, until they are just tender.
2. Meanwhile, whisk the lime juice and zest in with the oil, soured cream, salt and pepper.
3. Toss the celeriac in the sauce while it is still warm and serve.

Serves 4

🕐 25 mins

Don't save yourself — go for a total-walnut experience!

Avocado, Papaya and Smoked Tofu Salad

JUICE AND ZEST OF 2 LIMES

1 TABLESPOON SESAME OIL

PINCH OF SALT

¼ TEASPOON FRESHLY GROUND BLACK PEPPER

2 RIPE AVOCADOS, PEELED AND STONED

2 RIPE PAPAYAS, PEELED AND STONED

100G (4OZ) SMOKED TOFU, THINLY SLICED

RED LETTUCE LEAVES OR RADICCHIO

Serves 4

🕐 45 mins

Excellent in the dark!

1.   Mix the juice and zest of the limes with the sesame oil, salt and pepper in a wide, shallow dish.

2.   Thinly slice the avocados and papayas and lay them in the dish with the tofu slices. Leave to marinate for 30 minutes.

3.   Arrange the leaves on a serving platter and lift slices of avocado, tofu and papaya on to them. Drizzle a little of the lime marinade over each serving.

4.   This salad is excellent with a few croûtons scattered over each serving.

Variation

Dice 100g (4oz) of haloumi cheese into cubes and grill them briefly just before serving so that they are hot and sizzling. Scatter these over the salad.

Bread Salad (Fattoush)

1 SMALL CUCUMBER, SLICED

1 SMALL CRISP LETTUCE, SLICED

3 TOMATOES, CHOPPED

3 SPRING ONIONS, FINELY CHOPPED

1 GREEN PEPPER, FINELY CHOPPED

4 SLICES WHOLEMEAL BREAD

2 TABLESPOONS OLIVE OIL

1/4 TEASPOON PAPRIKA

For the dressing:

4 TABLESPOONS OLIVE OIL

JUICE OF 1/2 LEMON

1 CLOVE GARLIC, CRUSHED

1 TABLESPOON FINELY CHOPPED FRESH
CORIANDER

1 TABLESPOON FINELY CHOPPED FRESH PARSLEY

1/4 TEASPOON FRESHLY GROUND BLACK PEPPER

PINCH OF SALT

1. Mix all the vegetables together in a large salad bowl.
2. Slice the bread into cubes and arrange on a baking tray. Blend the oil and paprika and pour over the bread, moving the cubes to absorb the oil. Bake or grill until the bread is toasted.
3. Combine all the dressing ingredients in a screw-top jar and shake well. Pour the dressing over the salad, add the bread cubes and toss lightly.
4. Serve at once with a baked potato, bowl of soup or sandwich.

Serves 4

25 mins

Mint and Parsley Salad (Tabbouleh)

55-100G (2-4OZ) BULGHUR

BOILING WATER

2 RIPE TOMATOES, FINELY
CHOPPED

3 SPRING ONIONS, FINELY CHOPPED
(OPTIONAL)

1/2-1 TEASPOON FRESHLY GROUND BLACK
PEPPER

55G (2OZ) FRESH FLAT-LEAVED PARSLEY, FINELY
CHOPPED

25-55G (1-2OZ) FRESH MINT, FINELY CHOPPED

JUICE OF 2-4 LEMONS

1. Measure the bulghur into a saucepan and just cover with boiling water. Stir and cover the pan; leave to cool.
2. Turn the tomatoes, onions if you're using them, pepper and herbs into a large salad bowl. Stir well and add the bulghur when it is quite cool.
3. Dress with lemon juice so that the salad is just moist.
4. Serve cool or chilled with fresh pitta bread.

Serves 4-6

30 mins, plus
cooling time

Tip

Some people consider tabbouleh to be a grain dish, others a herb dish – which is why I've suggested different quantities of both ingredients. Use the smallest amount of bulghur and the greatest amount of fresh herbs if you want a really leafy salad and vice versa if you want a more substantial, grain salad. Some people add oil to the salad, but I prefer the clean taste of just lemon.

Greek Salad

225G (8OZ) FRESH BROAD BEANS
½ COS LETTUCE
2 LARGE TOMATOES, THICKLY SLICED
½ CUCUMBER, THICKLY SLICED
1 SMALL COURGETTE, CUBED
1 ONION, FINELY SLICED
85G (3OZ) BLACK OLIVES, STONED

100G (4OZ) FETA CHEESE, BROKEN AND CRUMBLED
½ TEASPOON DRIED OREGANO
PINCH OF SALT
¼ TEASPOON FRESHLY GROUND BLACK PEPPER
1 TABLESPOON LEMON JUICE
3 TABLESPOONS OLIVE OIL

Serves 4

⏱ 20 mins

1. Boil the fresh beans in salted water for 7-10 minutes; drain and immerse in cold water for 2 minutes.
2. Separate the leaves of the cos lettuce and lay them out in a bowl.
3. Mix all the vegetables, olives, the cooked beans and feta cheese together and pile on top of the lettuce.
4. Mix the oregano, salt and pepper, lemon juice and olive oil together in a jug and drizzle over the salad before serving.

Tip

1 tablespoon finely chopped fresh basil may be added to this salad instead of the oregano. Also, smoked or marinated tofu chunks may be substituted for the feta.

Greek Cucumber Salad (Tzatziki)

2 WHOLE CUCUMBERS, WASHED
AND CUBED

3 CLOVES GARLIC, CRUSHED

3 SPRING ONIONS, FINELY CHOPPED

1 TABLESPOON FINELY CHOPPED FRESH CHIVES

JUICE OF ½ LEMON

285ML (½ PINT) PLAIN YOGURT

SALT AND FRESHLY GROUND BLACK PEPPER, TO
TASTE

1. Mix all the ingredients together in a salad bowl and adjust the seasoning. Cover the bowl and chill the salad for at least 1 hour.
2. Serve with plenty of crisp lettuce, radish and celery as well as some black olives and fresh bread.

Serves 4

15 mins, plus chilling time

Variations

Here are two changes in method which produce subtle changes in the flavour and texture of this salad:

1. Try salting the cucumber before adding it to the salad: first peel or score the cucumber, cube it and sprinkle with 1-2 tablespoons salt. Leave it for 20-30 minutes then drain away the juice and proceed as above.

2. Alternatively, salt the cucumber first but also add the pepper and lemon juice at this time. After 30 minutes, drain away the juice and proceed as above, but add fresh juice of ½ lemon.

DRESSINGS AND SAUCES

Avocado Soured Cream Sauce

1 LARGE RIPE AVOCADO, STONED AND
PEELED
140ML (¼ PINT) SOUR CREAM
1 TABLESPOON CHOPPED FRESH PARSLEY
1 TABLESPOON CHOPPED FRESH CHIVES

2 CLOVES GARLIC, CRUSHED
SALT TO TASTE
JUICE OF ½ LEMON
¼ TEASPOON FRESHLY GROUND BLACK PEPPER

Makes approximately
285ml (½ pint)

⏱ 10 mins

It's all in the wrist movement

1. Blend all the ingredients together in a food processor or bowl and serve at once.
2. This is excellent served with crudités, crackers, toast or over salads.

Tip

Place a bowl of this sauce in a larger bowl containing ice-cubes to keep this sauce really at its most appetising.

Spicy Drizzle Dressing

1 TABLESPOON OIL
3 CLOVES GARLIC, FINELY CHOPPED
½ TEASPOON FRESHLY GROUND BLACK PEPPER

1 TEASPOON ARROWROOT OR CORNFLOUR
60ML (2 FL OZ) SOY SAUCE
ZEST AND JUICE OF 2 ORANGES

Makes approximately
140ml (¼ pint)

⏱ 15 mins

1. Heat the oil in a saucepan and sauté the garlic for 2-3 minutes over a medium heat. Stir in the black pepper for 1 minute then sprinkle the arrowroot over the sauté and stir to a thick paste, or roux.
2. Add the soy sauce, zest and orange juice, stirring after each addition to make a sauce. Add more orange juice or some vegetable stock to make a thinner sauce.

3. Remove from the heat and serve in a small jug or bowl. Use hot or cold, as a sauce for crudités, fritters, salads or steamed greens.

Variation

For a sauce that knocks your head off, substitute chilli powder for the black pepper.

French Lace Tarragon Dressing

1 TABLESPOON FINELY CHOPPED FRESH
TARRAGON
1 TABLESPOON FINELY CHOPPED FRESH CHIVES
2 TABLESPOONS FINELY CHOPPED FRESH PARSLEY

285ML (½ PINT) PLAIN YOGURT
JUICE OF 1 LEMON
SALT AND FRESHLY GROUND BLACK PEPPER, TO
TASTE

1. Mix the herbs and yogurt together in a bowl and add the lemon juice, a little at a time, stirring after each addition. Taste the dressing after you have added half the juice and add to taste thereafter.
2. Season the dressing and leave to stand in the fridge for 30-60 minutes.
3. Drizzle over salad, sandwiches or chilled soups for a really emphatic taste.

Makes approximately 285g (½ pint)

⏱ 15 mins, plus chilling time

Tahini Lemon Sauce

3 TABLESPOONS TAHINI
140ML (¼ PINT) PLAIN YOGURT
JUICE OF ½ LEMON
2 CLOVES GARLIC, CRUSHED

SALT, TO TASTE
2 TABLESPOONS FINELY CHOPPED FRESH
CORIANDER

1. Blend all the ingredients together in a jug or bowl and pour over salads, falafels, stuffed pitta breads – even baked potatoes.

Makes approximately 180ml (6 fl oz)

⏱ 10 mins

That Little Chiffon Thing

1/2 RIPE AVOCADO

2 TABLESPOONS OLIVE OIL

1 TABLESPOON HONEY OR BARLEY MALT
SYRUP

JUICE OF 1/2 LEMON

1 TABLESPOON FRESH FINELY CHOPPED FENNEL
LEAF

Makes approximately
180ml (6 fl oz)

⏱ 10 mins

1. Blend all the ingredients to a smooth, light consistency and serve with salads and crudités.

Variation

Add 25g (1oz) ground or slivered almonds to the mixture for a deeper flavour and a surprise texture.

THE FORBIDDEN FOODS OF LOVE

Can food really fan the flames of desire? Is it true that a lusty meal can arouse passions of a more physical kind? Do aphrodisiacs really exist?

The answer to all these questions is 'yes', but not in the way that most people believe. Ever since Eve offered Adam that first arousing apple, men and women have been engaged in a perpetual quest to discover delicacies which might ignite their lovers' sexual passions. From the very earliest times, the aphrodisiac power of food has been of great importance to humans – clearly demonstrated by the fact that they are twice mentioned in Genesis, the first book of the Bible. After that infamous episode with the apple, the second reference to aphrodisiacs occurs in the story of Jacob, Rachel and Leah. The plot is far more complex, and far more sexually explicit, than any of today's soap operas. Rachel implores her sister Leah to give her mandrake root (considered to be a potent aphrodisiac/fertility-enhancer) in order to conceive a child with Jacob. Jacob is Leah's husband, also shared with Rachel. Leah agrees to give Rachel mandrake, but only on condition that she can sleep with Jacob that night (she does, and gets pregnant). Be sure to tune in to next week's exciting episode . . .

When it comes to courtship, most animals (and that includes all men) rely on just a few basic come-ons. Whether he's a male spider trying to persuade a female spider to mate with him (not make a meal of him), or whether he's a management type making a play for his secretary, he's got three basic tricks up his sleeve: visual cues, sounds and scent. Visual cues help him to identify and (hopefully) attract members of the opposite sex, while the right sounds can sometimes help to put his prospective paramour in a suitable frame of mind: for example, the sound of a male pigeon's cooing stimulates ovulation in the female pigeon. But it's the third category of sexual weapon – scent – which really concerns us here.

Scent is, in fact, used by both male and female animals to attract a mate, and to get them in the mood for *lurve*, baby! Scents and smells are – in today's deodorised and sanitised environment – rather difficult for nice people to discuss. Anyone who's personal odour isn't, well, as *fresh* as it might be is usually considered offensive, if not downright unclean. Actually, the anti-perspirant, deodorant, toothpaste and perfume industries have made billions by exploiting our insecurities on this subject. This phenomenon is very recent – only three hundred years ago, Shakespeare felt moved to compose a romantic sonnet about 'the breath that from my mistress reeks' . . . How many poets would dare write about their lover's bad breath today?[1]

The extraordinary thing is, that while modern humans go to extreme lengths to

1 Shakespeare, *Sonnets* cxxx.

conceal their natural scents, human nature itself doesn't change. Just one example: in an experiment, scientists at a London Hospital have discovered that the merest hint of love juices applied to the chest of female partners will significantly increase the frequency of the couples' love-making. And although we've been conditioned to feel embarrassed about our animal aromas, the very same smells are considered to be positively attractive when they come from the food we eat! A ripe Camembert cheese, for example, is considered to be a gourmet's delicacy . . . but imagine how disgusted we'd feel if the same smell came from a stranger on a tube train. This is called 'displacement', and it explains the secret of the most powerful of all the food aphrodisiacs. To put it bluntly, they bring out the animal in us!

For a moment, let's get technical. Pheromones (from the Greek *pher*, 'to carry' and *horman* 'to stimulate') are chemical messengers released by many living creatures into the environment. For example, male dogs know when females are on heat because of a sex-attractant pheromone the females produce. The tiniest amounts of pheromones can send signals over extraordinary distances – a female moth can 'call' a male flying over two miles away! In humans, the pheromone androstenone has similarly bewitching properties, serving to set the female reproductive clock on 'moon time' and at the same time boost sexual appetite. Half the adult population can't detect androstenone.[2] To the other half, it has an odour which has been described as sweaty, musky or like sandalwood. Clearly,

any food which gives off aromas similar to these has a good chance of being a pretty powerful sexual turn-on! With androstenone, as with so many other things to do with love, research proves that persistence pays off. Because even among those people who can't initially smell it, scientists have shown that after just one exposure, 50 per cent of those who couldn't previously detect it begin to be aware of its presence.[3]

Another potent sexual messenger is the alcohol known as dodecanol. Smelling mildly soapy, scientists have found that dodecanol reaches its natural peak at the time of a woman's ovulation, and is quite easy to distinguish on her breath by her partner. When allied with another chemical known as DMS (faintly cabbage-like), these substances can prove to be effective aphrodisiacs for many men. Although smells such as 'soap' and 'cabbage' hardly seem to be the most romantic, you must remember that we're talking about the merest hints – in this, as in so many things, less is more!

Still further substances, identifed by scientists as 'copulins', are produced by the female hormone oestrogen. Smelling slightly sharp and sweaty, these substances intensify as the level of sexual excitement increases; some of them have a distinctive fishy odour about them, which probably accounts for the widespread belief that seafood is a persuasive aphrodisiac. All these smells – soapy, marine, sweaty and acidic – are also found in many of the foods readily available in restaurants and supermarkets. Choose your menu with this knowledge in mind, and you might just transform a dull meal into a night to remember!

2 'Chemical Senses'. Bartoshuk, L.M. and Beauchamp, G.K., *Annual Review of Psychology*, 1994.

3 'Ability to smell androstenone can be acquired by ostensibly anosmic people', Wysocki, C.J., Dorries, K.M. and Beauchamp, G.K., *Proceedings of the Natural Academy of Science*, USA, 1989.

THE CHEMISTRY OF ECSTASY

How do aphrodisiacs actually function? Probably by working their chemical magic on the sexiest organ in the human body – your brain. Beginning deep within the brain itself, then extending down the spinal cord, the body's nervous system divides itself into two main branches, called the sympathetic and parasympathetic nervous systems. The sympathetic system controls your response to stressful situations, including sexual arousal, with an increase in heart rate and respiration, pupil dilation, sweating and increased muscle tension. The parasympathetic system dominates the sympathetic system in less stressful situations, responding with a dilation of blood vessels, a decrease in heart rate accompanied by a reduction in blood pressure and a contraction of the pupils. Generally, these two systems operate in perfect balance with each another.

Both of these nerve systems communicate with the brain by using chemical messengers such as hormones (oestrogen, testosterone and progesterone) and other chemicals known as neurotransmitters. One hormone – testosterone – primarily controls the libido in both sexes (men have up to thirty times more testosterone than women). The neurotransmitters also have a key part to play in turning us on: for example, the neurotransmitter dopamine is essential for emotional arousal and excitement. These chemical messengers can be stimulated (or inhibited) by the protein, vitamins, minerals and other substances in the food we eat. Dopamine, for example, requires vitamins C and B6 as well as the amino acids tyrosine and phenylalanine to be present in the diet in order to be produced. And the hormone-like substances known as prostaglandins (which are so essential to the sexual response that they are often administered by local injection to impotent men to relax the blood vessel walls and allow blood flow into the genitals) are manufactured from omega-3 fatty acids, found in seafood and flaxseed/linseed oil. It is in ways such as these that food provides us with the chemical building-blocks we need to achieve sexual ecstasy!

THE TOP TEN FOODS FOR LOVERS

In the Amazon of central Brazil, men of the Mehinaku tribe rub needlefish against their private parts in the hope that their organs will become similarly sturdy. Needlefish are in pretty short supply in most Western supermarkets, but – luckily for us – there are plenty of other easily available foods which tradition – and science – affirm can fortify and invigorate our love lives . . .

1 APRICOTS

Traditionally, Chinese brides ate apricots to increase their fertility. Since apricots are very rich sources of manganese, a mineral required for the production of sex hormones, this Chinese tradition may well have some basis in fact. Dried apricots are also concentrated sources of iron and beta-carotene, a type of vitamin A which can help to boost sperm count and increase levels of sex hormones such as progesterone.

2 ASPARAGUS

An old English custom was to eat boiled asparagus each morning for three consecutive days to galvanise the libido, and one Arabian manual also suggests a daily dish of asparagus to heighten sexual prowess. The shape of the vegetable is reasonably suggestive (one of the visual cues mentioned above) but it is the smell which can prove to be a particularly powerful turn-on. Scientists have shown that just under half the population produce asparagus-smelling urine after eating the vegetable (strangely, this seems to be a genetically inherited trait). A proportion of those people – no one knows quite how many – find this particular scent to be a potent sexual stimulant. Remember – success is not guaranteed – but it's worth trying!

3 BEANSPROUTS

Not perhaps the most romantic of foods, you might think . . . but you'd be wrong! In fact, the fresh smell of beansprouts is identical to a pheromone known as IBA, one of the most potent of human sexual attractants. The same vigorous smell (which perfumiers sometimes, very appropriately, refer to as 'green') can be detected in champagne and, of course, in many of the most sensual (and expensive) perfumes we wear. To use beansprouts at their peak of freshness, you'll have to sprout them yourself . . . those sold in shops are often past their best.

4 CARROTS

Originating from Afghanistan, the carrot has been in cultivation in the Mediterranean area since at least 500 BC, and traditionally has been served at Middle Eastern feasts by members of royal families bent on seduction. Carrots are rich in the beta-carotene form of vitamin A (see Apricots). The British have always drastically under-rated this noble vegetable, which possesses both sweet and savoury characteristics, and is therefore exquisitely adaptable to a wide range of culinary uses. Freshly pressed carrot juice (organic if possible) is one of the most stimulating natural drinks you'll find.

5 CHOCOLATE

Chocolate has long been known as the food of love. The Aztec emperor Moctezuma II is reputed to have consumed fifty glasses of honey-sweetened chocolate each day to sustain his virility, and its arousing effects so impressed the explorer Hernán Cortés that he introduced the drink to Spain upon returning from his Mexican expedition in 1519. Casanova reputedly braced himself with oysters and a cup of chocolate before venturing into a lady's boudoir, and the Comtesse du Barry, mistress of King Louis XV of France, is said to have used chocolate on her lovers for the same naughty purpose. Apart from containing caffeine (see below), chocolate also provides the lover with a stiff dose of the amphetamine-like neurotransmitter known as phenylethylamine, which has been used to treat depression. Scientists also speculate that this is the chemical at least partly responsible for that topsy-turvy feeling we know as 'falling in love' – when you meet Mr/Ms Right, your phenylethylamine level rockets sky high!

6 COFFEE

Coffee is native to Ethiopia and has been cultivated and brewed in Arab countries for centuries. Soon after the drink was introduced into Europe in the mid seventeenth century, its stimulant – and aphrodisiac – properties were observed. This has recently been confirmed by scientists who surveyed several hundred adults living in and around Michigan, USA. They report that older women who drink at least one cup of coffee a day are much more sexually active than non-coffee drinkers. And as far as men are concerned, the news is equally good. Coffee-drinking men over sixty appear to suffer much less from impotence. The researchers speculate that coffee may have an effect because the caffeine it contains is a potent central nervous system stimulant that 'is known to enhance response to sensory stimulation and hasten response to normal reflexes'. In other words, caffeine can make you more sensitive to the touch as well as quicken your reaction time. Caffeine stimulates the release and action of epinephrine, one of the neurotransmitters that trigger sexual arousal. It also works as a smooth-muscle relaxant, enabling blood to flow more effectively into the male sexual organ, where it is needed for a man to maintain an erection. Sounds like a good reason to conclude that romantic dinner with a strong cup of java!

7 CORIANDER

A member of the carrot family, coriander (sometimes called cilantro or Chinese parsley) is a herb revered since Biblical times – the manna of the Old Testament was described as being similar to coriander.

Like parsley, its sexual attraction lies in the fact that it smells similar to the sex pheromone androstenone. It is probably for this reason that essential oils made from the green leaves are widely used in beverages, sweets, tobacco and perfumes.

8 FIGS

Figs were a favourite food of love for the ancient Greeks, and are a good source of niacin, which improves circulation to all parts of the body, and of magnesium, also needed to produce sex hormones.

9 PARSLEY

The most widely used flavouring and garnish for many dishes, parsley has recently been found to be one of the most concentrated sources of glutathione, an important antioxidant which helps to keep all the body's vital systems working. Apart from being an excellent source of folic acid, vitamin A and iron, parsley also has an odour which is strikingly similar to the sex pheromone androstenone, as have celery, celeriac, carrot tops and young parsnips. Lashings of parsley, or indeed any of these vegetables, can only bring you and your partner good health . . . and probably much more besides!

10 TRUFFLES

Irresistible to female pigs, who are used to retrieve these mysterious fungi from the roots of oak and beech trees, truffles have a pungent, almost carnal, musky flavour which has proven to be a potent sexual stimulant for many, including Madame de Pompadour, the Emperor Claudius and Louis XIV. Although the Perigord truffle of

France is perhaps the best known, the finest – and strongest in flavour – is the white truffle which grows in the Italian Piedmont area. Truffles are ruinously expensive, and although the price of love is never too high, you might like to know that many of the stronger-flavoured wild mushrooms (ceps, chanterelles, or morels) possess the same sexual, earthy scent.

VITAL ADVICE

HOW TO KEEP THOSE LOVE FIRES BURNING

'Without good eating and drinking' declared the Greek poet Eunuchus in 160 BC, 'love grows cold.' Here's a quick checklist to make sure the ardent flames of desire keep on scorching!

♡ Be sure to include lashings of naturally-occuring beta-carotene in your diet. Usually found in foods which are coloured yellow or orange, it helps to boost sex hormones and raises sperm count in men.

♡ Make sure you're consuming adequate amounts of omega-3 fatty acids – found in linseed, rapeseed (canola) and soya bean oil, and also in the food supplement spirulina – as they're essential for the production of prostaglandins (see above). Consuming omega-3 fatty acids may also reduce the risk of prostate cancer, a leading cause of death from cancer among men.

♡ Too much alcohol will suppress sensation and decrease nerve response needed for arousal . . . so no more than two glasses of red wine a day.

♡ Don't smoke. Nicotine increases the chance of infertility in women and impotence in men.

♡ Take gentle exercise – people who do are more lusty than their less active counterparts.

♡ Include food rich in B vitamins and vitamin C. Both of these nutrients are needed to make neurotransmitters associated with sexual arousal.

♡ Foods abundant in zinc – such as pumpkin seeds, wheatgerm, sesame seeds, peanuts, almonds and cashew nuts – will increase sperm motility, and reduce the risk of prostate inflammation.

♡ Keep off the meat – it makes you smell "off" and obscures those more pleasant and arousing scents your body manufactures.

♡ If you're taking medication, check with your doctor whether it may be acting to decrease your libido – many drugs do.

PART FOUR
Main Attractions

Well here we are, we've arrived at the centrepiece of your meal! There's so much choice on offer here I think I'll just let you browse your way through it . . . it's all so good, and my only advice would be to leave a little room for deserts!

STIR-FRIES

Stir-fried Seitan with Pepper and Onion Sauce

285G (10OZ) SEITAN (SEE BELOW),
TINNED OR FROZEN

3 TABLESPOONS OIL

3 CLOVES GARLIC, FINELY CHOPPED

1 LARGE ONION, THINLY SLICED

1 RED PEPPER, THINLY SLICED

1 GREEN PEPPER, THINLY SLICED

1 TABLESPOON PLAIN FLOUR

1/2 TEASPOON CHILLI POWDER

1/2 TEASPOON FRESHLY GROUND BLACK PEPPER

200ML (7 FL OZ) VEGETABLE STOCK
(SEE PAGE 87) OR WATER

5 SPRING ONIONS, VERY THINLY SLICED

1 x 285G (10OZ) TIN WATER CHESTNUTS,
SLICED OR QUARTERED

1 TABLESPOON SOY SAUCE

2 TABLESPOONS SHERRY OR RED WINE
(OPTIONAL)

Serves 4

⏱ 30 mins

Try this — you're in for a treat

1.   Drain or thaw the seitan and slice into thin strips. Place half of the oil in each of two frying pans. Sauté the seitan in one pan over a medium flame for 10-12 minutes, turning it often.

2.   Sauté the garlic and onion in the other pan over a medium heat for 5-7 minutes, until clear and tender. Add the peppers to the onion sauté and stir a further 3 minutes.

3.   Mix the flour, chilli powder and black pepper together and sprinkle over the onion sauté. Stir for 1 minute, then add the stock, a little at a time, stirring after each addition. The sauce will thicken.

4.   Add the remaining ingredients, including the sautéed seitan, to this pan and stir well. Cook for a further 5-7 minutes, adjusting the seasoning and liquid if necessary.

5.   Serve hot over rice or hot noodles.

Tip

Seitan is the ultimate, meaty, meat-replacement! Made from wheat gluten (don't even think about it if you're gluten-allergic), it was first developed centuries ago in China by Buddhist monks, then drifted over to Japan where it acquired the name seitan, literally 'gluten cooked in soy sauce'. It is high in protein, low in fat, and can be found in the refrigerated section of many health-food stores. It has a kind of chewy texture which some vegetarians find too meaty!

Cashew Stir-fried Rice

3 TABLESPOONS OIL

2 CLOVES GARLIC, CRUSHED

1 MEDIUM ONION, FINELY CHOPPED

2 STICKS OF CELERY, FINELY CHOPPED

100G (4OZ) MUSHROOMS, SLICED

100G (4OZ) MANGETOUT, TRIMMED

100G (4OZ) BABY SWEETCORN, WASHED

85G (3OZ) CASHEW NUTS, BROKEN OR CHOPPED

1 TABLESPOON SOY SAUCE

JUICE OF ½ LEMON

570ML (1 PINT/2 CUPS) COOKED BROWN RICE

1.   Heat 2 tablespoons of the oil in a frying pan or wok and gently sauté the garlic, onion and celery until they begin to soften, about 5 minutes.

2.   Add the remaining spoonful of oil and stir in the mushrooms, mangetout, sweetcorn and nuts. Continue to sauté, stirring often, for another 5-7 minutes.

3.   Sprinkle the soy sauce and lemon juice over the sauté and cover the pan.

4.   Drain the rice of any excess liquid then stir the cooked rice into the sauté. Continue cooking over a medium flame until the rice is hot.

5.   Serve immediately.

Serves 4

🕐 30 mins

Stir-fried Spring Vegetables with Smoked Tofu

450G (1LB) BROCCOLI

1 TABLESPOON SESAME OIL

450G (1LB) FRENCH BEANS, TRIMMED
AND SLICED

2 SMALL CELERIAC, PEELED AND VERY THINLY
SLICED

100G (4OZ) SMOKED TOFU, DICED

1 TABLESPOON SOY SAUCE

1 TABLESPOON DRY SHERRY

1 BUNCH WATERCRESS, DESTALKED AND
BROKEN INTO SPRIGS

1 TABLESPOON ROASTED SESAME SEEDS
(SEE TIP BELOW)

Serves 4

🕐 25 mins

*A stir-fry
sensation –
to water the
mouth and
tingle the
taste buds!*

1. Slice the florets from the broccoli stalks. Peel the stalks and slice them thinly.

2. Heat the oil in a wok over high heat and add the broccoli, beans and celeriac. Stir-fry for 3-5 minutes, stirring constantly. Add the tofu and stir for another 2 minutes, then add the soy sauce, sherry and watercress.

3. Stir for 1 minute then serve over rice with a garnish of roasted sesame seeds.

Tip

To roast sesame seeds, simply heat a dry, unoiled frying pan over a medium flame and add the sesame seeds to it. Agitate the pan as the seeds roast to a deep golden colour then immediately turn them into a shallow dish to cool. For best results keep cooking to the minimum.

Arame and Carrot Stir-fry with Ginger

25G (1OZ) DRIED ARAME SEAWEED

450G (1LB) CARROTS, PEELED

2 TABLESPOONS OIL

3 CLOVES GARLIC, FINELY CHOPPED

5 SPRING ONIONS, FINELY CHOPPED

2 TABLESPOONS GRATED FRESH GINGER

½ TEASPOON FRESHLY GROUND BLACK PEPPER

2 TABLESPOONS SOY SAUCE

1-2 TABLESPOONS ROASTED SESAME SEEDS (SEE PAGE 120)

1.   Rinse the seaweed under running water then immerse it in fresh, cold water for 15-20 minutes so that it rehydrates. Drain the water away and lift the soaked arame out of the bowl (leaving behind any sand, etc) and into a deep saucepan.

2.   Cover with fresh water and bring to a low boil. Arame creates a lot of foam at first, so watch the pan to ensure it doesn't boil over. Reduce the heat and simmer, partly covered, for about 15 minutes.

3.   Meanwhile, cut the carrots into thin strips. Heat the oil in a large pan and sauté the garlic for 3 minutes. Add the carrots, cover the pan and cook over a low to medium heat for about 15 minutes, stirring occasionally.

4.   Add the spring onions, ginger and black pepper and stir well.

5.   Drain the cooking water from the arame and immediately douse the hot seaweed with the soy sauce. Stir well.

6.   Now mix the arame and carrot mixtures together in the bigger of the two pans, cover and place over a low heat for 5 minutes.

7.   Serve hot or cold with a garnish of freshly roasted sesame seeds. This dish is excellent with rice or noodles.

Serves 4-6

45 mins

You don't need a bucket and spade to find this seaweed – just shimmy down to the supermarket

Tip

Arame is a black, slightly crunchy seaweed, which is lightly aromatic.

Mushroom and Pok Choi with Pimento

450G (1LB) MUSHROOMS,
CLEANED

2 TABLESPOONS OIL

5 CLOVES GARLIC, FINELY CHOPPED

¼ - ½ TEASPOON CHILLI POWDER

1 LARGE SWEET RED PEPPER (PIMENTO), THINLY
SLICED

1 TEASPOON ARROWROOT

140ML (¼ PINT) PINEAPPLE JUICE OR WATER

2 TABLESPOONS SOY SAUCE

450G (1LB) POK CHOI, TRIMMED, WASHED
AND DRAINED

Serves 4

30 mins

1. Trim the mushrooms and halve or quarter them to ensure they are all roughly the same size.

2. Heat the oil in a deep frying pan and sauté the garlic for 3 minutes. Add the chilli powder and sauté a further 1 minute. Now add the mushrooms and pimento, stir the sauté and cover the pan.

3. Reduce the heat and leave to cook for 5-7 minutes. Stir well and cook a further 3 minutes.

4. Meanwhile, blend the arrowroot and pineapple juice to a smooth paste. Add the soy sauce and pour the mixture over the sauté after it has cooked for 8-10 minutes.

5. Lay the pok choi over the sauté, cover the pan again and leave over a medium heat for 5 minutes. Remove the cover and stir the vegetables for a final 2-3 minutes to ensure an even cooking.

6. Serve immediately with rice or noodles and perhaps some fried tempeh.

Tip

Pok choi is used in Chinese cookery. It is instantly recognisable from its bright, deep-green leaf and white spine.

PIZZA AND PASTA

Linguine in Sun-dried Tomato Sauce

225G (8OZ) WHITE OR GREEN LINGUINE

SALT

For the sauce:

1 TABLESPOON OLIVE OIL

7-9 CLOVES GARLIC, FINELY CHOPPED

3-5 SPRING ONIONS, FINELY CHOPPED

½ TEASPOON CHILLI POWDER

125G (4½ OZ) SUN-DRIED TOMATOES,
   CHOPPED

2 X 500G (1LB 2OZ) CARTONS SIEVED
   TOMATO

1 HEAPED TABLESPOON FINELY CHOPPED FRESH
   BASIL OR 2 TEASPOONS DRIED BASIL

½ TEASPOON BROWN SUGAR

1 TEASPOON VEGETABLE PASTE OR YEAST
   EXTRACT

1. Heat the oil in a large saucepan over a low to medium flame. Add the garlic and sauté for about 5 minutes, until it begins to colour slightly. Add the spring onions and stir a further 2 minutes. Add the chilli powder and stir 1 minute.

2. Now add the sun-dried tomatoes and stir until they have absorbed the sauté juices. Add the remaining ingredients and stir for 3-5 minutes.

3. When the sauce begins to bubble, cover the pan and reduce the heat to a minimum. Leave the sauce to cook very slowly for at least 30 minutes. You may leave it longer or, better still, remove it from the heat after 30 minutes and leave it to cool in the pan. Reheat the sauce when you are ready to use it.

4. To cook the linguine, bring a large pan of salted water to the boil and add the linguine. Stir it into the water and boil for 7-8 minutes, until it is just tender.

5. Drain and serve immediately with a ladleful of the sauce.

Serves 4

⏱ 1 hr

Linger over your linguine

Tips

1. I like to pour the sauce over the pasta, but you may prefer to stir the two together. Go ahead, just make sure you do it quickly so as not to lose too

much heat in the process. Warmed plates or bowls help keep this delicious meal delicious.

2. This is a very rich sauce and you may find it is perfect all by itself; however, a garnish of Parmesan or other freshly grated cheese suits it wonderfully.

Conchiglie with Roasted Fennel and Tomato Sauce

1 MEDIUM MALE FENNEL BULB (SEE PAGE 129)

3 TABLESPOONS OLIVE OIL

8 TOMATOES

1-3 CLOVES GARLIC, FINELY CHOPPED

GRATED RIND OF ½ LEMON

PINCH OF SALT

½ TEASPOON FRESHLY GROUND BLACK PEPPER

225G (8OZ) CONCHIGLIE (SHELL-SHAPED PASTA)

2 TABLESPOONS FRESHLY GRATED PARMESAN CHEESE

Serves 2-4

🕐 45 mins

1. Preheat the oven to 200°C/400°F/Gas Mark 6.

2. Trim the fennel, wash it well and cut it into eight parts. Steam the fennel for 5-7 minutes, until just tender.

3. Transfer it to a roasting tin and drizzle 1 tablespoon of the oil over it. Roast for 15 minutes, until golden.

4. Meanwhile, peel the tomatoes and chop the flesh, discarding the seeds.

5. Heat the remaining oil in a saucepan and sauté the garlic over a low flame for 2-3 minutes. Add the chopped tomatoes and the lemon rind and sauté for a further 20 minutes.

6. When the fennel has roasted, chop it into small pieces and add to the sauce. Season with the salt and pepper and keep hot while you cook the pasta (see page 129).

7. Toss the cooked pasta and sauce together and serve hot with a sprinkling of Parmesan.

Avocado, Papaya and Smoked Tofu Salad (page 104)

Rich Vegetable Stew (page 140)

Rotolo Ripieno (page 132)

Tips

1. To peel tomatoes, cover them with boiling water for just under 1 minute then lift them with a slotted spoon and plunge them immediately into cold water. This will loosen, and sometimes even split, the skin and you may easily peel it off with a knife.

2. The flavour of male fennel differs quite noticeably from that of female fennel. A male fennel is long and thin with a strong flavour; the female fennel is bulbous, quite fibrous and has a less powerful flavour.

3. Conchiglie are easy to cook: bring a large pan of salted water to the boil and drop the pasta in it. Return to the boil then reduce the heat a little and boil for 10-12 minutes, depending on the size of the shells. Drain the cooked pasta immediately and serve.

Penne Rigate with Roasted Red Pepper Pesto

225G (8OZ) PENNE

SALT

For the pesto:

4 MEDIUM RED PEPPERS

70G (2½ OZ) GROUND ALMONDS

ZEST OF 1 LEMON

4 TABLESPOONS OLIVE OIL

1-3 CLOVES GARLIC

2 TEASPOONS BALSAMIC VINEGAR

55G (2OZ) PARMESAN CHEESE, FRESHLY GRATED

PINCH OF SALT

¼ TEASPOON FRESHLY GROUND BLACK PEPPER

1. Preheat the oven to 200°C/400°F/Gas Mark 6.

2. Place the peppers on a baking tray and roast them for about 20 minutes, turning them once during that time. The peppers will char slightly and lose their full shape. Cool them on a wire rack.

3. Peel the skin from the cool peppers, remove the seeds and discard. Perform this stage over a bowl or plate in order to catch any of the precious pepper juice. Turn the skinned peppers, their juice and the remaining pesto ingredients into a food processor and blend until smooth and thick.

4. Spoon the mixture into sterilised jars and pour a little more olive oil over to seal the contents.

Makes approximately 225ml (8 fl oz) pesto
Serves 4 with the penne

45 mins, plus cooling time

Easy to cook – not so easy to forget

5. Bring a large saucepan of salted water to the boil and cook the penne for 10-12 minutes.

6. Drain and serve, with a spoonful of this pesto directly on, and a garnish of fresh basil if desired.

Tips

1. The peppers may be prepared up to 24 hours before you wish to use them. Just be sure you reserve any juices they produce. Of course, the roasting may be done over charcoal if you are set up to do that. In that case, the flavour will be smokier and you may have to adjust the seasoning a little.

2. Penne are a straight, hollow (tube-like) pasta with a little pointy end, just perfect for holding a little of this pesto on each mouthful.

Rigatoni in Pine Nut and Gorgonzola Sauce

225G (8OZ) RIGATONI OR FUSILLI

SALT

For the sauce:
100G (4OZ) CAULIFLOWER FLORETS
100G (4OZ) BROCCOLI FLORETS
55G (2OZ) PINE NUTS

2 TABLESPOONS OLIVE OIL

1 RED ONION, FINELY CHOPPED

1 TEASPOON FRESH THYME, FINELY CHOPPED

¼ -½ TEASPOON FRESHLY GROUND BLACK
    PEPPER

100G (4OZ) GORGONZOLA CHEESE, CUBED

Serves 2-4

🕐 30 mins

1. Bring a pot of salted water to the boil and boil the rigatoni for about 12 minutes, until just tender.

2. Steam the cauliflower and broccoli for 7-8 minutes, until just tender but still brightly coloured.

3. Roast the pine nuts by laying them on some kitchen foil under a warm grill. Move them several times during roasting, about 3 minutes.

4. Heat the oil in a saucepan over a medium flame and sauté the onion until clear and tender, about 3 minutes. Add the thyme, pepper and a pinch of salt and stir for 1 minute longer.

5. Add the steamed cauli and broccoli, the roasted pine nuts and the cubed Gorgonzola and remove from the heat. Stir well.

6. Drain the pasta immediately it is cooked and stir into the sauce. Serve hot.

Tips

1. Rigatoni is a broad tube pasta with ridges. Fusilli are those pasta spirals which are sold just about everywhere.
2. Pine nuts are sometimes sold as pine kernels.
3. Red onions, apart from being very pretty, are less powerful in flavour than white onions. If you can't find one, use 3-5 spring onions instead.

Variation

Steam 450g (1lb) washed and trimmed spinach instead of the cauliflower and broccoli. When you stir it into the sauté, break it apart a little with the wooden spoon then continue as above.

Radicchio alla Trevigiono (Radicchio Lasagne)

3 RADICCHIOS, QUARTERED
3 TABLESPOONS OLIVE OIL
340G (12OZ) LASAGNE
1 MALE FENNEL BULB (SEE PAGE 129)
85G (3OZ) BUTTER OR MARGARINE
3 CLOVES GARLIC, FINELY CHOPPED

1 MEDIUM ONION, FINELY CHOPPED
PINCH OF SALT
¼ TEASPOON FRESHLY GROUND BLACK PEPPER
25G (1OZ) PLAIN FLOUR
570ML (1 PINT) MILK
140G (5OZ) DOLCELATTE CHEESE, CUBED

1. Preheat the oven to 200°C/400°F/Gas Mark 6.
2. Arrange the radicchio pieces on a tray and drizzle the oil over them. Grill them under a warm grill for 8-10 minutes, until they change colour and become slighly charred. Set aside.
3. Bring a large pot of salted water to the boil and boil the lasagne until just tender, about 12 minutes. Drain immediately and set aside.
4. Cut the fennel into eight parts and steam for 7-9 minutes. Cool slightly and chop quite finely.
5. Melt the butter in a saucepan over a medium heat and sauté the

Serves 4

⏱ 1 hr 15 mins

garlic and onion until just golden, about 5 minutes. Add the chopped fennel, salt and pepper and stir a further 1 minute.

6.   Sprinkle the flour over the sauté and stir while it thickens to a paste, or roux. Add the milk, a little at a time, stirring after each addition.

7.   Stir in the dolcelatte cubes and adjust the seasoning if necessary.

8.   Pour a little sauce into an oven dish, cover with some of the charred radicchio then cover that with a layer of lasagne. Repeat these layers – sauce, radicchio, lasagne – until the ingredients are used up. Finish with a layer of sauce.

9.   Bake for 20 minutes, until the top is bubbling and golden. Serve hot.

Rotolo Ripieno

For the filling:

900G (2LB) FRESH SPINACH

140G (5OZ) RICOTTA CHEESE

140G (5OZ) FRESH PLUM TOMATOES, PEELED, SEEDED AND CHOPPED

55G (2OZ) PECORINO CHEESE, GRATED

55G (2OZ) PINE NUTS, ROASTED (SEE PAGE 130)

2-3 CLOVES GARLIC, CRUSHED

PINCH OF SALT

1/4 TEASPOON FRESHLY GROUND BLACK PEPPER

1/2 TEASPOON GRATED NUTMEG

For the pasta:

340G (12OZ) STRONG, PLAIN FLOUR

PINCH OF SALT

3 EGGS, BEATEN

For the topping:

25G (1OZ) PECORINO CHEESE, GRATED

55G (2OZ) UNSALTED BUTTER OR MARGARINE

Serves 4

1 hr 15 mins, plus cooling time

1.   Mix all the filling ingredients together in a bowl and adjust the seasoning to taste.

2.   For the pasta, sift the flour and salt on to a board and make a well in the centre. Add the eggs and stir, then knead, to a smooth dough.

3.   Roll the dough to a rectangle of about 3mm (1/8 inch) thickness and spread the filling over it. Leave a space round the edges, about 2.5cm (1 inch) deep, that is clear of the filling. Roll the pasta as for a Swiss roll and then wrap the whole thing in a piece of butter

muslin. Tie the ends of the muslin with string and place the roll in a long, narrow casserole.

4.   Cover the roll with lightly salted cold water and place over a medium flame. Bring the water to a boil, reduce the heat and simmer for about 20 minutes.

5.   Remove the pan from the heat and put to one side, leaving the pasta roll to cool in the water for 5-10 minutes.

6.   Unwrap the muslin and slice the roll into 2.5cm (1 inch) slices. Arrange the slices in a buttered oven dish, sprinkle with the Pecorino and dabs of the butter.

7.   Place under a hot grill for 5 minutes then serve immediately.

Tip

Pecorino, when mature, is quite similar to Parmesan in that it can be grated and used in the same way.

Zucca di Pasta

450G (1LB) PASTA (PENNE, FUSILLI OR FARFALLE)

SALT

1 MEDIUM PUMPKIN

2 TABLESPOONS OLIVE OIL

3 CLOVES GARLIC, CRUSHED

PINCH OF SALT

1/4 TEASPOOON FRESHLY GROUND BLACK PEPPER

285ML (1/2 PINT) WATER

1 HANDFUL (ABOUT 140ML/1/4 PINT) FLAT-LEAVED PARSLEY, FINELY CHOPPED

3 TABLESPOONS GRATED PECORINO CHEESE

1.   Quarter the pumpkin and peel each quarter; also remove the seed pulp and discard. Dice or cube the flesh and weigh it so that you have 450g (1lb).

2.   Heat the olive oil in a large saucepan and sauté the pumpkin for 5-7 minutes over a medium flame. The pumpkin should brown slightly. Add the garlic, salt and pepper and stir 1 minute longer.

3.   Add the water, cover the pan and simmer for 10-12 minutes, until the pumpkin is very soft. Reduce the heat and add the parsley and Pecorino. You may wish to add another tablespoon of oil as well.

Serves 4

🕐 45 mins

4. Stir well and leave covered.

5. Meanwhile, bring a large pot of salted water to the boil and add the pasta. Boil the pasta for about 12 minutes, until just tender, then drain and stir into the hot pumpkin mixture.

6. Serve at once, with more parsley and/or cheese, if you like.

Cannelloni Florentine

450G (1LB) SPINACH, WASHED, DRAINED AND TRIMMED

2 TABLESPOONS OIL

3 CLOVES GARLIC, CRUSHED

1 SMALL ONION, FINELY CHOPPED

285G (10OZ) FIRM TOFU, DRAINED

¼ TEASPOON GROUND NUTMEG

FRESHLY GROUND BLACK PEPPER TO TASTE

12 SMALL CANNELLONI TUBES

25-55G (1-2OZ) DRIED BREADCRUMBS

1 TEASPOON DRIED BASIL

For the tomato sauce:

1 x 400G (14OZ) TIN TOMATOES

1 LARGE CARROT, GRATED

1 ONION, FINELY CHOPPED

2 STICKS CELERY, FINELY CHOPPED

1 TABLESPOON TOMATO PURÉE

1 TEASPOON RAW CANE SUGAR

1 TABLESPOON FINELY CHOPPED FRESH BASIL

FRESHLY GROUND BLACK PEPPER, TO TASTE

Serves 4

 45 mins

1. Preheat the oven to 400°F/200°C/Gas Mark 6.

2. Press the spinach into a saucepan without adding extra water. Cover and cook over a medium flame for 2-3 minutes, until wilted. Drain and finely chop.

3. Heat the oil and sauté the garlic and onion until clear and tender. Mash the tofu into the sauté with the nutmeg and black pepper. Mix well and cook 3 minutes more. Add the chopped spinach, stir well and remove from the heat.

4. Use this mixture to loosely stuff the cannelloni tubes. Lay them side by side in a lightly oiled ovenproof dish.

5. To make the sauce, combine all the sauce ingredients in a saucepan, and bring to a boil over a medium flame. Reduce the heat, cover the pan and simmer for 10 minutes.

6. Spread the sauce evenly over the stuffed cannelloni. Mix the breadcrumbs and dried basil and spread over the sauce.

7. Bake for 20 minutes. Serve hot.

Tip

Commercial cannelloni tubes vary in that some of them need to be cooked before they are filled; others can be filled straightaway. Check the instructions on the packet.

Variations

1. Add 450g (1lb) cooked chick peas to the stuffing and increase the amount of garlic, black pepper or both. You may also wish to buy larger cannelloni.

2. This dish is classically made with ricotta cheese and sometimes with pine nuts added. A mere 55g (2oz) pine nuts will suffice if you wish to add them to your version. Not so much pepper is needed when they are included.

Tender Mushroom Pizza

450G (1LB) MUSHROOMS, CLEANED AND THICKLY SLICED

1 TABLESPOON SOY SAUCE

2 TABLESPOONS OIL

3 CLOVES GARLIC, FINELY CHOPPED

1 SMALL ONION, THINLY SLICED

140G (5OZ) TOMATO PURÉE

3 TABLESPOONS WINE VINEGAR

285ML (½ PINT) WATER

1 TEASPOON DRIED OREGANO

¼ TEASPOON CHILLI POWDER

1 TEASPOON BROWN SUGAR

2 TABLESPOONS FINELY CHOPPED FRESH BASIL

100G (4OZ) GRATED PARMESAN CHEESE

For the base:

450G (1LB) PLAIN FLOUR

2 TEASPOONS BAKING POWDER

1 TEASPOON BICARBONATE OF SODA

285-425ML (½-¾ PINT) WATER

1. Preheat the oven to 220°C/425°F/Gas Mark 7.
2. Douse the sliced mushrooms in the soy sauce and put to one side.
3. Heat the oil in a large saucepan and sauté the garlic and onions until clear and tender. Add the mushrooms and soy sauce and sauté over a medium heat for 5-7 minutes, stirring often.
4. Add the remaining ingredients, except the Parmesan, to the sauté and stir-simmer while you make the pizza base.

Serves 4

⏲ 45 mins

5. Mix the dry ingredients together, make a well in the centre and gradually add the water, stirring after each addition. You want a firm but slightly sticky dough.

6. Divide the dough into two to four pieces and pour a little oil on your hands. Work the dough to the edges of the pizza 'bricks' or baking trays (these may be non-stick or lightly oiled) and spoon the mushroom sauce over, spreading nearly to the edges of the dough. Sprinkle with the Parmesan and bake for 15 minutes.

7. Slice and serve hot or cold.

CASSEROLES AND STEWS

Boston Baked Beans

225G (8OZ) HARICOT BEANS,
    WASHED AND SOAKED OVERNIGHT
2 TABLESPOONS OIL
2 ONIONS, FINELY CHOPPED
450G (1LB) TOMATOES, PEELED AND CHOPPED
1 SMALL TIN PIMENTOS, CHOPPED
285G (10OZ) TOMATO PURÉE
285ML (½ PINT) VEGETABLE STOCK
    (SEE PAGE 87)

2 TABLESPOONS BLACKSTRAP MOLASSES
2 TEASPOONS DRY MUSTARD
2 TABLESPOONS CIDER VINEGAR
½ TEASPOON GROUND CINNAMON
¼ TEASPOON GROUND CLOVES
1 TEASPOON FRESHLY GROUND BLACK PEPPER

Serves 4-6

4 hrs 30 mins, plus soaking beans overnight

1. Drain the beans and cover with fresh water. Bring to a boil in a large saucepan and boil for 10 minutes. Reduce the heat, cover the saucepan and simmer for 30 minutes.

2. Preheat the oven to 150°C/300°F/Gas Mark 2.

3. Heat the oil in a separate saucepan and sauté the onions until clear and tender. Mix in the remaining ingredients and stir over a medium heat for 10 minutes.

4. Drain the beans, add them to the tomato sauce and transfer the whole mixture to an ovenproof casserole dish. Cover the casserole and bake for 3-4 hours, until the beans are tender. Stir them occa-

sionally during this time, adding a drop of stock or water if they seem too dry.

5.   Serve hot or cold with fresh bread, toast, baked potatoes or cornbread.

Tip

Although you could simply use pre-cooked beans for this dish, the secret of a really tangy, deep flavour in baked beans is that long, slow cooking in the rich sauce.

Variation

If you don't have an oven, this can be made on the cooker-top. Use a thick-bottomed pan with a good, tight cover and cook as slow as you can without too much peeking.

Long, Slow, Comfortable Stew

225G (8OZ) HARICOT BEANS, WASHED, DRAINED AND SOAKED

2 LITRES (4 PINTS) WATER

3 TABLESPOONS OIL

5 CLOVES GARLIC, FINELY CHOPPED

2 MEDIUM ONIONS, THINLY SLICED

3 MEDIUM CARROTS, CHOPPED

2 LITRES (4 PINTS) VEGETABLE STOCK (SEE PAGE 87)

1 TEASPOON FRESHLY GROUND BLACK PEPPER

1 TEASPOON EACH OF DRIED THYME AND SAGE

2 TEASPOONS DRIED PARSLEY

3 SMALL ONIONS, PEELED AND QUARTERED

3 TOMATOES, CHOPPED

1.   Soak the beans overnight then rinse, drain and place in a large saucepan with the fresh water. Bring to a boil, cover the pan, reduce the heat and simmer briskly until the beans are nearly cooked, about 45 minutes. Drain the beans and discard the cooking water.

2.   Heat the oil in a large pan and sauté the garlic and onions until clear and tender. Add the carrots and continue to sauté for a further 5-7 minutes.

3.   Add the beans and vegetable stock and bring to a simmer over a low heat. Stir in the remaining ingredients and simmer gently until the beans are fully cooked, about 1-1½ hours: pop one in your

Serves 4-8

2-3 hrs, plus soaking beans overnight

mouth and press it against the roof of your mouth with your tongue. If it breaks easily, it is cooked. Don't rush this dish – it is improved by long, slow cooking. Serve hot in a large soup plate with plenty of croûtons, garlic bread or fresh wholemeal bread.

Backenoff Alsace

225G (8OZ) TVP CHUNKS OR QUORN

570ML (1 PINT) ALSACE WINE

2 SMALL ONIONS, COARSELY CHOPPED

6 WHOLE CLOVES

6 CLOVES GARLIC, QUARTERED

1 STICK CELERY, FINELY CHOPPED

1 TEASPOON FRESHLY GROUND BLACK PEPPER

1 TEASPOON FINELY CHOPPED FRESH THYME

1 TEASPOON FINELY CHOPPED ROSEMARY

2 BAY LEAVES

900G (2LB) POTATOES, SCRUBBED AND SLICED

2 LARGE ONIONS, THINLY SLICED

Serves 4

3-4 hrs, plus marinating time

One of my favourites – to hot you up on a cold day

1. Turn the TVP chunks into a large bowl and pour the wine over. Stir in the onion chunks, whole cloves, garlic, celery, pepper and herbs. Leave the mixture to marinate for at least 2 hours, but ideally all day or overnight. Add more wine or a little vegetable stock if it looks too dry.

2. Preheat the oven to 170°C/325°F/Gas Mark 3.

3. Arrange a layer of sliced potato in the bottom of a large casserole. Place a layer of the soaked TVP over the potato (leave the marinade behind for the moment), then arrange a layer of the sliced onions over that. Repeat these layers of potato, TVP and onion, finishing with a layer of potato.

4. Pour the marinade juices over the ingredients in the casserole until you can just see the juices beneath the potatoes. If you run out of juices, top them up with more of the wine or some vegetable stock.

5. Cover the casserole and bake for as long as you can, 2-3 hours is ideal.

6. Serve hot.

Cassoulet

675G (1½LB) COOKED BLACK-EYED
    BEANS, DRAINED
1 x 400G (14OZ) TIN TOMATOES
180ML (6 FL OZ) VEGETABLE STOCK
    (SEE PAGE 87)
3 CLOVES GARLIC, CRUSHED
2 LEEKS, CHOPPED
1 SMALL CAULIFLOWER, CUT INTO FLORETS

1 TEASPOON FRESHLY GROUND BLACK PEPPER
1 TEASPOON DRIED OREGANO
2 TABLESPOONS FINELY CHOPPED FRESH
    PARSLEY
55G (2OZ) DRIED BREADCRUMBS
1x 450G (1LB) TIN NUTTOLENE, FINELY
    CUBED

1. Preheat the oven to 180°C/350°F/Gas Mark 4 and lightly oil a casserole dish.

2. Gently mix all the ingredients, except a handful of cubed Nuttolene and the breadcrumbs, together in the casserole.

3. Sprinkle the reserved Nuttolene over the dish and top with the breadcrumbs. Bake for 45-50 minutes. Serve hot.

Serves 4

🕐 1 hr

Sobronade Serenade

225G (8OZ) FLAGEOLET BEANS,
    WASHED, DRAINED AND SOAKED
2 LITRES (4 PINTS) WATER
5 TABLESPOONS OIL
1 WHOLE BULB GARLIC, FINELY CHOPPED
3 STALKS CELERY, THINLY SLICED
1 TEASPOON FRESHLY GROUND BLACK PEPPER
¼ TEASPOON GROUND CLOVES

2 MEDIUM TURNIPS, PEELED AND CHOPPED
4 MEDIUM CARROTS, PEELED AND CHOPPED
3 SMALL ONIONS, QUARTERED
450G (1LB) POTATOES, PEELED AND CHOPPED
2 LITRES (4 PINTS) VEGETABLE STOCK
    (SEE PAGE 87)
1 LARGE BUNCH (APPROXIMATELY 55G/2OZ)
    FRESH PARSLEY, CHOPPED

1. Soak the beans overnight. Drain and rinse them, then turn into a large saucepan with the fresh water. Bring to a boil, cover the pan and reduce the heat. Simmer until the beans are nearly cooked, about 35 minutes. Drain away the cooking water.

2. Heat the oil in a large pan and sauté the garlic and celery for 7-10 minutes over a low to medium flame. Stir often.

3. Add the pepper and cloves and stir a further 1 minute. Add the

Serves 4-8

🕐 2 hrs, plus
soaking beans
overnight

turnips, carrots, onions and potatoes and stir into the sauté for 5 minutes.

4.   Now add the partly cooked beans, vegetable stock and parsley and bring to a simmer. Cover the pan and simmer very gently until the beans are fully cooked.

5.   Serve with toasted bread which you should dip and shovel into this wonderfully thick soup.

Rich Vegetable Stew

450G (1 LB) EACH OF CARROTS, PARSNIPS, POTATOES, SWEDES AND TURNIPS, PEELED AND COARSELY CHOPPED

3 TABLESPOONS OIL

5-7 CLOVES GARLIC, QUARTERED

4 MEDIUM ONIONS, QUARTERED

3 STICKS CELERY, THINLY SLICED

2 TEASPOONS FRESHLY GROUND BLACK PEPPER

1-2 TABLESPOONS DRIED PARSLEY

1 TEASPOON DRIED THYME

½ TEASPOON DRIED SAGE

450G (1 LB) CHESTNUT PURÉE

2 LITRES (4 PINTS) VEGETABLE STOCK (SEE PAGE 87) OR WATER

6-12 WHOLE CLOVES

Serves 4-8

🕐 7 hrs

Guaranteed to fill you up.

1.   Prepare the vegetables and turn them into a large bowl; mix them well.

2.   Heat the oil in a large pan and sauté the garlic, onions and celery for about 7 minutes, stirring constantly. Add the pepper and herbs and stir a further 1-2 minutes.

3.   Add the mixed vegetables and stir carefully to distribute the sauté through them.

4.   Blend the chestnut purée and stock together and pour over the vegetables. Turn the mixture into a large stewpot and garnish with the whole cloves.

5.   Cover the pot tightly and bake in a very cool oven for 6 hours (an Aga or Rayburn is ideal). The aroma of this stew will tell you when it's ready, but the longer it cooks, the more robust its flavour.

6.   Serve all on its own, with a lump or two of fresh bread to mop up the delectable juices.

PIES, FLANS AND QUICHES

Quickest Spinach Flan

180G (6OZ) PUFF PASTRY
1350G (3LB) FRESH SPINACH,
    WASHED AND DRAINED
85G (3OZ) BUTTER
PINCH OF SALT

½ TEASPOON FRESHLY GROUND BLACK PEPPER
¼ TEASPOON GROUND MACE
55G (2OZ) DRIED BREADCRUMBS
55G (2OZ) PARMESAN CHEESE, GRATED

1. Preheat the oven to 200°C/400°F/Gas Mark 6.
2. Roll out the pastry to about 5mm (¼ inch) thickness and line a 30cm (12 inch) flan dish.
3. Press the spinach into a large saucepan or steamer and cook for 3-4 minutes, until it has reduced. Drain the spinach and roughly chop it with 55g (2oz) of the butter and the salt, pepper and mace.
4. Turn the spinach mixture into the flan case and press into place.
5. Mix the breadcrumbs and Parmesan together in a bowl and sprinkle this mixture over the spinach. Bake for 20 minutes.
6. Slice and serve, hot or cold.

Serves 4-6

45 mins

Parsnip Pie

225G (8OZ) SHORTCRUST PASTRY
6 MEDIUM PARSNIPS, PEELED AND QUARTERED
1 TABLESPOON GRATED FRESH GINGER
1 TEASPOON GROUND CINNAMON

¼ TEASPOON CHILLI POWDER
ZEST AND JUICE OF 2 LEMONS
1 TABLESPOON TAHINI
285G (10OZ) FIRM TOFU

1. Preheat the oven to 200°C/400°F/Gas Mark 6.
2. Roll two-thirds of the pastry into a round of about 5mm (¼ inch) thickness and line a 30cm (12 inch) flan case. Roll the remaining pastry into a rectangle and cut into strips to make a latticework lid to the pie. Put to one side.
3. Steam the parsnips until tender, about 20 minutes. Mash them

Serves 4-6

55 mins

with the spices, lemon zest and juice and the tahini. The mash should be firm but fluffy.

4. Roughly mash the tofu and stir briefly into the parsnip mash.

5. Press the mixture into the pastry and cover with the lattice. Bake for 20 minutes.

6. Serve hot.

Variations

1. Other vegetables, such as peas or sweetcorn kernels, may be added to the mash.

2. The latticework lid may be left off and replaced by a topping of 55g (2oz) breadcrumbs mixed with 55g (2oz) grated cheese, such as Parmesan.

Leek and Cheese Meringue

180G (6OZ) PUFF PASTRY

225G (8OZ) LEEKS, TRIMMED AND CHOPPED

SALT

2 TABLESPOONS BUTTER OR MARGARINE

2 TEASPOONS CARAWAY SEEDS

1/2 TEASPOON FRESHLY GROUND BLACK PEPPER

1/2 TEASPOON GROUND CINNAMON

JUICE OF 1/2 LEMON

2 EGGS, SEPARATED

55G (2OZ) CHEDDAR CHEESE, GRATED

140ML (1/4 PINT) MILK

Serves 4-6

45 mins

Sounds strange but so does spotted dick!

1. Preheat the oven to 200°C/400°F/Gas Mark 6.

2. Roll the pastry into a round about 5mm (1/4 inch) thick and line a 30cm (12 inch) flan dish. Pour about 225g (8 oz) raw rice or beans into the pastry case. Bake for 12-15 minutes. Remove from the oven, remove the rice or beans and reduce the oven temperature to 170°C/325°F/Gas Mark 3.

3. Immerse the chopped leeks in a bowl of salty water and wash them for 2-3 minutes. Rinse and drain well.

4. Melt the butter in a frying pan over a medium heat and sauté the caraway seeds for 2 minutes. Add the pepper and cinnamon and stir for 1 minute. Now add the well-drained leeks and stir for 2 minutes.

5. Pour the lemon juice over the sauté, cover the pan and reduce the heat to very low. Leave for 3-5 minutes.

6. In a small mixing bowl, blend the egg yolks, cheese and milk. When the leeks have finished cooking, spread them into the flan case and pour the egg mixture over them.

7. Whisk the egg whites to a stiff peak stage and immediately spread over the flan.

8. Bake for 20 minutes. Cool for 5 minutes then slice and serve with a selection of vegetable side dishes.

Carrot and Turnip Flan

For the pastry:
180G (6OZ) ROLLED OATS
85G (3OZ) BUTTER OR MARGARINE
PINCH OF SALT
1/4 TEASPOON FRESHLY GROUND BLACK PEPPER
1/2 TEASPOON GROUND CINNAMON
25G (1OZ) SUNFLOWER SEEDS, COARSELY CRUSHED

For the filling:
550G (1 1/4 LB) CARROTS, PEELED AND CHOPPED
340G (12OZ) TURNIPS, PEELED AND CUBED
25G (1OZ) BUTTER OR MARGARINE
2 TABLESPOONS PLAIN FLOUR
285ML (1/2 PINT) MILK
1/4 TEASPOON FRESHLY GROUND BLACK PEPPER
1/2 -1 TEASPOON GROUND GINGER
PARSLEY TO GARNISH

1. Preheat the oven to 200°C/400°F/Gas Mark 6.

2. For the pastry, measure the oats into a bowl and rub in the butter. Add the spices and sunflower seeds, mixing so that they are well distributed.

3. Press this crumb-like mixture evenly into a lightly oiled 23cm (9 inch), flan dish. Set aside.

4. Steam the carrots and turnips until tender. Drain them and mash to a purée.

5. Melt the butter in a saucepan and sprinkle the flour over. Stir to make a thick paste, or roux. Add the milk, a little at a time, stirring after each addition while the sauce thickens. Blend the sauce with the vegetable purée, pepper and ginger.

6. Spoon the mixture into the prepared flan case and smooth the top.

7. Bake for 15 minutes, slice and serve with parsley to garnish and a selection of steamed vegetables or salads.

Serves 4-6

40 mins

Quick Spinach and Bean Tart

225G (8OZ) PUFF PASTRY

225G (8OZ) COOKED BLACK-EYED

BEANS

1 ONION, THINLY SLICED

1 SMALL PACKET FROZEN

SPINACH, THAWED

1 TABLESPOON BUTTER OR MARGARINE

1 TABLESPOON PLAIN FLOUR

140ML (¼ PINT) MILK

55G (2OZ) MATURE CHEDDAR CHEESE, GRATED

PINCH OF SALT

½ TEASPOON FRESHLY GROUND BLACK PEPPER

Serves 4-6

 55 mins

1. Preheat the oven to 200°C/400°F/Gas Mark 6.

2. Roll out the pastry to 5mm (¼ inch) thickness and line a 20-23cm (8-9 inch) flan dish.

3. Drain the beans, mix them with the sliced onion, and spread over the pastry base.

4. Leave the spinach to thaw and drain off any liquid from it. Arrange the thawed spinach over the beans and onions in the tart.

5. Melt the butter in a small saucepan and sprinkle the flour over it. Stir to make a thick paste, or roux. Add the milk, a little at a time, stirring after each addition to make a thick sauce. Stir in the cheese, salt and pepper and cook for a further 2-3 minutes to make a smooth sauce.

6. Pour the cheese sauce over the beans and bake the tart for 30 minutes.

Onion Tart

For the pastry:

85G (3OZ) WHOLEMEAL FLOUR

85G (3OZ) PLAIN FLOUR

85G (3OZ) COLD BUTTER OR MARGARINE

PINCH OF SALT

1 TABLESPOON ICED WATER

1 TABLESPOON LEMON JUICE

1 EGG WHITE, LIGHTLY WHISKED

For the filling:

45G (1½ OZ) BUTTER OR MARGARINE

4 LARGE ONIONS, THINLY SLICED

2 TABLESPOONS GREEN PEPPERCORNS

285ML (½ PINT) SOURED CREAM

1 EGG YOLK

25G (1OZ) GRUYÈRE CHEESE, GRATED

PINCH OF SALT

6 BLACK OLIVES, STONED

1. Preheat the oven to 220°C/425°F/Gas Mark 7.
2. For the pastry, sift the flours into a mixing bowl, then sprinkle the bran back into the mixture. Add the butter and salt and rub together until you have a crumb-like mixture. Add just enough iced water and lemon juice to make a paste then use immediately or cover the pastry with plastic wrap and refrigerate for 1 hour.
3. Roll the pastry to line a 30cm (12 inch) flan dish. Fill with raw rice or beans and bake blind for 10 minutes. Remove the beans, brush the pastry with the egg white and bake again for 3-5 minutes. Reduce the oven temperature to 200°C/400°F/Gas Mark 6.
4. Meanwhile, melt the butter in a large pan over a medium flame and sauté the sliced onions until clear and tender, 7-10 minutes.
5. Take from the heat and add the peppercorns, soured cream, egg yolk, Gruyère and salt. Stir thoroughly and pour into the tart.
6. Slice the olives in half and place them in a pattern into the onion mixture.
7. Bake for 20 minutes, until just brown on top.

Serves 4-6

🕐 1 hr 30 mins

Don't forget your toothbrush – need I say more?!

Onion and Apple Pie

225G (8OZ) SHORTCRUST PASTRY

1350G (3LB) APPLES, PEELED, CORED AND SLICED

450G (1LB) ONIONS, SLICED

85G (3OZ) PLAIN FLOUR

1 TABLESPOON FINELY CHOPPED FRESH SAGE

2 TEASPOONS FRESHLY GROUND BLACK PEPPER

1 TEASPOON GROUND ALLSPICE

2 TABLESPOONS FINELY CHOPPED FRESH PARSLEY

2 TABLESPOONS BUTTER OR MARGARINE

Serves 4-6

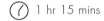 1 hr 15 mins

1. Preheat the oven to 200°C/400°F/Gas Mark 6.

2. Roll the pastry to a thickness of 5mm (¼ inch) and line a 23cm (9 inch) pie dish. Reserve any scraps of pastry, press them together and roll into a rectangle. Cut this pastry into strips for use later.

3. Prepare the apples and onions and have them ready on separate plates.

4. Mix the flour in a small bowl with the sage, pepper and allspice. Arrange a layer of sliced apples in the pie dish, cover with a layer of onion slices and sprinkle some of the flour mixture over this. Repeat these layers – apple, onion, flour mix – until all the ingredients are used.

5. Sprinkle the parsley over the pie and place dabs of butter over that.

6. Now arrange the pastry strips in a loose lattice over the pie, press the pastry edges together and bake for 45 minutes.

7. Serve at once, although you can eat it cold or reheated.

RICE DISHES

Sweet and Sour 'Chicken'

140G (5OZ) TVP CHUNKS OR QUORN	25G (1OZ) PLAIN FLOUR
3 TABLESPOONS OIL	285ML (½ PINT) PINEAPPLE JUICE
1 LARGE ONION, THINLY SLICED	60ML (2 FL OZ) WINE VINEGAR
1 LARGE GREEN PEPPER, THINLY SLICED	1 TABLESPOON SUGAR
½ TEASPOON FRESHLY GROUND BLACK PEPPER	½ TSP HOLBROOK'S WORCESTERSHIRE SAUCE
½ TEASPOON DRY MUSTARD	1-2 TABLESPOONS SOY SAUCE
1 TEASPOON DRIED PARSLEY	225G (8OZ) PINEAPPLE, CHOPPED
1 TEASPOON DRIED MARJORAM	1 SMALL BUNCH SEEDLESS GRAPES

1. Turn the TVP chunks into a bowl and cover with boiling water; stir well and leave to rehydrate.

2. Heat the oil in a pan and sauté the onion and pepper for 7-10 minutes, stirring often.

3. Mix the ground pepper, mustard and herbs into the flour and put to one side. Blend the pineapple juice, vinegar, sugar, Worcestershire and soy sauces together in a small jug.

4. Sprinkle the flour mixture over the sauté and stir as it cooks to a thick paste. Gradually add the liquid mixture, a little at a time, stirring after each addition. The sauce will thicken and become aromatic.

5. Drain the TVP chunks of any water and add to the sauce; stir in the pineapple and grapes. Simmer 10 minutes, stirring often.

6. Serve hot over rice.

Serves 4

🕐 45 mins

Tip

Holbrooks Worcestershire Sauce is made without anchovies for those of us who avoid eating fish.

Thai Tofu Curry

285G (10OZ) FIRM TOFU, CUBED

3-4 TABLESPOONS VEGETABLE OIL

2 LARGE ONIONS, THINLY SLICED

2 SHALLOTS, CHOPPED

2 CLOVES GARLIC, FINELY CHOPPED

1 TABLESPOON GRATED FRESH GINGER

2CM (3/4 INCH) STALK LEMONGRASS, CHOPPED

2 TEASPOONS CHOPPED CORIANDER ROOT OR
    2 TABLESPOONS CHOPPED FRESH CORIANDER

10 DRIED RED CHILLIES OR 2 TEASPOONS
    CHILLI PASTE

1/2 TEASPOON GRATED LIME PEEL

3 TEASPOONS ROASTED CORIANDER SEEDS

1 TEASPOON ROASTED CUMIN SEEDS

2 ROASTED CARDAMOM PODS

1/2 TEASPOON EACH OF GROUND NUTMEG,
    CINNAMON AND CLOVES

1/4 TEASPOON GROUND MACE

285ML (1/2 PINT) THICK COCONUT MILK

2 TABLESPOONS TAMARIND WATER OR LIME
    JUICE

1 LEVEL TABLESPOON RAW CANE SUGAR

FRESHLY GROUND BLACK PEPPER, TO TASTE

PINCH OF SALT

Serves 4

45 mins

1. Arrange the tofu on a tray and grill for 3-5 minutes, carefully turning twice in that time; set aside.

2. Heat half the oil in a small frying pan and sauté the onion until clear and tender; set aside.

3. Use a mortar and pestle to grind the shallots, garlic, ginger and lemongrass with the coriander root, chillies, lime peel, coriander seeds, cumin seeds and cardamom pods. Add the ground spices to this mixture then stir in a few spoonfuls of cold water to make a paste.

4. Heat the remaining oil in a small pan, add the paste and sauté for a few minutes, stirring frequently.

5. Pour in the coconut milk and bring to a boil. Add the tamarind water, sugar and seasoning. Bring to the boil again before stirring in the tofu and onions. Simmer for 10 minutes over a low flame.

6. Serve with rice.

Tip

Tamarind is traditionally used in Eastern cuisines; it has a slightly salty sour flavour which usually lifts the flavour of other spices it is combined with.

Creole Jambalaya

140G (5OZ) TVP CHUNKS

2-3 TABLESPOONS OIL

3 CLOVES GARLIC, CRUSHED

2 SMALL ONIONS, THINLY SLICED

1 GREEN PEPPER, THINLY SLICED

ALL THE CELERY LEAVES FROM 1 HEAD CELERY

450G (1LB) RIPE TOMATOES, COARSELY CHOPPED

3 TABLESPOONS TOMATO PURÉE

¼ TEASPOON HOLBROOK'S WORCESTERSHIRE SAUCE

225G (8OZ) LONG GRAIN WHITE RICE, WASHED

285-425ML (½ - ¾ PINT) VEGETABLE STOCK (SEE PAGE 87)

½ TEASPOON DRIED THYME

FRESHLY GROUND BLACK PEPPER, TO TASTE

FRESH PARSLEY, FINELY CHOPPED

1. Turn the TVP chunks into a deep bowl and cover them with boiling water; set aside to rehydrate.
2. Heat half the oil in a large pan and sauté the chunks for 7-10 minutes, turning occasionally, until they begin to colour. Remove them from the pan and set aside.
3. Add the remaining oil to the pan, then stir the garlic, onions and pepper until they soften. Add the celery leaves and stir a further minute or two. Add the tomatoes and the purée then stir in the Worcestershire sauce, then the rice, 285ml (½ pint) of the stock, the thyme and pepper.
4. Bring to a boil and add the TVP chunks. Cover the pan and cook over a low flame for about 20 minutes, until the rice is tender. Check during the cooking process to ensure the rice is not sticking and add a drop more stock if necessary.
5. Serve garnished with plenty of fresh parsley.

Serves 4-6

🕐 55 mins

Variation

Authentic Creole Jambalaya has prawns or shrimps in it. For a similar contrast in texture, sprinkle 55g (2oz) broken cashew nuts on to the prepared dish.

*A*lmond Vegetable Chop Suey

2 TEASPOONS ARROWROOT

60ML (2 FL OZ) COLD WATER

½ TEASPOON SOY SAUCE

2-3 TABLESPOONS OIL

3 SPRING ONIONS, VERY THINLY SLICED

1 STICK CELERY, THINLY SLICED

85G (3OZ) MUSHROOMS, SLICED

1 RED PEPPER, THINLY SLICED

⅛ SMALL WHITE CABBAGE, SHREDDED

1 BUNCH WATERCRESS, WASHED AND CHOPPED

85G (3OZ) ALMONDS

1 TABLESPOON DRY SHERRY

100G (4OZ) MUNG BEANSPROUTS

Serves 4

⏱ 25 mins

1. Whisk the arrowroot, water and soy sauce together in a small bowl.

2. Heat the oil in a large frying pan or wok. Add the spring onions, celery, mushrooms and pepper and cook for 3 minutes over a medium flame, stirring constantly.

3. Add the cabbage and stir 5 minutes more. Add the watercress and the almonds and cook a further 2 minutes.

4. Stir in the arrowroot mixture, then cook over a low flame until the sauce thickens.

5. Add the sherry and the beansprouts, cover the pan and leave over a medium flame for literally 1 minute to warm through.

6. Serve at once over rice.

Tip

For best flavour and texture, and to preserve the colour of your vegetables, heat your wok first, then add the oil and vegetables.

Parsnip and Pumpkin Curry

3 TABLESPOONS BUTTER OR GHEE

5-7 CLOVES GARLIC, FINELY CHOPPED

2 MEDIUM ONIONS, FINELY CHOPPED

6 MEDIUM PARSNIPS, PEELED AND CHOPPED

1 SMALL PUMPKIN, SEEDED, PEELED AND CUBED

2 MEDIUM POTATOES, PEELED AND DICED

140-285ML (¼ - ½ PINT) VEGETABLE STOCK (SEE PAGE 87) OR WATER

2 TEASPOONS CUMIN SEEDS

1 TEASPOON MUSTARD SEEDS

½ TEASPOON CHILLI POWDER

2 TEASPOONS TURMERIC

4-6 TABLESPOONS CHOPPED FRESH CORIANDER

1. Heat 2 tablespoons of the butter in a large pan over a medium heat and sauté the garlic and onions until clear and tender, about 7-10 minutes.

2. Add the parsnip, pumpkin and potato chunks and stir well. Reduce the heat, cover the pan and cook the vegetables for 15 minutes, stirring occasionally. As soon as they begin to stick, add a little of the vegetable stock.

3. The aim of this curry is to cook the vegetables 'dry', in their own juices, as much as possible before adding any liquid. When the vegetables are tender, add any additional stock you desire, but I encourage you to try this quite dry the first time you prepare it.

4. Heat the remaining butter in a small frying pan and sauté the cumin and mustard seeds for about 3 minutes, stirring constantly. Add the chilli powder and stir a further 1 minute. Add the turmeric and stir a final 1 minute then turn the sauté into the vegetables and stir well. Add the chopped coriander and stir once more.

5. Serve the curry at once or leave it to cool and mature for up to 4 hours, then reheat it and serve with rice, dhal and a yogurt sauce (Risqué Raita, see page 193).

Serves 4

⏱ 50 mins

You won't need 10 pints of lager to enjoy this!

Tip

Ghee is clarified butter, now mostly made from cow's milk butter.

Pepper and Sweetcorn Ragoût

2 TABLESPOONS OIL

3 CLOVES GARLIC, FINELY CHOPPED

1 LARGE ONION, THICKLY SLICED

2 RED PEPPERS, THICKLY SLICED

2 GREEN PEPPERS, THICKLY SLICED

285ML (½ PINT) VEGETABLE STOCK (SEE PAGE 87)

½ TEASPOON FRESHLY GROUND BLACK PEPPER

BOUQUET GARNI OF PARSLEY, THYME, MARJORAM AND BAY

100G (4OZ) SWEETCORN KERNELS

2 TABLESPOONS SHERRY

1 TABLESPOON PLAIN FLOUR

Serves 4

🕐 35 mins

1. Heat the oil in a large pan over a medium flame and sauté the garlic, onion and peppers for 5-7 minutes, stirring occasionally. Add the stock, black pepper and bouquet garni.

2. Bring to the boil, then cover the pan, reduce the heat and simmer gently for about 5 minutes.

3. Add the sweetcorn and cook a further 5-7 minutes. Remove the bouquet garni. Stir the sherry and flour together in a cup and add to the saucepan.

4. Simmer for 2-3 minutes more to thicken the sauce, stirring all the while.

5. Adjust the seasoning and serve at once over rice, steamed millet or baked potato.

Coconut Vegetable Rice

225G (8OZ) BROWN RICE, WASHED

3 SPRING ONIONS, FINELY CHOPPED

225G (8OZ) GREEN BEANS, TRIMMED AND SLICED

½ HEAD CAULIFLOWER, BROKEN INTO LARGE FLORETS

425ML (¾ PINT) HOT VEGETABLE STOCK (SEE PAGE 87)

55G (2OZ) CREAMED COCONUT, GRATED

1 TABLESPOON FINELY CHOPPED FRESH BASIL

1 TABLESPOON FINELY CHOPPED FRESH PARSLEY

¼ TEASPOON FRESHLY GROUND BLACK PEPPER

3 MEDIUM TOMATOES, CHOPPED

Serves 4-6

🕐 1 hr 30 mins

1. Soak the rice in hot water for an hour, then drain. Put it into a saucepan with the prepared vegetables and most of the stock.

2. Dissolve the coconut in the remaining stock and add it to the rice with the herbs and black pepper. Bring the stock to a boil

152

then cover the pan, reduce the heat, and cook until the rice and vegetables are just cooked, about 20 minutes.

3.   Stir in the chopped tomatoes and serve at once.

Variation

Add 1 teaspoon turmeric and 100g (4oz) slivered almonds to the vegetable mixture as you add the herbs. Stir well and proceed as above.

SENSATIONAL CENTREPIECES

Vegetable Chartreuse

FIRM CENTRE OF WHITE CABBAGE, QUARTERED AND HEART REMOVED

180G (6OZ) BABY CARROTS, SCRUBBED AND TRIMMED

180G (6OZ) BABY SWEETCORN

4 SMALL TURNIPS, PEELED AND VERY THINLY SLICED

4 SMALL COURGETTES, WASHED AND QUARTERED LENGTHWISE

225G (8OZ) SMALL FRENCH BEANS, TRIMMED

5 SPRING ONIONS, TRIMMED AND VERY THINLY SLICED

180G (6OZ) FRESH PODDED PEAS

180ML (6 FL OZ) MILK

2 EGGS, BEATEN

1/2 TEASPOON GROUND NUTMEG

4-6 LARGE CABBAGE LEAVES

1.   Preheat the oven to 190°C/375°F/Gas Mark 5.

2.   Steam the cabbage, carrots, sweetcorn, turnip, courgette, beans, onions and peas until just tender, about 7 minutes. They must neither wilt nor lose their colour.

3.   Arrange the small vegetables in a pattern round the edges of a deep well-buttered mould and use the remainder, specifically the cabbage quarters, to neatly fill the centre.

4.   Whisk the milk, eggs and nutmeg together to a light froth and pour over the vegetables. Place the mould in a large casserole with 2-5cm (1- 2 inches) of water in it. When the mould is placed in it the

Serves 4-6

1 hr

water should rise yet remain below the top edge of the mould. Cover the casserole, place in the oven and bake for 45 minutes.

5.   Meanwhile, blanch the cabbage leaves in a pot of boiling water for 2 minutes. Drain.

6.   When the chartreuse has cooked, drape the cabbage leaves over the top and press a serving platter over the cabbage. Turn the whole thing over and allow the chartreuse to unmould on to the platter. Tidy the cabbage leaves so that they form a handsome background and arrange more steamed vegetables or salad around the chartreuse.

7.   Slice or cut in wedges and serve hot or cold with iced butter and spicy sauces such as Spicy Drizzle Dressing (see page 108), French Lace Dressing (see page 109) or Risqué Raita (see page 193).

*S*unday Roast

100G (4OZ) RED LENTILS

1-2 TEASPOONS YEAST EXTRACT

180ML (6 FL OZ) BOILING WATER

570ML (1 PINT/2 CUPS) COOKED RICE (WHITE OR BROWN)

100G (4OZ) ROLLED OATS

1 TEASPOON FRESHLY GROUND BLACK PEPPER

1 TABLESPOON DRIED MIXED SWEET HERBS

2 TABLESPOONS PREPARED MUSTARD

2 TABLESPOONS TAHINI

2 TABLESPOONS SOYA FLOUR

140ML (¼ PINT) WATER OR VEGETABLE STOCK (SEE PAGE 87)

PLAIN FLOUR

55G (2OZ) DRIED BREADCRUMBS

FRESHLY GROUND BLACK PEPPER

Serves 4-8

 2 hrs

1.   Preheat the oven to 190°C/375°F/Gas Mark 5.

2.   Wash and drain the red lentils and put in a saucepan. Dissolve the yeast extract in the water and pour over the lentils. Leave to soak for 10 minutes then cook, covered, at a simmer over a medium heat for about 10 minutes, until the lentils soften.

3.   In a large mixing bowl, stir together the rice, oats, pepper and herbs. Whisk the mustard, tahini, soya flour and water together in a small bowl.

4.   When the lentils have cooked, stir them into the rice mixture along with the tahini mixture. Leave to stand for 10 minutes while you lightly oil a roasting tin and spread the surface of a pastry board with a little plain flour.

5.   Turn the roast mixture on to the board and shape it into a large cylinder. Roll the roast in the breadcrumbs, pressing as you do so, and place the roast in the centre of the tin. Sprinkle the top of the roast with fresh pepper then cover the tin with kitchen foil and bake for about 45 minutes.

6.   Uncover the roast for the final 5 minutes, to brown the top.

7.   Serve with your favourite vegetables and plenty of gravy and mustard.

Tips

1.   This roast will lose its shape a little during baking; you may wish to press the mixture into a loaf tin or mould to give it a different and more supported shape. Simply ensure that all sides of the loaf are covered in the bread-crumbs and that the tin or mould is well buttered.

2.   Parsnips, potatoes, carrots and small onions may be baked alongside this roast in the traditional way; however, the roast will not produce any juices. Make a little gravy or dilute yeast extract to pour over the roasting veg before you cover the tin.

Nori Ring Mould

2 SHEETS TOASTED NORI

1 TABLESPOON SOY SAUCE

1 TABLESPOON WATER

55G (2OZ) CREAM CHEESE

3 SPRING ONIONS, FINELY CHOPPED

2 MEDIUM POTATOES, PEELED AND STEAMED

25G (1OZ) BUTTER OR MARGARINE, SOFTENED

2 TABLESPOONS MILK

100G (4OZ) COOKED PEAS

55G (2OZ) BREADCRUMBS

PINCH OF SALT

1/4 TEASPOON FRESHLY GROUND BLACK PEPPER

1 RIPE AVOCADO, PEELED AND SLICED

450G (1LB) RIPE TOMATOES, CHOPPED

2 TABLESPOONS SOURED CREAM

2 TEASPOONS GREEN PEPPERCORNS

1.   Cut the nori sheets in half along their length and moisten them in a mixture of the soy sauce and water. Arrange the nori halves in a 23cm (9 inch) ring mould, leaving some overhang.

2.   Mix the cream cheese, onion, potato, butter and milk together

Serves 4-8

🕐 45 mins, plus chilling time

in a mixing bowl, working to a light consistency. Add the peas, breadcrumbs and seasoning and stir well.

3.   Prepare the avocado. Press half of the potato mixture into the nori moulds then arrange the avocado slices over the potato. Press the remaining potato over the avocado and fold the overhanging nori over to cover the potato.

4.   Seal the nori edges by dampening them and pressing gently with your fingers. Refrigerate the mould for a few hours.

5.   To serve, slice the chilled mould with a serrated knife and place the slice on a serving plate. Arrange tomato chunks on or around the slice and top with a dollop of soured cream garnished with green peppercorns.

_A_sparagus Soufflé

450G (1LB) ASPARAGUS, TRIMMED

4 EGGS, SEPARATED

55G (2OZ) GRUYÈRE CHEESE, GRATED

PINCH OF SALT

¼ TEASPOON FRESHLY GROUND BLACK PEPPER

25G (1OZ) BUTTER OR MARGARINE

25G (1OZ) PLAIN FLOUR

285ML (½ PINT) SINGLE CREAM

Serves 4-6

⏱ 55 mins

This is one soufflé that won't do a flip!

1.   Steam-boil the asparagus in a little salted water for 8 minutes, until tender. Roughly mash the asparagus and place it in a mixing bowl with the egg yolks, Gruyère and seasoning; stir well.

2.   Melt the butter in a saucepan over a medium flame and sprinkle the flour over. Stir to make a thick paste, or roux, then remove from the heat and stir in the cream to make a smooth sauce. Leave aside to cool.

3.   Preheat the oven to 220°C/425°F/Gas Mark 7.

4.   Pour the cooled sauce over the asparagus mixture and mix thoroughly.

5.   Whip the egg whites until stiff then fold them into the asparagus mixture. Pour immediately into a 20cm (8 inch) lightly buttered soufflé dish and bake for 20 minutes.

6.   Serve hot.

Tip

A soufflé is not at all difficult to make provided everything is at the right temperature at the right time! Make sure the cream sauce is well cooled before mixing it with the asparagus mixture. And don't whip the egg whites until the last minute – if they sit around, they lose their whip. Finally, don't over-mix in the final stage and make sure the oven is really preheated. Get these things right and your soufflé will rise well, form a crisp top and keep a soft, delectable centre.

MARINADES

Dried Tomato Marinade

55G (2OZ) SUN-DRIED TOMATOES

1 TABLESPOON DRIED GARLIC FLAKES OR 5-7 CLOVES GARLIC, FINELY CHOPPED

2 TEASPOONS DRIED OREGANO

1 TEASPOON DRIED BASIL

JUICE OF 2 LEMONS

60ML (2 FL OZ) OLIVE OIL

1. Decide how you want to serve the tomatoes: leave them whole or slice them into thin strips. Turn them into a deep bowl, add the remaining ingredients and stir well. Add a little more lemon juice or olive oil if necessary to ensure all the tomatoes are covered.

2. Marinate for at least 3 hours, though all day or overnight is ideal.

3. Drain the tomatoes to serve in salads, as a garnish to soups or flans, or spoon on to toast with a little of the marinade. Their use is limited only by your imagination.

Serves 4

20 mins, plus 3 hrs or more to marinate

Variations

1. To cook the tomatoes, and serve them hot, add 180ml (6 fl oz) water to the marinade and turn the whole into a saucepan. Simmer gently for 12-15 minutes and serve with a spoonful of the juice.

2. To serve as a rich tomato sauce for pasta:

2 TABLESPOONS OIL

5-7 CLOVES GARLIC, FINELY CHOPPED

1 MEDIUM ONION, FINELY CHOPPED

1 DRIED TOMATO MARINADE (ABOVE), WITH
    SLICED TOMATOES AND ALL MARINADE
    JUICES

285G (10OZ) TOMATO PURÉE

570ML (1 PINT) WATER OR VEGETABLE STOCK
    (SEE PAGE 87)

2 TABLESPOONS FINELY CHOPPED FRESH PARSLEY

1 TEASPOON BROWN SUGAR

2 TEASPOONS SOY SAUCE

Serves 4-6

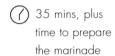 35 mins, plus
time to prepare
the marinade

1. Heat the oil in a saucepan and sauté the garlic and onion until clear and tender, about 7 minutes.

2. Add the remaining ingredients and simmer gently for 15-20 minutes. Adjust the flavours and thickness to suit your taste and serve over pasta.

Tempeh Marinade

2 x 225G (8OZ) BLOCKS TEMPEH,
    DEFROSTED

1 MEDIUM ONION, THINLY SLICED

1 BULB GARLIC, FINELY CHOPPED

1 APPLE, PEELED AND COARSELY CHOPPED

140ML (¼ PINT) OLIVE OIL

285ML (½ PINT) GOOD VINEGAR
    (TRY RASPBERRY, CIDER OR TARRAGON)

60ML (2 FL OZ) SOY SAUCE

1 TABLESPOON FRESH GINGER, GRATED

2 TEASPOONS FRESHLY GROUND BLACK PEPPER

12 WHOLE CLOVES

1 TEASPOON MUSTARD SEEDS

½ DRIED CHILLI

Serves 4

 at least 4 hrs
45 mins

1. Slice or cube the tempeh (see page 266 to find out what it is) and arrange in a casserole with the onion, garlic and apple nicely interspersed.

2. Mix the remaining ingredients together in a jug and pour over the tempeh. Cover and leave to marinate for at least 4 hours, but best all day or overnight. Agitate the casserole once or twice during this time if possible.

3. Lift the tempeh from the marinade and sauté or bake or, as is my preference, leave it covered and in the marinade and bake in a medium oven (180°C/350°F/Gas Mark 4) for about 45 minutes.

4. Serve hot over rice with plenty of green and yellow veg to accompany.

Bean and Broccoli Marinade

3 TABLESPOONS OIL

5 CLOVES GARLIC, FINELY CHOPPED

1 MEDIUM ONION, FINELY CHOPPED

1 RED PEPPER, FINELY CHOPPED

½ TEASPOON CHILLI POWDER

1 x 7.5CM (3 INCH) PIECE CINNAMON STICK, BROKEN

3 CARDAMOM PODS, SLIGHTLY CRUSHED

2 TEASPOONS FENNEL SEEDS

285ML (½ PINT) CIDER VINEGAR

60ML (2 FL OZ) SOY SAUCE

450G (1LB) GREEN BEANS

450G (1LB) COOKED KIDNEY BEANS

450G (1LB) COOKED CHICK PEAS

450G (1LB) BROCCOLI, TRIMMED AND CUT INTO FLORETS

1. Heat the oil in a large saucepan over a medium heat. Sauté the garlic and onion until clear and tender, about 7 minutes.

2. Now stir in the red pepper and the spices and sauté a further 3-5 minutes, stirring often. Add the remaining ingredients, bring to a low simmer, cover the pan and cook for 12-15 minutes.

3. Stir the marinade, cover the pan and remove from the heat. Leave to cool in the pan, then transfer to a container you can seal and leave in the fridge. Chill and serve.

4. This dish will keep about four days in the fridge, if you don't eat it all in the first day. It is excellent as a standby snack or meal. Serve it with some of the delicious marinade for maximum enjoyment.

Serves 8

45 mins, plus chilling time

Refreshing Tofu Marinade

550G (1¼ LB) FIRM TOFU

JUICE AND ZEST OF 3 ORANGES

JUICE AND ZEST OF 1 LEMON

3 SPRING ONIONS, FINELY CHOPPED

2 TABLESPOONS FINELY CHOPPED FRESH CORIANDER

1 TABLESPOON FINELY CHOPPED FRESH PARSLEY

6 WHOLE CLOVES

½ TEASPOON FRESHLY GROUND BLACK PEPPER

1. Cut the tofu into four 'steaks' or into 2.5cm (1 inch) cubes and place in a casserole or gratin dish.

2. Mix the remaining ingredients together in a jug and pour over the tofu. Cover the dish and leave to marinate for at least 4 hours, though all day or overnight is ideal.

Serves 4

25 mins, plus marinating time

3.   Turn the tofu at least once during this time to ensure an even marination and agitate the dish once or twice more, as well.

4.   Drain the marinade juices and serve the tofu immediately, cold, or cook it in your favourite manner (i.e. sauté, breaded and grilled).

5.   The marinade may be used again the same day or as part of a dressing or broth.

All-purpose Robust Marinade

4 TABLESPOONS OIL

5-7 CLOVES GARLIC, FINELY CHOPPED

1 MEDIUM ONION, FINELY CHOPPED

1 TEASPOON FRESHLY GROUND BLACK PEPPER

100-225G (4-8OZ) QUORN OR TVP CHUNKS

285ML (½ PINT) GOOD VINEGAR (I.E. CIDER, RASPBERRY, TARRAGON)

60ML (2 FL OZ) SOY SAUCE

JUICE AND ZEST OF 1 ORANGE

1 TABLESPOON GRATED FRESH GINGER

2 BAY LEAVES

1 TEASPOON DRIED THYME

½ TEASPOON GROUND ALLSPICE OR CLOVES

Serves 4-8

🕐 40 mins, plus cooling time

1.   Heat the oil in a large saucepan and sauté the garlic and onion until clear and tender, about 7 minutes over a medium flame.

2.   Add the pepper and sauté a further 1 minute then stir in the Quorn or TVP and reduce the heat. Stir often to sauté the Quorn, about 7 minutes, then add the remaining ingredients. Bring to a simmer, cover the pan and leave over a low heat for 12-15 minutes.

3.   Let the marinade cool in the pan then strain the Quorn or TVP from the juices and add to salads, flans, potato dishes, soups or stews.

Variation

This marinade may be used for foods other than TVP or Quorn. It is excellent for: a mixture of beans and vegetables; a 'sauerkraut' of shredded cabbage, turnips, beetroot and onion; a pot full of vegetarian sausages with baby onions and sweetcorn; a 'pickle' of sliced cucumber, red pepper and sweet onions.

Asparagus Soufflé (page 156)

PART FIVE

On the Side

These quick and easy side dishes are just as creative – and sensually pleasing – as the main courses you've just browsed. Mix and match, pick and choose to your heart's delight. And don't forget that the Ingredient Finder on page 280 can help you find recipes for which you've already got good food in your larder – in a flash!

Potato Fans with Rosemary and Chives (page 166)

POTATO DISHES

Superlative Parsley and Dill Potatoes

900G (2LB) POTATOES, SCRUBBED OR
PEELED
55G (2OZ) BUTTER
PINCH OF SALT
½ TEASPOON FRESHLY GROUND BLACK PEPPER
(OPTIONAL)

3 TABLESPOONS FINELY CHOPPED FRESH
PARSLEY
2 TABLESPOONS FINELY CHOPPED FRESH
DILLWEED

1. Steam the potatoes until tender, but not falling apart.
2. Melt the butter in a large saucepan and stir in the salt, pepper, parsley and dill. Stir for 1 minute then add the cooked potatoes and gently toss them in the butter sauce over a medium heat.
3. Turn immediately into a warmed serving dish and pour any remaining herb butter over. Serve hot.

Serves 4-6

🕐 30 mins

Tip

New potatoes are excellent in this dish as they hold their shape so well and have such a strong flavour of their own. However, any potato will do provided it is not overcooked. Large potatoes may be quartered.

Rösti

900G (2LB) POTATOES, SCRUBBED
1 MEDIUM ONION, VERY THINLY
SLICED

100G (4OZ) BUTTER OR MARGARINE
100G (4OZ) BROCCOLI, FINELY CHOPPED
(OPTIONAL)

1. Steam or boil the potatoes in their skins until they are three-quarters cooked, about 20 minutes. They should feel tender but must not be breaking apart. Allow the potatoes to cool so that you

Serves 2-4

🕐 40 mins

can handle them, then grate them into a large bowl. Add the sliced onion and mix gently.

2.   Melt half the butter in a large frying pan and add the potato mixture to it. Move the rösti with a wooden spoon as it cooks then, when it is nearly cooked, add the broccoli if you are including it.

3.   Shape the mixture into a firm, round cake in the pan and press it down. Leave it to brown on the underside, adding a little more butter if necessary.

4.   Now use a spatula to lift and turn the rösti. Add the remaining butter, brown the other side then serve on to a hot plate.

5.   You may make one large rösti and divide it, or a smaller cake for each serving. Excellent for a hot breakfast, a potato accompaniment to a salad or grilled meal, or as a meal all on its own.

Potato Fans with Rosemary and Chives

4 BAKING POTATOES, SCRUBBED

4 TABLESPOONS BUTTER OR MARGARINE

1 TEASPOON SALT

FRESHLY GROUND BLACK PEPPER, TO TASTE

1 TEASPOON DRIED ROSEMARY, LIGHTLY GROUND

1 TABLESPOON FINELY CHOPPED FRESH CHIVES

Serves 4

1 hr

1.   Preheat the oven to 200°C/400°F/Gas Mark 6.

2.   Slice the potatoes into thin slices but cutting only seven-eighths of the way through the potato. Place each potato on a sheet of kitchen foil.

3.   Blend the remaining ingredients together and spread a little of the herb butter blend between each potato slice.

4.   Wrap the buttered potatoes so the edges of the foil are sealed and on top of the potato and bake for about 45 minutes, until the potato is tender. Open the foil and brown the potatoes by baking a further 5-10 minutes.

5.   Serve immediately.

Rich Potato Garlic Bake

900G (2LB) POTATOES, PEELED AND THINLY SLICED

1 BULB GARLIC, CRUSHED OR THINLY SLICED

1 TEASPOON FRESHLY GROUND BLACK PEPPER

100G (4OZ) BUTTER OR MARGARINE

1. Preheat the oven to 180°C/350°F/Gas Mark 4.
2. Rinse the potato slices and dry with a clean tea towel. Arrange a layer of sliced potatoes in a casserole dish and sprinkle some garlic and ground pepper over them.
3. Dab some of the butter over the layer and repeat layers of potato, garlic, pepper and butter until all the ingredients are used.
4. Cover the casserole and bake for 45 minutes. Uncover the dish and bake a further 10 minutes to give a golden crust.
5. Serve hot with greens.

Serves 4

⏱ 1 hr

Yes, really — one whole bulb of garlic! You won't regret it!

Creamed Potato Cakes

450G (1LB) POTATOES, PEELED AND QUARTERED

450G (1LB) BROCCOLI, CHOPPED

2 TABLESPOONS FINELY CHOPPED FRESH PARSLEY OR CORIANDER

1 TEASPOON DRIED THYME

140ML (¼ PINT) MILK

100G (4OZ) PLAIN FLOUR

1 TEASPOON FRESHLY GROUND BLACK PEPPER

2-4 TABLESPOONS BUTTER OR MARGARINE

1 SMALL ONION, FINELY CHOPPED

1. Steam the potatoes and broccoli until just tender then mash them together in a mixing bowl. Add the herbs and milk and whisk to a fairly smooth consistency. Aim for a thick paste: you may not need all the milk.
2. Mix the flour with the ground pepper and drop large spoonfuls of the mixture into it. Roll these gently so that most of the surface is covered and lift carefully into a frying pan in which the butter has melted.
3. Press the cakes with a wooden spoon to flatten them a little and cook for 3-5 minutes. Turn them over and cook the other side.

Serves 2-4

⏱ 40 mins

4. When all the cakes are cooked, add the chopped onion to the hot pan and sauté briefly.

5. Serve the cakes on a warmed plate with the onions tipped over them. Delicious with salads or a plate of steamed vegetables and rice.

Virgin's Tears

2 LARGE POTATOES, SCRUBBED

2 PICKLED GREEN CHILLIES, VERY FINELY
   CHOPPED

2 CLOVES GARLIC, CRUSHED OR VERY FINELY
   CHOPPED

2 SPRING ONIONS, FINELY CHOPPED

½ BUNCH FRESH CORIANDER, RINSED AND
   FINELY CHOPPED

2 TABLESPOONS TOMATO PURÉE

JUICE OF 1 LEMON

2 LARGE POTATOES

Serves 2-4

🕐 50 mins

1. Preheat the oven to 200°C/400°F/Gas Mark 6, and bake the potatoes for 45 minutes.

2. Blend all the ingredients together in a mixing bowl and leave to stand while the potatoes bake.

3. Slice the potatoes open and pile on this scorching hot relish.

Clarke Gables

2 LARGE POTATOES, BAKED
   (SEE ABOVE)

140ML (¼ PINT) MILK

2 TABLESPOONS BUTTER OR MARGARINE

2 TABLESPOONS GRATED PARMESAN CHEESE

SALT AND FRESHLY GROUND BLACK PEPPER,
   TO TASTE

1 TABLESPOON PREPARED MUSTARD

1 TEASPOON HORSERADISH SAUCE

4 TABLESPOONS FINE BREAD OR CRACKER
   CRUMBS

4 TABLESPOONS GRATED CHEESE, SUCH AS
   CHEDDAR OR MOZZARELLA

Serves 2-4

🕐 55 mins

1. Slice the baked potatoes in half and scoop out the flesh into a mixing bowl. Blend the flesh with the milk, butter, Parmesan and seasoning. Add a little more milk if necessary to make a fairly smooth mash.

168

2.   Blend the mustard and horseradish in a small bowl and spread thinly over the inside of each potato shell. Pile the mash back into the shells and top with a mixture of the breadcrumbs and grated cheese.

3.   Toast under the grill or bake in the hot oven for 5-7 minutes, until the top is bubbling hot.

4.   Serve at once. Just like Clarke, these are crusty, smooth and hot.

Skin Fetishes

2 LARGE POTATOES, BAKED (SEE OPPOSITE)

2 TABLESPOONS OIL

1 MEDIUM ONION, CHOPPED

1 TEASPOON FRESHLY GROUND BLACK PEPPER

100G (4OZ) FRESH PEAS

2 TABLESPOONS BUTTER OR MARGARINE

1 TABLESPOON FINELY CHOPPED FRESH MINT

2 TABLESPOONS FINELY CHOPPED FRESH PARSLEY

1.   Slice the baked potatoes in half and scoop out the flesh; place to one side.

2.   Heat the oil in a frying pan and sauté the onion until clear and tender. Stir in the pepper and sauté a further 1 minute. Add the potato flesh and peas and cook the mixture over a low heat while you prepare the potato skins.

3.   Brush the inside of the skins with butter or margarine and place under a hot grill for 5-7 minutes. Turn the skins, brush a little butter on the outsides and grill a final 3 minutes.

4.   Meanwhile, remove the sauté from the heat and stir in the fresh herbs.

5.   Serve the Fetishes with the sauté piled high in the crisped skins.

Serves 2-4

🕐 1 hr

Cowpoke's Dream

2 LARGE POTATOES, BAKED
(SEE PAGE 168)

1 TABLESPOON BUTTER OR MARGARINE

1 TABLESPOON PLAIN FLOUR

½ TEASPOON PREPARED MUSTARD

285ML (½ PINT) MILK

140ML (¼ PINT) SINGLE CREAM OR SOYA
CREEM

85G (3OZ) CHEDDAR OR OTHER STRONG
CHEESE, GRATED

GARNISH OF CHOPPED SPRING ONION OR
FRESH PARSLEY

Serves 2-4

 1 hr

1. Make the sauce to coincide with the potatoes being ready. Melt the butter in a saucepan over a low heat and stir in the flour to make a smooth paste or roux. Now stir in the mustard and then add the milk, a little at a time, stirring after each addition to make a smooth paste. Keep the sauce over a low heat throughout.

2. Add the cream (adjust the thickness of the sauce if necessary by adding a little more milk) and then stir in the grated cheese. Cover the pan and remove from the heat.

3. Immediately slice the baked potatoes in half and roughly break open the flesh.

4. Serve at once on a warmed plate, topped with a generous helping of sauce and garnish.

GREENS

*L*emon Garden Greens

1350G (3LB) MIXED GREENS (SEE TIPS)
55G (2OZ) BUTTER OR MARGARINE
5-7 CLOVES GARLIC, FINELY CHOPPED
1 TEASPOON FRESHLY GROUND BLACK PEPPER

JUICE AND ZEST OF 1 LEMON
1 LEMON, QUARTERED
1 TABLESPOON FRESH MARIGOLD FLOWERS
(OPTIONAL)

1. Wash the greens really well by immersing them in a bowlful of cold water. Agitate them in the water to loosen sand and grit then lift from the water and rinse them under running water. Drain and then dry them by spinning them in the salad spinner or dabbing them with a tea towel.

2. Now you may trim and coarsely chop the greens. Place them in a steamer and steam for 5 minutes, until they are wilted.

3. Meanwhile, melt the butter in a large saucepan and sauté the garlic for 3 minutes. Add the pepper and stir a further 1 minute.

4. Now lift the greens into the sauté and stir, toss and roughly chop with a wooden spoon over a medium flame for 5 minutes. About half way through, add the lemon zest and juice.

5. Serve the greens immediately on to warmed plates with a wedge of lemon to accompany. Garnish with fresh marigold flowers if you have any in your garden (see also page 227).

Serves 4

25 mins, including washing time

give your taste buds a thrill !

Tips

1. This recipe is especially for the greens that many of us don't seem to use any longer, but that are really healthy and flavourful. A mixture of greens is best and I recommend these: dandelion (before they have flowered), carrot tops, mustard greens, beet greens, sorrel, kale and, of course, simple spring greens. The secret is to keep the amount of water to a minimum and to never overcook the greens. They should still have some bright green colour left when you eat them, so expect a little tiny bit of crunch left in each mouthful, not the squidgy mess we have got so used to eating!

2. Black pepper is a wonderful accompaniment to rich greens, but you

may wish to reduce the quantity somewhat or to add the same amount of ground nutmeg to the sauté.

3.   If you don't have a steamer, simply turn the greens into a large saucepan after you have drained them but before you have dried them. Don't add extra water, though you may need to stir the greens once during the first 5 minutes of cooking.

Spring Greens

900G (2LB) SPRING GREENS

2 TABLESPOONS OIL

3 CLOVES GARLIC, FINELY CHOPPED

1 LARGE ONION, THINLY SLICED

1/2 TEASPOON FRESHLY GROUND BLACK PEPPER

1/4 TEASPOON GROUND NUTMEG

60ML (2 FL OZ) WINE OR RASPBERRY VINEGAR

30ML (1 FL OZ) SOY SAUCE

JUICE OF 1 ORANGE

Serves 4

🕐 20 mins

1.   Wash and drain the greens and chop coarsely. Make sure you use the dark outer leaves, however unsightly they seem at first glance.

2.   Heat the oil in a large saucepan and sauté the garlic and onion until clear and tender, about 5 minutes. Add the pepper and nutmeg and stir 1 minute longer over a medium flame. Add the chopped greens to the sauté and cover the pan.

3.   Cook over a medium flame for 3 minutes. Stir the greens, cover the pan and cook a further 3 minutes. The greens should be wilted, soft and still rather bright in colour.

4.   Mix the remaining ingredients in a jug and add these to the greens. Increase the heat and cook until the liquid boils. Stir for 2 minutes, remove from the heat and turn into a warmed serving dish.

5.   Serve immediately.

Tips

1.   Serve with a dollop of soured cream or plain yogurt or a dab of herb butter (see page 175).

2.   If you like a bit of a sauce with your greens, add 140ml (1/4 pint) vegetable stock (see page 87) to the liquid then stir in 2 teaspoons arrowroot

which has been softened in 1 tablespoon cold water. Cook for an extra 5 minutes while it thickens, then serve.

*H*erbed Spinach Salad in Filo Baskets

4 SHEETS FILO PASTRY

25ML (1 FL OZ) MELTED BUTTER
  OR OIL

225G (8OZ) YOUNG SPINACH LEAVES,
  WASHED AND DRAINED

1 TABLESPOON CHOPPED FRESH TARRAGON

1 TABLESPOON CHOPPED FRESH CHIVES

1 TABLESPOON CHOPPED FRESH BASIL

FRENCH DRESSING, OR DRESSING OF YOUR
  CHOICE

CROÛTONS (SEE PAGES 23 AND 101)

25G (1OZ) HAZELNUTS, COARSELY CHOPPED

1.   Preheat the oven to 180°C/350°F/Gas Mark 4.

2.   Use some of the butter or oil to moisten the outside of four small ovenproof dishes (ramekins work well). Stand them upside down on a lightly oiled baking sheet.

3.   Cut the sheets of pastry in half to make eight squares. Lightly brush the first square with butter or oil, then lay it over the top of an upturned dish, oiled side up. Cover with another square of pastry, turned through 180 degrees so that the points of the square do not adjoin. Brush the upper surface with oil. Use the remaining sheets in pairs on the other dishes.

4.   Bake for 5 minutes or until crisp. Leave to cool slightly then remove the filo baskets carefully from the upturned dishes.

5.   Shred the spinach. Mix it with the fresh herbs and stir in just enough dressing to moisten. Divide the salad between the filo baskets, and sprinkle each one with croûtons and nuts.

6.   Serve at once.

Serves 4

⏲ 25 mins

Tip

This is a very handsome way of serving this strong green salad. The basket is surprisingly robust so go ahead and add a bit of bean or tofu to the salad if you wish.

Chicory au Brézier

4 HEADS CHICORY (WITLOOF), TRIMMED
1 LARGE RED PEPPER
140ML (¼ PINT) VEGETABLE STOCK
(SEE PAGE 87)
JUICE OF ½ LEMON
¼ TEASPOON FRESHLY GROUND BLACK PEPPER
¼ TEASPOON GROUND NUTMEG

For the sauce:

140ML (¼ PINT) TOMATO PURÉE
60ML (2 FL OZ) WATER OR VEGETABLE STOCK
1 TEASPOON FINELY CHOPPED FRESH BASIL
1 TABLESPOON FINELY CHOPPED FRESH PARSLEY
¼ TEASPOON FRESHLY GROUND BLACK PEPPER

Serves 4

⏱ 35 mins

1.   Preheat the oven to 170°C/325°F/Gas Mark 3 and lightly butter an oven dish.
2.   Cut the chicory heads in half along their length; slice the pepper into thin strips. Arrange the vegetables in the oven dish.
3.   Mix the vegetable stock with the lemon juice, black pepper and nutmeg and pour over the vegetables. Cover the dish and bake for 25 minutes.
4.   Mix the remaining ingredients in a small saucepan and bring to a simmer. Pour this sauce over the vegetables and serve at once with a light drizzle of single cream or plain yogurt.

Sautéed Lettuce Chiffonade in Parsley Garlic Butter

1 LARGE COS LETTUCE, WASHED,
DRAINED AND TRIMMED
85G (3OZ) BUTTER OR MARGARINE
7-9 CLOVES GARLIC, FINELY CHOPPED

55G (2OZ) FINELY CHOPPED FRESH PARSLEY
SALT TO TASTE
FRESHLY GROUND BLACK PEPPER, TO TASTE

Serves 4

⏱ 25 mins

1.   When the lettuce leaves are prepared, roll several together in a bunch and slice the bundle into very thin, narrow strips. The lettuce will look very lacey indeed.
2.   Melt the butter in a large saucepan over a medium flame and sauté the garlic for 2-3 minutes. Add the parsley, reduce the heat and sauté a further 3-5 minutes, stirring constantly.

3. Now add the lettuce and cook, increasing the heat a little, until the lettuce is wilted and its juices have evaporated somewhat, about 3-5 minutes.

4. Season to taste and serve immediately.

Tip

This is delicious as a small side dish, especially with a little soured cream or plain yogurt placed to one side. It is excellent as one of several vegetable dishes served over a plate of steamed rice.

Short and Curly Kale Well-dressed

450G (1LB) CURLY KALE, WASHED AND DRAINED

2 TABLESPOONS BUTTER OR MARGARINE

5 CLOVES GARLIC, FINELY CHOPPED

1 SMALL ONION, FINELY CHOPPED

1/2 TEASPOON FRESHLY GROUND BLACK PEPPER

JUICE OF 1 LEMON

1. Prepare the kale and slice into coarse strips just before you are ready to use it.

2. Melt the butter in a deep saucepan over a medium heat and sauté the garlic and onion until clear and tender. Add the ground pepper and stir a further 1 minute.

3. Turn the prepared kale into the pan and cover. Reduce the heat and leave to cook for about 5 minutes then stir the greens, cover the pan again and leave a further 3-5 minutes.

4. The secret of this dish is to keep a low heat so the greens cook without losing flavour, texture and colour. When the kale is tender but still bright green, remove it from the heat and pour the lemon juice over.

5. Serve at once.

Serves 2-4

⏱ 25 mins

Variation

For those who like buttery greens, blend the lemon juice with 2 tablespoons butter or margarine and 1 tablespoon finely chopped fresh fennel leaf. Dab each serving with a bit of this butter blend and serve immediately.

VEGETABLES

Spiced Okra

225G (8OZ) OKRA, WASHED

3 TABLESPOONS OIL

1 TEASPOON EACH MUSTARD SEEDS AND
CRACKED FENUGREEK SEEDS

½ TEASPOON CHILLI POWDER

5 CARDAMOM PODS, CRUSHED

½ TEASPOON EACH OF GROUND CUMIN AND
CORIANDER

140ML (¼ PINT) VEGETABLE STOCK
(SEE PAGE 87) OR WATER

2 TABLESPOONS SOY SAUCE

25G (1OZ) CREAMED COCONUT, GRATED

Serves 2-4

⏱ 45 mins

1.   Top and tail the okra.

2.   Heat the oil in a large pan over a medium heat and add all the spices. Sauté for 3-5 minutes, until the mustard seeds pop.

3.   Reduce the heat and add the okra. Stir for 2-3 minutes, then add the stock. Simmer, covered, over a low heat for 15 minutes.

4.   Add the soy sauce and then the coconut. Stir until it has thickened, about 2 minutes, then take from the heat.

5.   You may add a little more stock or soy sauce to adjust the consistency of the sauce. Serve at once over rice.

Parsnip Fritters

450G (1LB) PARSNIPS, PEELED AND
CUBED

1 TABLESPOON BUTTER OR MARGARINE

2 TABLESPOONS PLAIN FLOUR

2 FREE-RANGE EGGS, LIGHTLY BEATEN

25G (1OZ) WALNUTS, COARSELY CHOPPED

1 TEASPOON BAKING POWDER

VEGETABLE OIL FOR DEEP-FRYING

1 TABLESPOON CHOPPED FRESH PARSLEY

Serves 4

⏱ 45 mins

1.   Steam the parsnips for 10 minutes, until tender. Drain them and mash to a thick purée.

2.   Blend the parsnip purée with the butter, flour, eggs, nuts and baking powder in a large bowl and mix thoroughly.

3.   Drop tablespoons of the mixture into hot oil and fry until

puffed up and golden. Drain them well and keep them warm until all the mixture has been used.

4. Pile the fritters round the edges of a serving platter and garnish with the parsley.

5. Put a favourite sauce into a bowl in the centre and serve.

Tip

Serve with a simple sauce of plain yogurt blended with fresh chives and chopped parsley. For other sauce ideas, see pages 193-4.

Spiced Cauliflower

2 TABLESPOONS OIL

½ TEASPOON EACH OF GROUND CORIANDER, CUMIN AND TURMERIC

¼ TEASPOON CHILLI POWDER

3-5 CLOVES GARLIC, FINELY CHOPPED

1 MEDIUM ONION, THINLY SLICED

1 TABLESPOON PLAIN FLOUR

2 MEDIUM CAULIFLOWERS, BROKEN INTO LARGE FLORETS

1 LARGE CARROT, PEELED AND DICED

1 LARGE COOKING APPLE, PEELED, CORED AND DICED

180-285ML (6-10 FL OZ) COLD WATER

FRESHLY GROUND BLACK PEPPER, TO TASTE

285G (10OZ) CARTON SOURED CREAM OR PLAIN YOGURT

4 TABLESPOONS COOKED (OR TINNED) CHICK PEAS, WARMED

1 TABLESPOON FINELY CHOPPED FRESH PARSLEY

1. Heat the oil in a large pan and gently sauté the spices for 3-5 minutes, stirring frequently. Add the garlic and onion and sauté a further 3 minutes.

2. Sprinkle the flour over the sauté and stir as the sauté thickens. Add the cauliflower, carrot and apple, plus just enough water to cover the bottom of the pan.

3. Bring to the boil, cover the pan and cook over a reduced heat for about 10 minutes, until the vegetables are just tender. Top up the water if necessary to prevent sticking. Season to taste and remove the pan from the heat.

4. Add the soured cream or yogurt, stir well and turn the cauliflower into a warmed serving dish.

5. Garnish with the warm chick peas and parsley and serve hot.

Serves 4

⏱ 45 mins

Cauliflower will never be the same again!

Deep-fried Mushrooms

85G (3OZ) PLAIN FLOUR

¼ TEASPOON SALT

1½ TABLESPOONS OIL

7 TABLESPOONS WARM WATER

1 FREE-RANGE EGG WHITE

180G (6OZ) BUTTON MUSHROOMS, CLEANED

A LITTLE EXTRA FLOUR

VEGETABLE OIL FOR DEEP-FRYING

Serves 4

⏱ 55 mins

1. Sift the flour and salt together into a mixing bowl, add the oil and warm water, and stir well.

2. Whisk the egg white until very stiff and then fold this into the batter.

3. Dust the mushrooms with a little flour, dip them into the batter and deep-fry a small batch in hot oil until golden. Drain well and keep them warm whilst cooking the remaining mushrooms.

4. Serve on a platter with a favourite sauce in a dish in the middle.

Tip

Any favourite sauce will do with these mushrooms. See pages 193-4 for some ideas.

Fennel à la Grecque

3 TABLESPOONS OLIVE OIL

3 CLOVES GARLIC, COARSELY CHOPPED

1 MEDIUM ONION, FINELY CHOPPED

1 LARGE FENNEL BULB, COARSELY CHOPPED

½ TEASPOON FRESHLY GROUND BLACK PEPPER

2 TABLESPOONS TOMATO PURÉE

JUICE OF 1 LEMON

60ML (2 FL OZ) RED WINE VINEGAR

3 TABLESPOONS WATER

3 TABLESPOONS FINELY CHOPPED FRESH PARSLEY

55G (2OZ) BLACK OLIVES, STONED

25G (1OZ) FLAKED ALMONDS

Serves 4

⏱ 30 mins, plus chilling time

1. Heat the oil in a large saucepan and sauté the garlic and onion until clear and tender, about 5 minutes. Add the chopped fennel and stir for 7-10 minutes, sprinkling in the black pepper for the last minute or two.

2. Blend the tomato purée, lemon juice, vinegar and water togeth-

er in a jug and pour over the sauté. Stir until the liquid begins to bubble, then remove the mixture from the heat. Cover the pan and leave to cool.

3.   Turn into a serving dish with the parsley and olives and stir well. Chill for at least 4 hours, though all day or overnight is ideal.

4.   Serve garnished with the flaked almonds.

Sesame Glazed Carrots

450G (1LB) CARROTS, PEELED AND
CUT INTO STICKS

25G (1OZ) BUTTER OR MARGARINE

1 TABLESPOON SUGAR

25G (1OZ) SESAME SEEDS

1.   Steam the carrots for 10 minutes.

2.   Melt the butter in a large frying pan, add the sugar and cook until lightly browned, stirring constantly. Add in the carrots and stir over a low flame for 5-7 minutes. Add the seeds and cook for 3 more minutes or until the carrots are tender and lightly glazed.

3.   Serve hot as an accompaniment to your main dish.

Serves 4

🕐 20 mins

Tip

For a slightly roasted flavour, turn the glazed carrots and their juices into an oven dish and bake, uncovered, in a hot oven, at 190°C/375°F/Gas Mark 5, for 10 minutes.

Sweet and Sour Celery

225G (8OZ) FRESH OR TINNED
    PINEAPPLE PIECES IN NATURAL JUICE
1 TABLESPOON SUGAR OR HONEY
2 TABLESPOONS CIDER VINEGAR
1 SMALL ONION, FINELY CHOPPED
1 LARGE RED PEPPER, COARSELY CHOPPED

1 SMALL HEAD CELERY, COARSELY CHOPPED
½ TEASPOON FRESHLY GROUND BLACK PEPPER
55G (2OZ) FLAKED ALMONDS, ROASTED
1 TABLESPOON ROUGHLY CHOPPED FRESH
    PARSLEY

Serves 4

🕐 30 mins

1.   Drain the pineapple pieces, put the chunks aside and pour the juice into a small saucepan. Add the sugar, vinegar, onion, red pepper and celery to the saucepan. Bring to the boil over a medium flame, then sprinkle in the black pepper, cover the pan, reduce the heat and simmer for 12-15 minutes.

2.   Stir in the pineapple chunks and cook for 3 minutes longer.

3.   Serve, sprinkled with the nuts and parsley, over steamed rice.

Coconut Aubergine

2 MEDIUM AUBERGINES
SALT
2 LARGE RED OR GREEN PEPPERS,
    SLICED
2 TABLESPOONS OIL
1 MEDIUM ONION, FINELY CHOPPED

1 TABLESPOON CURRY PASTE, OR TO TASTE
100G (4OZ) CREAMED COCONUT
200ML (7 FL OZ) VEGETABLE STOCK
    (SEE PAGE 87)
450G (1LB) COOKED CHICK PEAS

Serves 4

🕐 1 hr 30 mins

A temptation for nibblers!

1.   Cut the aubergines into slices, sprinkle with salt and leave on a plate for 30 minutes. Rinse them in cold water and pat dry.

2.   Preheat the oven to 200°C/400°F/Gas Mark 6 and lightly oil an oven dish.

3.   Arrange the aubergine slices alternately with the pepper slices in the oven dish and bake for 20 minutes.

4.   Heat the oil in a saucepan over a medium flame and sauté the onion until clear and tender, about 3 minutes. Add the curry paste and stir a further 1 minute.

5.   Crumble or grate the coconut and add to the sauté along with

the stock and the chick peas. Stir over a low to medium flame until the coconut dissolves. If the sauce seems too thick, add a drop more stock. Pour the sauce over the aubergine.

6. Cover the dish and bake a further 20 minutes; remove the lid and bake for a final 10 minutes.

7. Serve hot with rice or couscous and steamed greens.

Parsnips with Walnuts

675G (1½ LB) PARSNIPS, PEELED
90ML (3 FL OZ) OLIVE OIL
SEA SALT

FRESHLY GROUND BLACK PEPPER
55G (2OZ) WALNUTS, BROKEN

1. Preheat the oven to 200°C/400°F/Gas Mark 6.
2. Cut the parsnips into 10cm (4 inch) slices and steam for 5-7 minutes.
3. Pour the oil into a gratin dish and arrange the parsnips in it. Season generously with salt and pepper and turn the parsnips in the oil. Bake for 20 minutes.
4. Sprinkle the walnuts over the top and bake for another 10 minutes.
5. Serve hot with steamed rice, greens and your favourite sauce.

Serves 4

🕐 55 mins

Tip

Don't skimp on the salt and pepper as this dish really comes into its own when the flavour of walnuts offsets a peppery bite.

Pickled Cabbage

1 SMALL WHITE CABBAGE, SHREDDED

1 TABLESPOON SALT

2 TEASPOONS CASTOR SUGAR

2 TABLESPOONS SESAME OIL

25G (1OZ) GRATED FRESH GINGER ROOT

¼-½ TEASPOON CHILLI POWDER

1 TEASPOON WHITE AND BLACK PEPPERCORNS, ROUGHLY CRUSHED

90ML (3 FL OZ) DRY VERMOUTH

Serves 4

1 hr 20 mins, plus maturing time

1. Place the shredded cabbage in a bowl, sprinkle with the salt and toss the cabbage to distribute the salt. Leave for 1 hour, then squeeze and knead the cabbage with your hands. Lift the cabbage into a clean bowl, leaving any liquid behind, and sprinkle with the sugar.

2. Heat the oil in a frying pan over a low flame and stir in the ginger and chilli. Sauté for 1-2 minutes, then pour over the cabbage.

3. Add the peppercorns and vermouth and stir well. Stir a little of the cabbage round the sauté pan to collect all of the precious oil and spices.

4. Refrigerate all day or overnight.

5. Serve cool, as a salad, in sandwiches or as a filling for baked potatoes.

Cipolline in Agrodolce

750G (1LB 10OZ) SHALLOTS

55G (2OZ) BUTTER OR MARGARINE

1 TABLESPOON OLIVE OIL

2 TABLESPOONS SUGAR

90ML (3 FL OZ) WHITE WINE VINEGAR

PINCH OF SALT

½ TEASPOON FRESHLY GROUND BLACK PEPPER

285ML (½ PINT) VEGETABLE STOCK (SEE PAGE 87) OR WATER

Serves 4

1 hr 20 mins

1. Boil the shallots in their skins for 1-2 minutes. Lift from the water with a slotted spoon and peel whilst still warm.

2. Melt the butter and oil together in a pan and dissolve the sugar in it. Add the vinegar, seasoning and the shallots. Pour in just enough stock or water to show through the mixture.

3. Stir, cover the pan and cook over a low flame for 1 hour, adding more water if necessary to prevent the shallots from sticking.

4. Adjust the seasonning and serve hot or cold.

Variations

1. Thicken the cooking juices by stirring in 2 teaspoons cornflour or arrow-root dissolved in 60ml (2 fl oz) water. Stir while the sauce thickens; serve hot.
2. Add 1-2 tablespoons tomato purée to the cooking juices and a handful of fresh chopped herbs such as basil, rosemary and savory.
3. Prepare as above but increase the sugar to 3 tablespoons and add 55g (2oz) each of raisins and pine nuts about half way through the cooking process.

True Love Truffles

2 LARGE TRUFFLES
140ML (¼ PINT) VERY DRY WHITE WINE
(SUCH AS FRASCATI)
PINCH OF SALT

1 TEASPOON LIGHTLY CRUSHED PEPPERCORNS
4 ARTICHOKE HEARTS
ZEST AND JUICE OF 1 LEMON
25G (1OZ) WELL-ICED BUTTER

1. Clean and trim the truffles and put in a bowl or ramekin. Pour the wine over, add the salt and pepper and leave for at least 1 hour.
2. Stir occasionally. Coarsely chop the artichoke hearts and make a nest of them on two small serving plates.
3. Lift the truffles from the wine and place them over the hearts. Sprinkle a little of the zest on each truffle and a little over the hearts.
4. Drizzle about 1 teaspoon of lemon juice over each serving and place the remaining lemon juice in a tiny cream pot next to the serving.
5. Serve at once with a round of iced butter and the salt and pepper near to hand. It's up to you what you do with all that spiced wine. . .

Serves 2

🕐 1 hr 20 mins

BEANS

Kidney Beans Bourguignon

225G (8OZ) DRIED KIDNEY BEANS,
    SOAKED OVERNIGHT

3 TABLESPOONS BUTTER OR MARGARINE

1 TABLESPOON OLIVE OIL

7 CLOVES GARLIC, COARSELY CHOPPED

2 LARGE ONIONS, COARSELY CHOPPED

450G (1LB) MUSHROOMS, CLEANED AND
    QUARTERED

1 TEASPOON FRESHLY GROUND BLACK PEPPER

570ML (1 PINT) RED WINE

1 X 7.5CM (3 INCH) PIECE CINNAMON STICK

Serves 4

🕐 2 hrs, plus
soaking
overnight

*Better than
the real
thing...*

1.   Drain the beans, rinse and turn into a pressure cooker. Cover with fresh water and cover the pan. Cook at full pressure for 25 minutes; cool the cooker immediately and drain the beans of all but the thickest cooking juices.

2.   Meanwhile, heat the butter and olive oil together in a large saucepan and sauté first the garlic then the onion until tender and slightly golden. Add the mushrooms and continue to sauté, stirring often. When the mushrooms begin to release their juices, sprinkle the pepper over all and cover the pan. Reduce the heat and cook for 5 minutes.

3.   Stir well then add the cooked beans and their juices, the red wine and the cinnamon stick. Stir, cover the pan and leave to cook over a low heat for at least 1 hour.

4.   Stir occasionally, adding a little stock or water if necessary to prevent sticking. This dish may be allowed to cool and then reheated later if you prefer.

5.   Serve hot over rice or roast potatoes with side dishes of steamed pumpkin and spring greens.

184

Yellow Dhal

225G (8OZ) DRIED SPLIT YELLOW PEAS
710ML (1¼ PINTS) WATER
1 TEASPOON SALT
1 TABLESPOON OIL
5 CLOVES GARLIC, FINELY CHOPPED

1 TEASPOON FRESHLY GROUND BLACK PEPPER
1 TEASPOON CUMIN SEEDS, SLIGHTLY CRUSHED
½ TEASPOON CHILLI POWDER
1 TABLESPOON FINELY CHOPPED FRESH
    CORIANDER

1. Pour the peas into a large frying pan and place over a medium heat. Roast the peas, stirring constantly, to a golden colour. Do not let them brown. Turn them into a bowl, cover with water and leave to soak overnight.

2. Drain and rinse the peas and place them in a saucepan with the measured fresh water and the salt. Bring to the boil, reduce the heat, cover the pan and simmer for about 30 minutes, until the peas become tender.

3. Heat the oil in a small frying pan and sauté the garlic until just golden. Add the spices, stir for a further 1 minute then add the sauté to the peas.

4. Simmer the peas for a further 10 minutes until the peas are mushy and have lost their form.

5. Stir in the fresh coriander and serve hot over rice.

Serves 2-4

🕐 50 minutes, plus soaking overnight

Green Beans in Garlic and Tomato Sauce

900G (2LB) GREEN BEANS,
    FRESH, FROZEN OR TINNED
2 TABLESPOONS OLIVE OIL
1 BULB GARLIC, FINELY CHOPPED
1 LARGE ONION, QUARTERED AND THINLY
    SLICED

2 X 400G (14OZ) TINS PEELED TOMATOES
1½ TEASPOONS DRIED OREGANO
2 TABLESPOONS FINELY CHOPPED FRESH BASIL
1 TEASPOON FRESHLY GROUND BLACK PEPPER

1. Prepare the beans by trimming them and slicing into 2.5cm (1 inch) pieces.

2. Heat the oil in a large saucepan and sauté the garlic over a low to medium flame until the garlic begins to turn golden. Do not

Serves 2-4

🕐 45 mins

brown. Add the onion and sauté a further 5-7 minutes, stirring often.

3.   Add the remaining ingredients and bring to a low simmer, stirring often. Finally, add the green beans and cover the pan. Reduce the heat and cook for 15 minutes.

4.   Serve immediately over freshly boiled rice. Alternatively, leave the dish to cool so that the flavours mature.

5.   Reheat the same day if possible.

Variation

For a more substantial dish, add 450g (1lb) chopped carrots to the sauté after the onions are tender. Sauté a further 7 minutes, then proceed as above.

Chick Pea and Onion Ambrosia

225G (8OZ) DRIED CHICK PEAS,
SOAKED OVERNIGHT
2 TABLESPOONS OLIVE OIL
5-7 CLOVES GARLIC, FINELY SLICED

900G (2LB) SHALLOTS, HALVED AND
QUARTERED
FRESHLY GROUND BLACK PEPPER, TO TASTE
1 LEMON, QUARTERED

Serves 4

 1 hr, plus
soaking
overnight

1.   Drain the chick peas then rinse and turn into a pressure cooker. Just cover with water and cook at pressure for about 25 minutes (see instructions for your pressure cooker). Drain the cooked chick peas, keeping only the thick liquor at the bottom of the pan.

2.   Meanwhile, heat the oil in a large pan over a low heat and sauté the garlic until just golden. Stir the shallots into the sauté, cover the pan and cook for 5 minutes.

3.   Stir again then add the cooked chick peas, about 140ml (¼ pint) of the liquor and some freshly ground pepper. Cover the pan and cook for 5 minutes, then uncover and cook over a medium flame for 2-3 minutes.

4.   Serve immediately over rice, millet or couscous, or with plenty of fresh pitta breads. Give each serving a wedge of lemon, which should be squeezed over the chick peas just before eating.

Baked Tofu Steaks in Mushroom Sauce

550G (1¼ LB) FIRM TOFU

1 TABLESPOON PREPARED MUSTARD

25G (1OZ) DRIED BREADCRUMBS

450G (1LB) MUSHROOMS, TRIMMED AND CLEANED

½ BUNCH SPRING ONIONS, TRIMMED

2 MEDIUM TOMATOES, COARSELY CHOPPED

2 TABLESPOONS BUTTER OR MARGARINE

1 TEASPOON FRESHLY GROUND BLACK PEPPER

1. Preheat the oven to 180°C/350°F/Gas Mark 4.
2. Dry the tofu on a clean tea towel then slice it into thick steaks and spread each with a little prepared mustard.
3. Carefully dredge the steaks in the breadcrumbs and put to one side. Thickly slice or halve the mushrooms, according to the texture you prefer, and put to one side. Slice the onions into thin strips and prepare the tomatoes.
4. Melt the butter in an oven dish, ensuring that it spreads across the bottom of the pan. Place the tofu steaks on it and season with half the pepper. Arrange the mushrooms, onions and tomato pieces around and over the steaks and sprinkle with the remaining pepper.
5. Cover the oven dish and bake for 35 minutes. Uncover, gently stir the vegetables and bake uncovered for a final 5-7 minutes.
6. Serve immediately over dry toast, rice, noodles or steamed potatoes.

Serves 4

50 mins

Tip

You can marinate the tofu first for a deeper flavour.

GRAINS

*T*ortillas

450G (1LB) FINE CORNMEAL
100G (4OZ) PLAIN FLOUR
1 TEASPOON SALT

180-225ML (6-8 FL OZ) WARM WATER
A LITTLE PLAIN FLOUR

Serves 4

⏱ 20 mins

Go on, roll up your sleeves – get stuck in, hombre!

1. Stir the cornmeal, flour and salt together in a mixing bowl. Gradually add the warm water, stirring to make a ball of dough. Knead the dough for about 5 minutes, then cover and leave to stand for 15-20 minutes.

2. Place the dough on a floured board and divide into twelve portions. Work the pieces into thin, flat circles about 15cm (6 inches) across: traditionally this is done entirely with the hands in a sort of patting movement. You may, of course, prefer to try a lightly floured rolling pin.

3. Heat a large, ungreased frying pan or griddle over a medium heat and cook the tortillas for 1-2 minutes on each side.

4. Serve immediately or wrap in a cloth to keep them warm and soft.

Tip

Tortillas are used to lift food to the mouth, or are sometimes wrapped around food (burritos) or arranged under toppings (tostados).

Pretty and Simple Risotto

55G (2OZ) BUTTER OR MARGARINE

2 MEDIUM ONIONS, FINELY CHOPPED

225G (8OZ) RISOTTO RICE

570ML (1 PINT) VEGETABLE STOCK
(SEE PAGE 87)

SALT, TO TASTE

¼-½ TEASPOON FRESHLY GROUND BLACK
PEPPER

85G (3OZ) PARMESAN CHEESE, GRATED

1. Melt the butter in a large saucepan over a low flame. Sauté the onions slowly until they are clear and tender; allow 10-12 minutes if you can.

2. Add the rice to the sauté and stir constantly while it absorbs the butter. The rice should become nicely clear, like pearls.

3. Increase the heat to a medium flame and add the stock, a little at a time, stirring after each addition while it comes to a simmer. After you have added about half the stock in this way, turn the remainder into the pot, cover the pan and simmer until all the liquid is absorbed; allow 20 minutes.

4. Remove the rice from the heat and leave for 5 minutes.

5. Fluff it out into a serving dish, sprinkle the Parmesan over it and serve immediately.

Serves 4

 1 hr

Variations

1. Add 1-2 tablespoons of fresh, chopped herb (such as parsley, chives or a mixture of basil and parsley) to the risotto as you turn it into a serving dish. Simply fluff it all together with a fork.

2. Add slivered almonds or tiny cubes of Nuttolene to the risotto at the same time as you add the remaining stock.

3. Add 1 teaspoon turmeric to the sauté just before stirring in the rice. The risotto will turn out a lovely lemon colour.

4. Which brings me to lemons: add the zest of 1 lemon to the topping of Parmesan as you serve the risotto.

Special Quinoa

225g (8oz) QUINOA, WASHED AND
    DRAINED (SEE PAGE 266)
850ML (1½ PINTS) BOILING VEGETABLE
STOCK (SEE PAGE 87) OR WATER
1 TEASPOON YEAST EXTRACT

1 TABLESPOON FINELY CHOPPED FRESH PARSLEY
2 TEASPOONS FINELY CHOPPED FRESH BASIL
1 TEASPOON FINELY CHOPPED FRESH THYME
3 SPRING ONIONS, FINELY CHOPPED
3 CLOVES GARLIC, CRUSHED

Serves 4

⏲ 30 mins

A South American grain – say it 'Keen-nah'

1. Measure the quinoa into a saucepan, pour over the boiling stock, stir in the remaining ingredients and simmer, covered, over a medium to low heat for 20 minutes.
2. Serve instead of rice or potatoes.

Variations

1. Prepare as above but stir in 100g (4oz) cooked peas and 55g (2oz) slivered almonds or pine nuts.
2. Cool the quinoa and toss it with a mixture of chopped vegetables to make a salad. Dress the salad as usual.
3. Use instead of rice to stuff peppers, marrow and squashes.

Mixed Grain Pilaf

85g (3oz) WILD RICE,
    WASHED AND DRAINED
85g (3oz) BUCKWHEAT,
    ROASTED
85g (3oz) MILLET
225g (8oz) FRESH GARDEN PEAS
1 GREEN PEPPER, DICED
1 RED PEPPER, DICED

4 TABLESPOONS BUTTER OR MARGARINE
2 ONIONS, THINLY SLICED
JUICE OF 2 LEMONS
1 HANDFUL MINT, FINELY CHOPPED
PINCH OF SALT
½ TEASPOON FRESHLY GROUND BLACK PEPPER
PAPRIKA TO GARNISH

Serves 4-8

⏲ 45 mins, plus cooling time

1. Cover the rice with twice its volume of fresh water and bring to a boil over a medium flame. Reduce the heat and simmer, covered, for 25 minutes, until the grains are burst and tender.
2. In separate pans, simmer the buckwheat and millet in twice

their volumes of water for 15-20 minutes, until all the liquid is absorbed. Leave the grains in their pans, uncovered, for a further 5-10 minutes.

3.   Boil or steam the peas for 7-8 minutes, until just tender.

4.   Combine all the grains in a large bowl, fluffing them together with a fork. Add the peas and diced peppers to the grains.

5.   Melt the butter in a frying pan and sauté the onions until clear and tender, about 7-10 minutes. Pour this over the grain mixture and add all the remaining ingredients except for the paprika.

6.   Stir well and press firmly into a lightly buttered ring mould. Leave to cool, then carefully turn out of the mould on to a serving platter.

7.   Garnish with paprika and serve in thick slices.

Tip

To roast the buckwheat, heat a clean dry pan over a medium flame. Measure the buckwheat into the hot pan and shake the pan over the flame while the buckwheat deepens in colour and becomes aromatic – a lovely earthy, nutty aroma which makes your mouth water. The roasting process takes about 5 minutes, depending on the quantity of grain to be roasted. The amount in this recipe can be roasted all at once; larger quantities may need to be done in batches. You may cool the grains after roasting or turn them immediately into boiling water to cook.

Sesame Noodles

285G (10OZ) CHINESE NOODLES	25G (1OZ) SESAME SEEDS
1 TABLESPOON OIL, PREFERABLY SESAME	FRESHLY GROUND BLACK PEPPER, TO TASTE
1 TABLESPOON FINELY CHOPPED FRESH GINGER	

1.   The noodles will need to be cooked in boiling water for a short time – check instructions on pack. When just tender, drain them well and set aside.

2.   Heat the oil in a saucepan, add the ginger and cook for 2

Serves 4

⏱ 20 mins

minutes. Add the seeds and cook a further 2 minutes. Stir in the noodles and continue cooking gently until heated through.

3.   Sprinkle with the freshly ground black pepper and serve hot. This dish is excellent with a variety of vegetable dishes.

Wild and Carefree Rice with Chestnuts

180G (6OZ) DRIED CHESTNUTS, RINSED AND SOAKED

100G (4OZ) WHOLEGRAIN BROWN RICE, WASHED AND DRAINED

100G (4OZ) WILD RICE, WASHED AND DRAINED

1 LARGE RED ONION, COARSELY CHOPPED

1 ORGANIC LEMON, FINELY CHOPPED

2 BAY LEAVES

Serves 4-6

🕐 1 hr 15 mins, plus soaking time

1.   Soak the chestnuts all day, overnight or at least 4 hours.

2.   Mix the washed rices, chopped onion and lemon and the chestnuts together in a large bowl. Turn the mixture into a deep saucepan and add the bay leaves and twice the volume of cold water.

3.   Place over a medium heat and bring the water to a boil. Reduce the heat, cover the pan and simmer gently for about 50 minutes, until all the liquid is absorbed and the rice and chestnuts are tender.

4.   Serve hot with a knob of butter melted over it or cold with plenty of seasoning.

Tips

1.   All of the organic lemon may be used so all you need do is wash it well, chop finely and turn everything but the pips into the rice mixture. Don't forget to add the juice!

2.   When the rice mixture is in the saucepan, push your finger into it and touch the bottom of the pan. Measure how deep the mixture is and then add water to twice that height.

SAUCES AND GRAVIES

Risqué Raita

285G (10OZ) PLAIN YOGURT

3 CLOVES GARLIC, CRUSHED

2 SPRING ONIONS, FINELY CHOPPED

1 FRESH CHILLI, FINELY CHOPPED, OR

¼ TEASPOON CHILLI POWDER

2 TABLESPOONS FINELY CHOPPED FRESH CORIANDER

1. Mix all the ingredients together in a bowl and serve immediately, or chill, covered, until ready to serve.

Serves 4

🕐 15 mins, plus chilling time

Scrumptious Sweet and Sour Sauce

2 TABLESPOONS BUTTER OR MARGARINE

1 SMALL ONION, FINELY CHOPPED

¼ - ½ TEASPOON CHILLI POWDER

285G (10OZ) PINEAPPLE, CHOPPED INTO

SMALL CHUNKS

2 SPRING ONIONS, TRIMMED AND VERY THINLY

SLICED

1 EATING APPLE, PEELED AND FINELY CHOPPED

2 TEASPOONS ARROWROOT

285ML (½ PINT) SWEET FRUIT JUICE

(E.G. PINEAPPLE, APPLE, APRICOT)

1-2 ORGANIC LEMONS, FINELY CHOPPED

1. Melt the butter in a saucepan and sauté the onion over a low heat until clear and tender. Add the chilli powder and stir a further 1 minute then add the pineapple chunks, spring onions and the eating apple. Stir well, cover the pan and leave over a low heat for about 5 minutes.

2. Meanwhile, stir the arrowroot with 1-2 tablespoons of the fruit juice to make a thin paste. Add half of the remaining fruit juice to the sauté and stir well. When it begins to bubble, stir in the arrowroot paste and stir constantly while the sauce thickens.

3. Gradually add the remaining juice and the chopped organic lemons, stirring well after each addition.

4. Serve the sauce in a gravy boat or pour immediately over each portion of a stir-fry and serve.

Makes approximately 570ml (1 pint)

🕐 30 mins

Royal Rich Gravy

3 TABLESPOONS OIL

1 MEDIUM ONION, FINELY CHOPPED

½ TEASPOON FRESHLY GROUND
BLACK PEPPER

55G (2OZ) MUSHROOMS, FINELY CHOPPED

2 MEDIUM TOMATOES, FINELY CHOPPED

1 TABLESPOON CORNFLOUR OR PLAIN FLOUR

140ML (¼ PINT) MILK

285ML (½ PINT) VEGETABLE STOCK (SEE PAGE 87)

120-180ML (4-6 FL OZ) RED WINE

Makes approximately
570ml (1 pint)

🕐 1 hr

1. Heat the oil in a saucepan and sauté the onions over a low heat until they begin to caramelise: they will become deep-golden in colour and slightly sticky. Allow 20 minutes.

2. Add the pepper, mushrooms and tomatoes, stir well and cover the pan. Keep over a low heat for 15 minutes, stirring once or twice in that time. If the sauté begins to stick (it shouldn't), add a tablespoon or two of water.

3. Sprinkle the flour over the sauté and stir well. Add the milk, a little at a time, stirring after each addition. Add the stock, stir well and raise the heat to medium.

4. Stir often while the gravy thickens then add the wine, stir well and remove from the heat.

5. Serve very hot over just about anything!

Peanut Sauce

2 TABLESPOONS BUTTER OR MARGARINE

5 CLOVES GARLIC, FINELY CHOPPED

1 SMALL ONION, FINELY CHOPPED

½ -1 TEASPOON CHILLI POWDER

1 TABLESPOON SMOOTH PEANUT BUTTER

425ML (¾ PINT) VEGETABLE STOCK
(SEE PAGE 87)

55G (2OZ) FRESHLY GROUND PEANUTS

JUICE OF 4 ORANGES

2 TABLESPOONS FINELY CHOPPED FRESH CORIANDER

Makes approximately
570ml (1 pint)

🕐 20 mins

1. Melt the butter in a saucepan and sauté the garlic and onion until clear and tender, about 5 minutes over a medium heat. Add the chilli powder to taste and stir a further 1 minute.

2. Stir the peanut butter into the sauté and then add the stock, a little at a time, stirring after each addition. The sauce will thicken.

3. Add the ground peanuts, orange juice and the coriander and stir for 2 minutes.

4. Remove from the heat and serve immediately with a rice dish or stir-fry.

5. Alternatively, let the sauce cool and serve cold or reheat for use later: the spiciness will usually increase during this time.

VEGETABLE PURÉES

Spinach and Almond Purée

675G (1½ LB) FRESH SPINACH, WASHED AND DRAINED

55G (2OZ) GROUND ALMONDS

1 TEASPOON FRESHLY GROUND BLACK PEPPER

1 TABLESPOON OIL

1 TEASPOON TURMERIC

1 TABLESPOON FINELY CHOPPED SPRING ONIONS

285G (10OZ) FIRM TOFU

1. Shred the washed spinach and put it into a heavy-based pan with just the water that remains on the leaves. Cover the pan and cook over a medium flame until the spinach wilts, about 4 minutes.

2. Lift the spinach from the pan and let it drain; discard its juices or use in a home-made vegetable stock. Lift the drained spinach into a food processor and purée with the ground almonds and black pepper.

3. Meanwhile, heat the oil in a large pan over a medium flame and sauté the turmeric for 1 minute. Add the spring onion and sauté for 2 minutes.

4. Add the tofu and roughly mash it into the sauté for 2 minutes – it will assume a lovely yellow colour. Finally, add the spinach and almond mixture and stir well while the mixture heats.

5. Serve hot.

Makes approximately 570ml (1 pint)

30 mins

I've even put this in toasted sandwiches

Tip

This purée is excellent as a filler for baked potatoes, flans or pasties, or as a component of an omelette or galette. Try it over a serving of steamed rice with a chutney to one side for a quick and simple meal.

Garlic Potato Purée

340G (12OZ) POTATOES, PEELED AND CUBED	1 TABLESPOON OLIVE OIL
	1 TABLESPOON PREPARED MUSTARD
225G (8OZ) BROCCOLI, SLICED	140ML (¼ PINT) MILK
3 CLOVES GARLIC, CRUSHED	1 TABLESPOON FINELY CHOPPED FRESH PARSLEY

Makes approximately 570ml (1 pint)

🕐 40 mins

1. Steam the potatoes and broccoli until very soft, then mash or blend them with the other ingredients, adding just enough milk to make a thick purée.
2. Serve hot or cold.

Tip

Serve this purée with warm pitta, dry toast or crudités. It is also delicious spread on toast, topped with fresh sliced tomatoes and grilled for 5-7 minutes.

Pumpkin Purée

675G (1½ LB) FRESH PUMPKIN	½ TEASPOON GROUND ALLSPICE OR CINNAMON
2 TABLESPOONS OIL	
1 MEDIUM ONION, FINELY CHOPPED	¼ TEASPOON GROUND NUTMEG
1 TEASPOON GROUND GINGER	SOY SAUCE, TO TASTE

Makes approximately 570ml (1 pint)

🕐 30 mins

1. Peel the pumpkin and cube the flesh. Steam for 10-12 minutes, until tender, then drain.
2. At the same time, heat the oil in a large pan over a medium flame and sauté the onion until it begins to caramelise, about 12 minutes. Add the spices to the onion and cook for 1 minute longer.
3. Stir the cooked pumpkin into the onion mixture and blend, in a food processor or mouli, to make a thick purée.
4. Add soy sauce to taste.

Tip

This purée is excellent as it is when served as a sauce for pastries, rice dishes or even pasta. It may also serve as the basis for a soup.

Herbed Spinach Salad in Filo Baskets (page 173)

PART SIX

Baked Goods

Roll up, roll up, roll up . . . It's the greatest flour show on earth, featuring all manner of comestibles, from the deliciously dainty to the delectably delightful! Just a note before you dive in: remember that natural flours differ greatly, and depending on what you use, some recipes may need rather more or less liquid.

Irish Soda Bread (page 203)

SWEET AND SAVOURY QUICK BREADS

Carrot Muffins

2 FREE-RANGE EGGS, WELL BEATEN
55G (2OZ) SUGAR
140ML (¼ PINT) OIL
1 LARGE COOKING APPLE, PEELED AND GRATED
2 MEDIUM CARROTS, PEELED AND GRATED
55G (2OZ) SULTANAS

55G (2OZ) WALNUT PIECES
180G (6OZ) PLAIN FLOUR
2 TEASPOONS BAKING POWDER
1 TEASPOON GROUND CINNAMON
½ TEASPOON ALLSPICE

1. Preheat the oven to 190°C/375°F/Gas Mark 5 and lightly oil or line a twelve-hole muffin tin.
2. Beat the eggs, sugar and oil until smooth in a large mixing bowl. Stir in the carrot, apple, sultanas and walnuts.
3. Sift the dry ingredients together and use a metal spoon to fold these lightly into the first mixture.
4. Fill each muffin case two-thirds full.
5. Bake for 15 minutes, until well risen and golden.

Makes 12 muffins

⏱ 30 mins

Another day, another carrot...

Just Perfect Banana Bread

3 LARGE, VERY RIPE BANANAS, PEELED AND MASHED
90G (3OZ) BUTTER OR MARGARINE
55G (2OZ) BROWN SUGAR
285ML (½ PINT) PINEAPPLE JUICE

450G (1LB) PLAIN FLOUR
25G (1OZ) WHEATGERM
1 TABLESPOON BAKING POWDER
1 TEASPOON GROUND ALLSPICE
1 TEASPOON GROUND CINNAMON

1. Preheat the oven to 180°C/350°F/Gas Mark 4.
2. Mash the bananas, butter and brown sugar together in a mixing bowl. Add the pineapple juice and purée the mixture with a hand-held blender.

Makes 2 large loaves

⏱ 1 hr, plus cooling time

3. In a separate bowl, mix the remaining ingredients so the spices are well distributed. Turn the dry mix into the banana mix and stir well but briefly.

4. Now spoon the batter into two lightly oiled large bread tins (about 20 x 10cm/8 x 4 inch). Bake for 45 minutes, leave to cool in the pans for 10 minutes, then turn on to a wire rack to cool completely. Slice thickly and serve.

Date and Walnut Loaf

90G (3OZ) BUTTER OR MARGARINE
55G (2OZ) BROWN SUGAR
285ML (½ PINT) APPLE JUICE
225G (8OZ) CHOPPED PITTED DATES
100G (4OZ) CHOPPED WALNUTS
55G (2OZ) WHOLEWHEAT FLOUR

450G (1LB) PLAIN FLOUR
1 TABLESPOON BAKING POWDER
1 TEASPOON GROUND CINNAMON
½ TEASPOON GROUND CLOVES
¼ TEASPOON GROUND NUTMEG

Makes 2 loaves

1 hr 5 mins, plus cooling time

1. Preheat the oven to 180°C/350°F/Gas Mark 4 and lightly oil two large (20 x 10cm/8 x 4 inch) bread tins.

2. Cream the butter, sugar and apple juice in a mixing bowl with a hand-held blender.

3. Mix the dates and walnuts together in a small bowl and stir in the wholewheat flour. Stir well to ensure the dates and walnuts are well coated. Mix the remaining dry ingredients in with the dates and walnuts and stir well.

4. Turn the dry mix into the creamed mixture and stir briefly. Spoon the batter into the loaf tins and bake for 45 minutes.

5. Cool in the tin for 10 minutes then turn on to a wire rack to cool completely. Serve cool, thickly sliced.

Orange Oat Bread

100G (4OZ) DRIED APRICOTS OR
    CURRANTS, FINELY CHOPPED
    OR MINCED
285-425ML (½ -¾ PINT) ORANGE JUICE
85G (3OZ) SUGAR
85G (3OZ) TAHINI OR OIL

100G (4OZ) ROLLED OATS
450G (1LB) PLAIN FLOUR
1 TABLESPOON BAKING POWDER
55G (2OZ) CANDIED ORANGE PEEL
2 TEASPOONS GROUND GINGER

1. Preheat the oven to 180°C/350°F/Gas Mark 4 and lightly oil two large (20 x 10cm/8 x 4 inch) bread tins.
2. Stir the apricots, most of the orange juice, sugar and tahini together in a large mixing bowl. Leave to stand for 10 minutes.
3. Mix the remaining dry ingredients together in a bowl and then add them to the apricot mixture; stir well. Adjust the consistency by adding more orange juice, if necessary, to make a wet, thick batter.
4. Spoon into the loaf tins and bake for 35-40 minutes. Cool in the tins for 10 minutes, then turn out on to a wire rack to cool completely.
5. Serve in thick slices.

Makes 2 large loaves

 1 hr 5 mins, plus cooling time

Irish Soda Bread

OIL
55G (2OZ) COARSE CORNMEAL
340G (12OZ) PLAIN FLOUR
340G (12OZ) WHOLEWHEAT FLOUR
25G (1OZ) WHEAT GERM

2 TEASPOONS BAKING POWDER
2 TEASPOONS BICARBONATE OF SODA
850ML (1½ PINTS) BUTTERMILK OR
    DAY-OLD MILK

1. Preheat the oven to 190°C/375°F/Gas Mark 5 and lightly oil a baking tray.
2. Sprinkle the cornmeal over the oiled tray. Mix the dry ingredients together in a bowl. Whisk 60ml (2 fl oz) oil and the buttermilk together then add to the dry mix. Stir well then knead for 3-5 minutes on a well-floured board.
3. Divide the dough into two parts and shape each into a round

Makes 2 loaves

 1 hr

loaf. Place the loaves on the baking tray and cut a cross in the top of each – to a depth of about 2.5cm (1 inch).

5.   Bake for 30 minutes, until the loaf sounds hollow when you tap the bottom crust.

6.   Cool on a wire rack before serving slightly warm with butter, jam and tea.

Favourite Teatime Scones

450G (1LB) PLAIN FLOUR

1 TABLESPOON BAKING POWDER

100G (4OZ) DRIED CURRANTS OR RAISINS

60ML (2 FL OZ) BARLEY MALT SYRUP

90ML (3 FL OZ) OIL

140ML (¼ PINT) MILK

140ML (¼ PINT) PLAIN YOGURT

Serves 4

🕐 30 mins

go on - pile on the jam

1.   Preheat the oven to 200°C/400°F/Gas Mark 6.

2.   Mix the flour, baking powder and currants together in a mixing bowl. Whisk the syrup, oil, milk and yogurt together in a separate bowl. Add the syrup mixture to the dry mix and stir briefly, adding a little more milk if necessary to make a firm batter.

3.   Turn the batter on to a well-floured board and roll to 2cm (¾ inch) thickness. Cut into rounds and place on a lightly oiled baking sheet.

4.   Bake for 12-15 minutes, then lift on to a wire rack to cool.

5.   Serve cool or just warm with jam and all the rest.

Sage and Onion Roll

2 TABLESPOONS BUTTER OR MARGARINE

1 MEDIUM ONION, VERY FINELY CHOPPED

½ TEASPOON FRESHLY GROUND BLACK
PEPPER

2 TEASPOONS DRIED SAGE OR 1 TABLESPOON
FINELY CHOPPED FRESH SAGE

450G (1 LB) PLAIN FLOUR

1 TABLESPOON BAKING POWDER

1 TEASPOON DRIED PARSLEY

½ TEASPOON DRIED THYME

3 TABLESPOONS OIL

180-285ML (6-10 FL OZ) MILK

½ TEASPOON COARSE SALT

1. Preheat the oven to 200°C/400°F/Gas Mark 6.
2. Melt the butter in a frying pan and sauté the onion over a low heat until clear and tender, about 10 minutes. Add the pepper and sauté a further 1 minute. Now stir in the sage and remove the pan from the heat.
3. Mix the flour, baking powder and dried herbs together in a bowl, make a well in the centre and add the oil and milk. Stir well and adjust the liquid to make a thick, sticky dough.
4. Turn the dough on to a well-floured board and roll into a rectangle of 2cm (¾ inch) thickness. Spread the sauté to the edges of the dough, leaving one long edge clear. Sprinkle the salt over the sauté and then roll the dough as you would a Swiss roll, sealing the long, clear edge of the rectangle with water or milk.
5. Place the roll sealed edge down on a non-stick or lightly oiled baking tray. Lightly score the top of the roll to mark slices of about 4cm (1½ inch) thick. Brush the top with milk and bake for 20-25 minutes, until golden.
6. Leave to cool on a wire rack then slice and serve cool or slightly warm with soup, salad or simply your favourite spread.

Serves 4-8

⏱ 55 mins

Tip

Add garlic or caraway seed to the sauté for a very wild flavour.

Yogurt Soda Bread

340G (12OZ) WHOLEMEAL FLOUR

100G (4OZ) UNBLEACHED WHITE FLOUR

PINCH OF SALT

2 TEASPOONS BICARBONATE OF SODA

285ML (½ PINT) PLAIN YOGURT

140ML (¼ PINT) WARM WATER

55G (2OZ) COARSE CORNMEAL

Makes 1 large loaf

 1 hr

1.   Preheat the oven to 200°C/400°F/Gas Mark 6.

2.   Stir the two flours, salt and the bicarbonate of soda together in a large bowl. Gradually stir in the yogurt, then add just enough of the water to make a moist but still fairly firm dough.

3.   Transfer this to a lightly floured board and knead briefly. Shape the dough into a round, and place it on a lightly oiled baking sheet which has been dusted with the cornmeal. Flatten the loaf slightly, use a sharp knife to make a deep cross on top of the loaf and brush with a little water or milk.

4.   Bake at the above heat for 20 minutes, then lower the heat to 180°C/350°F/Gas Mark 4 and continue cooking for 15 minutes, until the crust feels firm.

5.   Cool on a wire rack. This is best eaten on the day it is made.

YEAST BREADS

Granary Baps

15G (½ OZ) FRESH YEAST OR

7G (¼ OZ) DRIED YEAST

425ML (¾ PINT) WARM WATER

1 TEASPOON SUGAR, MOLASSES OR HONEY

675G (1½ LB) GRANARY FLOUR

PINCH OF SALT

1 TABLESPOON OIL

25G (1OZ) ROLLED OATS

Makes 8 baps

about 2 hrs 30 mins, plus cooking time

1.   Crumble the yeast into a small bowl with 140ml (¼ pint) of the water and the sugar. Stir and leave in a warm place to soften, about 10 minutes. Mix the flour and salt together in a mixing bowl and make a well in the centre. When the yeast has softened, stir the oil

into it and add this mixture to the flour. Add the remaining water and mix thoroughly to make a heavy dough.

2.   Turn the dough on to a well-floured board and knead it for 5-7 minutes, adding extra flour if necessary to make a firm, elastic dough.

3.   Place the dough in a lightly oiled bowl, cover with a clean cloth and keep in a warm place until it has doubled in volume – about 1 hour.

4.   Preheat the oven to 200°C/400°F/Gas Mark 6.

5.   Return the dough to a floured board, punch back, and knead briefly. Divide into eight pieces, shape into rounds and then flatten slightly on to a greased baking sheet. Brush the tops of the baps with water and sprinkle with the oats. Set aside in a warm spot and leave until doubled in size, about 30 minutes.

6.   Bake for 20 minutes. Cool on a wire rack.

*T*hree-seed Bread

15G (½ OZ) FRESH YEAST OR
7G (¼ OZ) DRIED YEAST
425ML (¾ PINT) WARM WATER
1 TEASPOON SUGAR, MOLASSES OR HONEY
675G (1½ LB) WHOLEMEAL FLOUR
PINCH OF SALT
85G (3OZ) POPPY SEEDS

1 TABLESPOON OIL
1 FREE-RANGE EGG, LIGHTLY BEATEN, OR
   1 TEASPOON TAHINI MIXED WITH
1 TABLESPOON WATER
25G (1OZ) PUMPKIN SEEDS
25G (1OZ) SUNFLOWER SEEDS

1.   Crumble the yeast into a small bowl with 140ml (¼ pint) of the water and the sugar. Stir and leave in a warm place to soften, about 10 minutes. Mix the flour, salt and poppy seeds together in a mixing bowl and make a well in the centre. When the yeast has softened, stir the oil into it and add this mixture to the flour. Add the remaining water and mix thoroughly to make a heavy dough.

2.   Turn the dough on to a well-floured board and knead it for 5-7 minutes, adding extra flour if necessary to make a firm, elastic dough. Place the dough in a lightly oiled bowl, cover with a clean cloth and keep in a warm place until it has doubled in volume – about 1 hour.

Makes 2 small loaves

about 2 hrs 45 mins, plus cooling time

3.   Preheat the oven to 200°C/400°F/Gas Mark 6 and lightly oil two small loaf tins.

4.   Knead the dough again, then divide it into two portions, shape roughly into oblongs, and press them into the tins. Brush the tops with beaten egg and sprinkle half of the pumpkin and sunflower seeds over each loaf. Set aside in a warm spot and leave until the dough reaches the top of the tins, about 30 minutes.

5.   Bake at the above heat for 10 minutes. Lower the heat to 180°C/350°F/Gas Mark 4 and bake for 30 minutes more. Cool on a wire rack.

Garlic and Rosemary Focaccia

25G (1OZ) FRESH YEAST

1 TEASPOON SUGAR

240-300ML (9-11 FL OZ) TEPID WATER

450G (1LB) PLAIN FLOUR

4 TABLESPOONS OLIVE OIL

3-5 CLOVES GARLIC, FINELY CHOPPED

2 TEASPOONS ROSEMARY LEAVES

2 TEASPOONS COARSE SALT

Serves 4

at least 3 hrs

1.   Dissolve the yeast and sugar in 120ml (4 fl oz) of the tepid water and leave in a warm place for 10 minutes.

2.   Measure the flour into a bowl and make a well in the centre. Pour half the oil, the softened yeast mixture and some of the remaining tepid water into the well and begin to work it into the flour. The dough should be firm and stiff enough to knead but still very pliable. Adjust the liquid to achieve the right texture then knead the dough on a floured board for about 10 minutes. Roll into a ball, place in a clean bowl and cover with a cloth. Leave for 2-8 hours.

3.   Preheat the oven to 200°C/400°F/Gas Mark 6.

4.   Knead the dough for 3 minutes then roll into two to four rounds of about 2cm (¾ inch) thickness. Brush each round with the remaining olive oil and sprinkle with garlic, rosemary and salt. Prick the surface of the bread with a fork, leave in a warm place for 30 minutes then bake for 20 minutes, until nicely golden.

5.   Cool on a wire rack and serve very fresh, either cool or warm.

Flat Bread with Olives

55G (2OZ) FRESH YEAST OR
25G (1OZ) DRIED YEAST
1 TEASPOON SUGAR
340ML (12 FL OZ) TEPID WATER
400G (14OZ) BLACK OLIVES (PRESERVED IN
OIL), STONED

900G (2LB) PLAIN FLOUR
OLIVE OIL
140ML (¼ PINT) DRY WHITE WINE
1 TABLESPOON CHOPPED FRESH THYME
2 TABLESPOONS CHOPPED FRESH OREGANO
COARSE SALT

1. Dissolve the yeast and sugar in 140ml (¼ pint) of the tepid water and place in a warm place for 15 minutes. Roughly chop the olives while the yeast works.
2. Measure the flour into a large bowl and make a well in the centre. Add the yeast mixture, 140ml (¼ pint) olive oil, the wine and half of the remaining water. Work together, at first with a wooden spoon, to make a soft but non-sticky dough. Add more water as necessary to achieve this.
3. Now add about two-thirds of the olives, thyme and oregano, turn the dough on to a floured board and knead for 7-10 minutes. Turn the dough into a clean bowl, cover with a cloth and leave to prove for 1-2 hours.
4. Preheat the oven to 200°C/400°F/Gas Mark 6.
5. Turn the dough on to a board and knead for 2 minutes then divide into two to four pieces and roll each into a round of about 2cm (¾ inch) thickness. Brush the rounds with a little olive oil, about 1 tablespoon, then sprinkle with the remaining olives, thyme, oregano and salt. Gently prick the surface of the round with a fork and lift the breads on to lightly oiled baking trays. Leave the rounds in a warm place to rise, about 30 minutes.
6. Bake for 20-25 minutes, until golden. Serve warm.

Serves 4-8

about 3 hrs

Layered Grape Bread

200G (7OZ) RAISINS

1 x 120-180ML (4-6 FL OZ) GLASS
SWEET DESSERT WINE

25G (1OZ) FRESH YEAST

1 TEASPOON SUGAR

140ML (¼ PINT) TEPID WATER OR MILK

340G (12OZ) PLAIN FLOUR

85G (3OZ) SUGAR

450G (1LB) BLACK GRAPES, SEEDED AND
HALVED

Serves 4

 about 3 hrs

1.   Measure the raisins into a bowl and cover with the wine. Leave to soak all day, overnight or for at least 2 hours.

2.   Dissolve the yeast and sugar in the tepid water and leave in a warm place for 15 minutes.

3.   Measure the flour and most of the sugar into a mixing bowl and stir well. Make a well in the centre and add the yeast mixture. Work to a soft but non-sticky dough, adding a little more tepid water or milk if necessary to achieve this. Turn the dough on to a well-floured board and knead for 7-10 minutes. Turn the dough into a clean bowl, cover and leave in a warm place to rise, about 1 hour.

4.   Preheat the oven to 180°C/350°F/Gas Mark 4.

5.   Turn the dough back on to a board and knead for 2-3 minutes. Divide the dough into two pieces and roll to equal sizes, about 23cm (9 inches) in diameter and 2cm (¾ inch) thickness. Place one round on a lightly oiled baking tray.

6.   Drain the raisins (drink the wine!) and spread half the raisins and half the grapes on the round. Dampen the edge of the round and place the other round of dough over it. Spread the remaining grapes and raisins on top and leave the bread in a warm place to rise, about 30 minutes.

7.   Sprinkle the remaining sugar over the bread and bake for about 45 minutes, until golden.

8.   Cool on a wire rack and serve warm at any time of day.

CAKES

Carrot Cake

100G (4OZ) BUTTER OR MARGARINE

100G (4OZ) BROWN SUGAR

3 EGGS, BEATEN

3 LARGE CARROTS, PEELED AND GRATED

100G (4OZ) WALNUTS, FINELY CHOPPED

55G (2OZ) RAISINS OR CURRANTS

GRATED ZEST OF 2 ORANGES

225G (8OZ) PLAIN FLOUR

1 TABLESPOON BAKING POWDER

1 TEASPOON GROUND ALLSPICE OR MIXED SPICE

1 TEASPOON GROUND GINGER

140-225ML (5-8 FL OZ) WATER OR FRUIT JUICE

1. Preheat the oven to 180°C/350°F/Gas Mark 4 and lightly oil a 23 x 36cm (9 x 13 inch) cake tin.

2. Cream the butter and sugar together in a large mixing bowl then add the beaten eggs and blend well. Stir in the carrots, walnuts, raisins and orange zest. Mix the flour, baking powder and spices together in a large bowl then add to the creamed mixture and stir well, adding enough water to make a soft batter.

3. Turn the batter into the cake tin and bake for 35-40 minutes, until a cocktail stick inserted comes out clean. Cool in the tin for 10 minutes then turn on to a wire rack to cool completely.

4. Slice and serve.

5. This cake is delicious iced with Cream Cheese Icing (page 258) or topped with Perfect On Everything Sauce (page 257). A little desiccated coconut is a very appealing garnish for the iced cake.

Serves 4-8

1 hr, plus cooling time

Warm Plum Cake

100G (4OZ) BUTTER OR
MARGARINE
85G (3OZ) BROWN SUGAR
2 EGGS
225G (8OZ) PLAIN FLOUR
4 TABLESPOONS WHEATGERM

2 TEASPOONS BAKING POWDER
450G (1LB) RIPE, SWEET PLUMS, STONED
AND QUARTERED
55G (2OZ) HAZELNUTS, CHOPPED
ICING SUGAR

Serves 4

🕐 1 hr.

Warm, squidgy and delicious!

1. Preheat the oven to 190°C/375°F/Gas Mark 5 and lightly oil a 20-23cm (8-9 inch) flan dish or cake tin.
2. Cream the butter and sugar together in a mixing bowl then beat in the eggs, with a hand-held blender if possible.
3. Mix the flour, wheatgerm and baking powder together and fold into the creamed mixture.
4. Carefully fold in the plums and turn the mixture immediately into the prepared dish. Sprinkle the hazelnuts over the top and bake for 45 minutes, until the top is golden and firm.
5. Cool in the dish then turn on to a serving plate, dust with the icing sugar and serve cool or slightly warm.
6. This is delicious with a bowl of fruit salad or fruit yogurt.

You're Kidding!
Aubergine and Chocolate Cake

1 LARGE AUBERGINE
SALT
55G (2OZ) PLAIN FLOUR
3 EGGS, BEATEN
2-4 TABLESPOONS OLIVE OIL

400G (14OZ) DARK CHOCOLATE
55G (2OZ) BUTTER OR MARGARINE
4 TABLESPOONS CHERRY CONSERVE OR JAM
ICING SUGAR

Serves 4-8

🕐 1 hr, plus
cooling and
setting time

1. Slice the aubergine into very thin rounds, lay them on a platter and sprinkle with salt. Leave to one side for about 30 minutes. Rinse the slices in fresh water and pat them dry with a clean tea towel.
2. Dust the slices with a little flour and dip each into the beaten

egg. Fry in the olive oil over a medium flame for 1-2 minutes each side. Drain on kitchen towels and leave to one side.

3. Break the chocolate into the top of a double boiler, add the butter and melt over boiling water. Stir well.

4. Place a layer of fried aubergines in a buttered, loose-bottomed 18cm (7 inch) cake tin. Spread a little of the chocolate over them and a little jam over the chocolate. Repeat these layers (there are usually four), ending with a chocolate layer.

5. Leave the cake to set then sprinkle with a little icing sugar and decorate with a cherry or two, if desired.

6. Serve in small slices with your favourite hot drink.

Go on - double dare you!

Carob Cake

180G (6OZ) WHOLEMEAL FLOUR
180G (6OZ) RAW CANE SUGAR
3 TABLESPOONS CAROB POWDER
1 TEASPOON BICARBONATE OF SODA
¼ TEASPOON SALT
1 TEASPOON VANILLA ESSENCE
6 TABLESPOONS OIL

200ML (7 FL OZ) WATER

For the lemon curd:
55G (2OZ) BUTTER OR MARGARINE
180G (6OZ) RAW CANE SUGAR
JUICE OF 2 LARGE LEMONS
85G (3OZ) ARROWROOT

1. Preheat the oven to 180°C/350°F/ Gas Mark 4 and lightly oil a 23cm (9 inch) cake tin.

2. Mix the flour, sugar, carob, bicarbonate of soda and salt together in a large mixing bowl. Stir in the vanilla, oil and water, mixing them well to make a thick, moist batter.

3. Pour into the tin, smooth the top and bake for 30-35 minutes, until a skewer comes out clean. Cool in the tin for 10 minutes then turn carefully out of the tin and on to a wire rack.

4. To make the lemon curd, melt the butter and sugar together in a small saucepan, then add the lemon juice and the arrowroot. Cook over a low flame, stirring constantly, until the mixture thickens. Set aside to cool.

5. Carefully slice the cake into two layers, spread the lower half with the lemon curd and replace the top half. Serve the same day.

Serves 4-8

🕐 1 hr, plus cooling time

*L*inzertorte

100G (4OZ) GROUND ALMONDS OR
    HAZELNUTS
100G (4OZ) PLAIN FLOUR
½ TEASPOON GROUND CINNAMON
85G (3OZ) BUTTER OR MARGARINE
55G (2OZ) SUGAR

1 TEASPOON GRATED LEMON PEEL
15G (½ OZ) SOYA FLOUR
60ML (2 FL OZ) WATER
½ TEASPOON OIL
225G (8OZ) RASPBERRY JAM

Serves 4-8

🕐 1 hr 15 mins,
    plus chilling time

1. Mix the nuts, flour and cinnamon together in a mixing bowl. Rub the butter into the dry ingredients to make a crumb-like texture. Stir in the sugar and grated lemon peel.

2. Whisk the soya flour into the water, pour into a small saucepan and heat gently, stirring, for 2-3 minutes. Add the oil.

3. Combine the two mixtures to make a firm dough (use a drop more water if necessary). Knead briefly then chill in the fridge for an hour or two.

4. Preheat the oven to 190°C/375°F/Gas Mark 5 and lightly oil a medium, 23cm (9 inch) flan dish.

5. Roll the dough on a lightly floured board to a thickness of about 5mm (¼ inch) and press it into the bottom and sides of the flan dish. Trim the edges and save these scraps. Spread the jam over the base of the flan. Roll out the scraps of dough, cut into strips and use these to make a latticework pattern over the jam. Press the edges of the lattice into the sides of the flan case.

6. Bake for 35-45 minutes, until the pastry is golden. Cool in the dish for 10 minutes, then slide on to a serving platter.

7. Serve warm or cold.

COOKIES AND BISCUITS

hocolate Nut Clusters

225G (8OZ) PLAIN CHOCOLATE
1 TABLESPOON OIL
85G (3OZ) ROASTED HAZELNUTS,
COARSELY CHOPPED

85G (3OZ) CRYSTALLISED GINGER, FINELY
CHOPPED

1. Break or grate the chocolate and place in the top of a double boiler over a medium flame.
2. Stir the chocolate while it melts then stir in the oil, remove the chocolate from the heat and immediately add the nuts and ginger, mixing well so that they are evenly distributed.
3. Drop spoonfuls of the mixture on to a lightly oiled baking sheet and place aside to cool.

Serves 4

⏲ 45 mins

lain Chocolate Digestive Biscuits

Why make your own, when you can buy them at the supermarket? Because these are better, that's why!

100G (4OZ) WHOLEMEAL FLOUR
100G (4OZ) FINE OATS
PINCH OF SALT
100G (4OZ) BUTTER OR MARGARINE

25G (1OZ) RAW CANE SUGAR
1 TEASPOON BICARBONATE OF SODA
2-3 TABLESPOONS MILK
100G (4OZ) PLAIN CHOCOLATE

1. Preheat the oven to 200°C/400°F/Gas Mark 6 and lightly oil a baking tray.
2. Mix the flour, oats and salt together in a mixing bowl. Rub the butter into the dry mix to a crumb-like consistency. Stir in the sugar.
3. Dissolve the bicarbonate of soda by whisking it into the milk. Add this to the dry ingredients to make a stiff dough (you may need a drop more liquid).

Makes 18-24 biscuits

⏲ 35 mins, plus cooling and setting time

4. Knead briefly on a lightly floured board. Roll out the dough to about 3mm (⅛ inch) depth and cut into 6cm (2½ inch) circles. Arrange on baking sheets and prick with a fork.

5. Bake for 10-15 minutes, until crisp and golden. Set aside to cool.

6. Coarsely grate the chocolate into the top of a double boiler. When it has melted, dip the biscuits to coat one side in the chocolate. Leave to set.

azelnut Shortbread

180G (6OZ) PLAIN FLOUR	100G (4OZ) RAW CANE SUGAR
2 TEASPOONS BAKING POWDER	100G (4OZ) ROASTED HAZELNUTS, CHOPPED
180G (6OZ) BUTTER OR MARGARINE	

Serves 4-8

🕐 45 mins, plus cooling time

1. Preheat the oven to 150°C/300°F/Gas Mark 2 and lightly oil a 2cm (8 inch) square cake tin.

2. Sift the flour and baking powder together in a mixing bowl. Rub the butter into the flour to make a fine, crumb-like texture. Stir in the sugar then the nuts. Mix well.

3. Turn the mixture into the cake tin and press down firmly, smoothing the top as you do so. Bake for 25-30 minutes, until just golden.

4. Cut the shortbread into slices while hot, but leave to cool on a wire rack before removing the slices.

Peanut Butter Cookies

100G (4OZ) PEANUT BUTTER,
SMOOTH OR CHUNKY

85G (3OZ) BROWN SUGAR

140ML (¼ PINT) ORANGE JUICE

GRATED RIND OF 2 ORANGES

340G (12OZ) PLAIN FLOUR

2 TEASPOONS BAKING POWDER

1 TEASPOON BICARBONATE OF SODA

1.   Preheat the oven to 180°C/350°F/Gas Mark 4.

2.   Cream the peanut butter and brown sugar together in a mixing bowl. Add the orange juice and rind and whisk to a smooth consistency, preferably with a hand-held blender.

3.   Mix the dry ingredients together in a separate bowl, then fold them into the creamed mixture to make a firm dough.

4.   Place walnut-sized balls of dough on a lightly oiled baking tray and flatten them by twice pressing a floured fork across to make a criss-cross pattern.

5.   Bake for 12-15 minutes, until lightly browned. Cool on a wire rack and serve.

Makes approximately
24 cookies

⏱ 45 mins

Nearly Black Brownies

100G (4OZ) COCOA POWDER

100G (4OZ) BUTTER OR MARGARINE

3 EGGS, BEATEN

140ML (¼ PINT) MILK

100G (4OZ) SUGAR

450G (1LB) PLAIN FLOUR

2 TEASPOONS BAKING POWDER

55G (2OZ) CHOPPED NUTS

55-100G (2-4OZ) PLAIN (NON-MILK)
CHOCOLATE CHIPS

1.   Preheat the oven to 180°C/350°F/Gas Mark 4.

2.   Stir the cocoa and butter together in a small saucepan over a medium heat, or in the top of a double boiler. The butter and chocolate must melt together; leave to cool.

3.   Beat the eggs, milk and sugar together and, when cool, add the chocolate mixture. Blend well.

4.   Stir the remaining ingredients together in a bowl then add this dry mixture to the egg mixture. Stir briefly and turn into a lightly oiled 23 x 33cm (9 x 13 inch) baking tin.

5.   Bake for 30 minutes. Cool in the tin then slice and serve.

Serves 4-8

⏱ 1 hr, plus
cooling time

Spicy Molasses Cookies

100G (4OZ) BUTTER OR MARGARINE

55G (2OZ) DARK BROWN SUGAR

½ JAR (ABOUT 225G/8OZ) BLACKSTRAP
MOLASSES

2 EGGS

285ML (½ PINT) FRUIT JUICE (SUCH AS
PINEAPPLE OR APPLE)

550G (1 ¼ LB) PLAIN FLOUR

1 TABLESPOON BAKING POWDER

1 TEASPOON BICARBONATE OF SODA

2 TEASPOONS GROUND GINGER

1 TEASPOON GROUND CLOVES

1 TEASPOON GROUND CINNAMON

1 TEASPOON GROUND ALLSPICE

Makes approximately
3 dozen cookies

⏱ 30 mins, plus
cooling time

1. Preheat the oven to 180°C/350°F/Gas Mark 4.
2. Cream the butter and sugar together in a large mixing bowl or blender. Add the molasses and eggs and blend well then add the fruit juice and blend to a smooth consistency.
3. In a separate bowl, mix the remaining ingredients then add this dry mix to the creamed mixture and stir well.
4. Turn the dough on to a well-floured board and roll to 1cm (½ inch) thickness. Use a cutter to cut out rounds or gingerbread-man shapes and place these on lightly oiled baking trays.
5. Bake for 9-11 minutes, then lift and cool on a wire rack. Decorate the men if making gingerbread men.

HOT TIPS:
Getting Fresh with your Food

The world's top cooks all know that by far the most important basic rule of sensual cooking consists of just one word: *freshness*. Fresh food requires less manipulation in the kitchen to bring out its flavour; and conversely, the more a foodstuff is processed, the greater its loss of natural flavours and vital nutrients.

When possible, buy organic food – or have a go at growing your own! Organic food is more likely to have its nutrients intact and, if it is from a local grower, it won't have been in prolonged storage during transit. Organic food is:

♡ Grown without artificial pesticides and fertilisers.

♡ Tastes good rather than just looks good.

♡ Is never irradiated.

♡ Contains no artificial hormones, genetically manipulated organisms or unnecessary medication.

♡ Is not over-processed to remove the goodness.

♡ Does not contain flavourings, dyes and other additives.

♡ Is nutritious, living food which promotes positive health and well-being.

Of course, the biggest single drawback with organic food is still its substantially higher price. The truth is, though, that organic agriculture is *not* necessarily any more expensive for the farmer. In 1983, the first well-documented scientific study was published which showed that an organic farm can achieve crop yields comparable to conventional farms at less cost, and with half the pollution and soil erosion produced by orthodox farming methods. The study, undertaken by the independent Rodale Research Center of Emmaus, Pennsylvania, demonstrated that farming costs were slashed by between 10 and 30 per cent – because organic farming doesn't use expensive chemical fertilisers. At the same time, crop yields equalled or exceeded state averages. For example, corn yields averaged 108 bushels per acre, compared to 85.3 bushels produced by conventional chemical farming.[1] Knowing this, we consumers should ask some hard questions about the pricing policies of organic foods.

As a parent, I'd just like to add a note here regarding my concern for the particular effect that pesticides and other chemical residues may have specifically on children. A recent American report suggests that children may consume about four times more cancer-causing substances than adults – and one child out of 3,000 may develop cancer from eating chemical residues.[2]

Another panel set up by the highly-respected National Academy of Sciences has also indicated that children may be

1 UPI, 21 November, 1983.
2 *Ibid*, 25 February, 1989.

more sensitive to pesticides than adults.[3] The panel recommended that the US government improve the way it calculates pesticide risks to include the difference between children and adults, and also to collect more detailed data on the amount of food children actually eat. Clearly, if these figures are even remotely accurate, there is major cause for parental concern. If you can't afford to eat organic food all the time (and it *can* be very expensive), at least try to make sure that your children eat as organically as possible.

Organic food is also better for the environment. Intensive agriculture is responsible for about 50 per cent of all water pollution (such as high nitrate levels). It has been clearly established that modern biological-organic farming methods lead both to lower leaching of nitrates into the water supply, and to lower nitrate content in vegetables.

THE SENSUAL SHOPPER
TOP TIPS FOR THE FRESHEST FOOD

♥ Do check the use-by date on the food's label. Old produce will have suffered severe nutritional and taste decay. Shopkeepers always put older stock at the front of the display – it's called stock rotation – so disarrange their display, and buy from the back!

♥ Remember that canning and bottling reduce the levels of vitamin C, thiamin and folic acid. Vitamin C loss continues during storage. If you have to buy canned food, do not keep it overlong. Although it may be safe to eat, its nutrients may be considerably depleted.

♥ Foods which contain sulphur dioxide as a preservative will have almost entirely lost their thiamin (vitamin B1) content.

♥ Freeze-dried foods are relatively good since there is no heating to deplete nutrients.

♥ Frozen foods suffer some thiamin and vitamin C loss. However the loss is less than in fresh food which has been kept for a number of days. If shopping for fresh food is a problem for you, frozen foods are probably the next best alternative, but be extra careful not to overcook them (see below).

♥ Choose unrefined monounsaturated oils – preferably olive oil – for cooking. Pure, refined polyunsaturated oils turn rancid more easily.

♥ Don't buy tinned goods which are damaged – no matter how good a bargain they appear to be. Small cracks in the lining inside the cans affect the contents which will certainly affect the delicate vitamins and other nutrients and may even cause the food itself to turn bad.

♥ Take chilled or frozen food home as quickly as possible, particularly in the summer. Bacteria thrive in the heat. So putting supermarket food into the back of a car on a hot day is like putting it into a greenhouse. It's well worth investing in a cool-bag.

3 The Associated Press, 28 June, 1993.

STORING AND COOKING

♡ Buy a thermometer for your fridge. It's been estimated that 80 per cent of UK fridges are too warm, which can make your food spoil very quickly, and helps food poisoning bacteria thrive. The recommended temperature is no more than 5°C.

♡ Although it may seem to be the safest thing to keep eggs in the refrigerator, it isn't. Condensation can unplug tiny, porous holes in the shell, allowing dangerous bacteria to penetrate. And the lowered temperature of the yolk means it needs even longer cooking.

♡ Never eat raw eggs in any form (e.g. mayonnaise) – always make sure they're thoroughly cooked.

♡ Cook everything thoroughly! If you still eat meat, you should buy a meat thermometer and check that cooking times and temperature are adequate.

♡ Be particularly careful if you use a microwave oven. The evidence suggests that you shouldn't rely on them to kill off bacteria in your food. Always follow the recommended standing times.

♡ Discard the packaging from chill foods – whether you're heating them in a microwave or a conventional oven. You don't want to take a chance on poisonous chemicals melting and finding their way into your food.

♡ Wash food before you eat it – even if you've grown it yourself. Vegetables and fruit can harbour bacteria from the soil.

♡ Never reheat food more than once. Make sure it's not underheated.

♡ Don't take chances! If your food smells off, throw it out!

♡ Be certain that frozen food is thoroughly defrosted before cooking.

♡ Be sure all kitchen towels, sponges, surfaces, food equipment and cutting boards are kept clean. When you're preparing a meal, it's also prudent to wash utensils and worktops between stages – never allow anyone to use the same knife or chopping board for raw meat and other foods without thorough washing in between.

♡ Put all rubbish and scraps of food straight into the waste bin – and always keep the lid securely down, so that flies can't get in and germs can't get out.

♡ Store oils, fats and oily foods like cheeses and shelled nuts in the refrigerator. This will help to slow down the process of oxidation which turns them rancid.

♡ Vitamin C, thiamin, riboflavin and folic acid all decay quickly in air. Once vegetables are harvested, the damaged tissues release an enzyme which starts to destroy the vitamin C. Blanching inhibits the enzyme, which is why freezing fresh vegetables is much better than keeping them unfrozen and eating them many days later.

♡ Vegetables lose around 70 per cent of their folic acid content within three days if they are stored in daylight. Store vegetables in the refrigerator until you are ready to use them, or freeze them straightaway.

♡ Store grains and cereals whole and in a dry, cool place.

♡ Cooking is generally harmful to the nutrients in food. However, it also changes starches, proteins and some vitamins into accessible forms for us as well as releasing nutrients in some foods which are otherwise bound in, like the amino acid tryptophan in cornmeal. Cooking is necessary for other foods to destroy toxic substances such as those found in soya beans and kidney beans. Cooking also makes some foods, like meat, palatable to eat. However, there are some ways in which you can reduce the nutrient loss in foods during the cooking process, as outlined below.

♡ Steaming is the best method of cooking most vegetables and grains. A simple steamer insert for your saucepans is inexpensive and the time needed to cook in this way is often shorter than traditional boiling. After steaming, pressure cooking is perhaps the best way to reduce nutrient loss. Invest in a non-aluminium pressure cooker which, because of the reduced cooking times, will also reduce energy consumption and therefore the size of your fuel bills.

♡ After pressure cooking, the next healthiest options are:

Stir-fry and sautéing
Baking and grilling
Roasting
Microwave
Deep-frying

♡ If you cook with fat don't let it become so hot that it starts to smoke. At this temperature the essential fatty acid linoleic acid is destroyed immediately. In fact, the rule to remember when cooking a stir-fry, for instance, is to heat your pan first then add cold oil and immediately add your vegetables. This simple guideline will help prevent loss of flavour and nutrients in your cooking.

♡ Fats which have been used for cooking once must be discarded since the linoleic acid and vitamins A and C will have been lost.

♡ If you boil food, do so for the minimum amount of time and then use the water for stock afterwards. The fragile water-soluble vitamins as well as some minerals leach into cooking water, which is why soups are so nutritious.

♡ Don't add bicarbonate of soda to cooking water, even if you see it recommended in recipes for cooking pulses. It destroys valuable B vitamins.

♡ Prepare food immediately before cooking – remember that vitamin C is destroyed once cells are damaged in vegetables – and for the same reason try not to chop them too finely. Scrubbing vegetables is better than peeling them.

♡ Once food is cooked, eat it straightaway. Keeping it warm will only result in further nutrient loss, which is why eating out too frequently may be less than healthy for you.

If you lead a hectic lifestyle, and consider that you don't have time for some of the advice given above, think again. The life you lead is totally dependent on a good nutritional support system – without which, you're just running on empty. And you can only do that for so long. Shopping regularly for fresh foods can appear to present a problem – if you don't attach a very high priority to it. But just think – no sensible person buys a Rolls Royce then tries to run it on two-star petrol! It's the same with your body – the better the fuel, the better the performance you'll receive.

THE KITCHEN SINK GOURMET
HOW TO GROW IT YOURSELF, WITHOUT A GARDEN!

The freshest food of all is the food you grow yourself: nothing, repeat nothing, can match that exquisite fresh-from-the-garden taste sensation. There's just one problem, though – you might not have a garden! Even so, you don't have to miss out on the delights of your very own home-grown fresh food. The tiniest square of land or narrowest window ledge is a potential hotbed of home-produced vegetables, herbs and even edible flowers!

Home-grown vegetables taste quite unlike shop-bought ones and stay fresh right up to the time of eating. As well as having the luxury of an instant supply of completely fresh produce, growing your own vegetables means you can be certain they are 100 per cent organic. And, of course, there is the all-important question of cost. Don't you begrudge paying over the odds for produce that is chemically treated and probably less than fresh? If so, then here are some really easy foods for you to try.

Sprouts

You can have a year-round supply of highly nutritious sprouts for little effort and not much cost. Don't dismiss them as exotic and rather tasteless salads. The term sprouts covers much more than just Chinese mung beansprouts. Any seed will sprout, but the best are legumes like peas, beans, fenugreek, alfalfa and clover, seeds such as pumpkin and sunflower and grains such as wheat and barley. Mustard and cress are in fact sprouts, and you probably know how easy they are to grow. An incredible source of concentrated nutrition, high in protein, amino acids, vitamins A, E, K, and especially B and C, sprouts do not need soil or sunshine. All that is required is air, moisture and a jar. So there is no reason why you should not soon have your own crop of this invigoratingly healthy and versatile food.

HOW TO GROW THEM

1. Use a container with some sort of drainage, such as a colander, strainer, mesh tray, or even a flowerpot with a net over the hole. A jar with a piece of cheesecloth or muslin held in place around the top with a rubber band is perhaps the simplest and most effective. The size of the jar depends on how many seeds you are sprouting, but it should be at least 500ml (about 18 fl oz).

2. Seeds can be bought from health-food stores and some supermarkets. Pick out all the clean, whole ones and throw out the rest.

3. For every 1dl or 100ml (3½ fl oz) the jar holds, use up to 2 or 3 tablespoons of seeds. First, they must be soaked in four times their own volume of water, ideally mineral water, until their bulk is doubled. This normally takes about 8 hours, or overnight. After this time, pour off the water. It contains a lot of the seeds' goodness and so should be used in cooking if possible.

4. The sprout container should be kept in darkness – just throw a teatowel over the jar. The seeds must be rinsed two or three times a day through the mesh of the jar. Make sure you drain them thoroughly each time by turning the container upside down, or the sprouts will rot.

5. Throw away any seeds that have not sprouted after two days. The rest will be ready to eat after four or five days. On the last day they can be put into the light, but only for a few hours or they will become bitter.

6. Most sprouts will need a final rinsing and draining before being put in the fridge in a covered container for storage. Some varieties, however, have loose husks which need to be removed. Place them in a large bowl of water and agitate until the husks float to the top and you can skim them off.

COOKING SPROUTS

Any grain or vegetable sprout will not require cooking, but bean or pea sprouts should be simmered quickly to make them easier to digest.

> Mung bean sprouts – 3 minutes.
> Lentil bean sprouts – 10-15 minutes.
> Peas – 5 minutes.
> Chick peas – 8 minutes.
> Fenugreek – 3 minutes.
> Soya beans – soak for just 2 hours,
>   rinsing frequently and then cook for
>   10-15 minutes.

Vegetable sprouts are good in salads and sandwiches, or as a garnish for any dish. Grain sprouts can be used in bread – just mix into the dough before baking. Bean sprouts can be steamed with other vegetables or stir-fried for a couple of minutes.

Yogurt

Do you like the idea of having a continuous, cheap supply of delicious protein? It is simple; for every cup of yogurt you want, simply expose the same amount of milk to bacteria in a warm place and wait for it to culture. You must sterilise all equipment first by putting 1 tablespoon of 5 per cent chlorine bleach to 2 gallons of warm, but not hot, water and soak for at least 30 seconds. Rinse well.

1. Fill 4 x 140ml (¼ pint) jars (with lids) with water at a temperature of about 38°C/100°F to within 5cm (2 inches) from the top in order to sterilise them.

2. Put a heating pad (such as those used for arthritic pain) on a moderate heat in a warm place and cover with a towel.

3. Pour 1 cup of warm water into an electric blender. Turn the blender on low and add 1 cup of non-instant dried skimmed milk and ¼ cup of 'starter' yogurt (simply commercial plain yogurt, but make sure it does not contain any stabilisers).

4. As soon as the mixture becomes smooth, turn off the blender and put it back into the jar. Do the same with the other jars and put them all on the heating pad with a towel over the top.

5. Just leave the jars for about 3 hours, and then check them. When the yogurt is set, put it in the fridge, making sure it does not get moved or knocked. It is ready to eat when it slightly resists a gentle finger touch.

TROUBLE-SHOOTING

♡ The yogurt does not set. In this case the milk powder probably was not fresh enough. Make sure you buy it from a shop with a fast turnover and smell it to check it has no odour. It could also mean that the temperature was too high; at 49°C/120°F the bacteria cannot live, so check with a thermometer. If the starter yogurt contained stabilisers, the bacteria would be inactivated, so buy a different make. It is also possible some liquid was left in the container during sterilisation which would kill the bacteria.

♡ The yogurt does not taste right. If it tastes cheesy, the cause may be some left over bacteria, so sterilise all containers and change the culture. If it is chalky, the powdered milk was probably too concentrated. If foam builds up, just skim it off. If the yogurt separates and tastes sour, it may have been exposed to too much heat, so do not leave it on the pad for so long next time. Alternatively, it may not have been exposed to enough cold air – ensure there is space around the container in the fridge.

Herbs

You can grow herbs almost anywhere as they are so hardy and thrive with constant picking. In a garden, their best position is on a border, all planted together. Paving slabs laid corner to corner on the earth make a super chequer-board herb garden. Each square of bare earth gives good breathing space and root room for a single herb species. And with the paving stones, you can get to the most remote plant without having to put on your wellies! Start them in the spring, in a sunny spot. If you do not have a garden, make up the right soil using an equal quantity of sand, leaf-mould and soil. Put in containers such as troughs or flowerpots on a sunny window-sill and keep well watered. It is even possible to grow taller varieties as they will conveniently become dwarfed in a confined space. Mint may be a little more difficult as it has spreading roots, so plant it in a separate pot.

Do not rule out indoor space – you can grow a bay tree in your sitting-room, for example! Make use of patios, balconies and walls with hanging pots. It is a good idea to use strawberry pots with a small herb planted in each pocket and a bigger one in the middle. Do not forget to put stones or pieces of slate in the bottom for drainage.

DRYING HERBS

Pick just before the buds open into flowers as they will be more flavoursome. Make sure not to do this when the weather is damp or the plants are wet from dew. Put them in bundles and hang them upside down, either in an airy, but fairly dark place, or in a cupboard. They will be ready in between twelve days and three weeks, depending on how much moisture there is in the atmosphere. When your herbs are fully dried, take the leaves off the stalks and put them in jars which are both clean and dry, making sure they are airtight. It is a good idea to label the contents of each container. When using dried herbs in cooking you will only need about one-third the amount you would use of fresh herbs.

Flowers

Flowers are a neglected food! Fun, flavoursome and attractive, they well deserve any growing space you may have. Use them with vegetables, salads or preserved in pickles. Just cook as you would vegetables. In this country, we originally cultivated flowers for use in cooking and medicine; the idea to grow them as beautiful plants came from abroad.

NASTURTIUMS

Sometimes called Indian cress, the name of these flowers comes from the Latin for 'twisted nose' because of their pungent smell. They are in fact very peppery and so can be used in salads and sandwiches for added flavour. The pods, especially the orange and red ones, can be used instead of capers, or for flavouring vinegar. Grow them indoors in a sunny window or in pots trailing down. Just make sure the compost is moist and then forget about them.

CARNATIONS

Use them crystallised or pickled in conserves or sauces.

ELDERS

The young shoots or blossoms can be used in pickles and the berries in chutney or wine.

ROSES

Use old-fashioned perfumed roses, such as Queen of Denmark (white), Cardinal Richelieu (red) or Madame Hardy (damask). The leaves of rose-geranium, either fresh or dried, can be used to give a subtle flavour to sweets, jams and jellies.

PANSIES

Great for decorations of any sort, especially on cakes when crystallised.

MARIGOLDS

Good for seasoning generally, marigold can also be used in place of saffron. The fresh or dried petals can be put in salads and soups.

Honey

Anyone can keep bees. All you need is a little patience and a sense of danger! A big garden is not necessary, as long as you ensure the hives are a suitable distance from neighbours and animals. To look after one hive, expect to spend about an hour a week. Although honey yields vary considerably, an average is about 18kg (40 lb) from each hive. Bear in mind the initial outlay to buy the necessary equipment and be careful in choosing a position that is away from both wind and sun. You can have great fun watching the incredible activities of your bees as well as the satisfaction of producing this miracle food in your own back garden. To store your honey, use screw-top jam jars labelled with the date, and put in a cool, dark place.

PART SEVEN
Just Desserts

FRUIT DESSERTS

Burgundy Pears

2 LARGE PEARS
140ML (1/4 PINT) WATER
55G (2OZ) CASTOR SUGAR
RIND OF 1 LEMON, IN LARGE PIECES

1 x 5CM (2 INCH) PIECE CINNAMON STICK
1 TEASPOON CORNFLOUR
2 TEASPOONS COLD WATER
140ML (¼ PINT) BURGUNDY WINE

Serves 2

🕐 35 mins, plus chilling time

1. Carefully peel the pears, leaving the stalks on.
2. Place the water, sugar, lemon rind and cinnnamon stick in a saucepan over a medium flame.Bring to the boil and simmer, stirring until the sugar is dissolved.
3. Mix the cornflour with the cold water and add to the syrup, heating and stirring until it thickens. Add the burgundy and remove from the heat.
4. Place the pears in a glass serving dish.
5. Discard the lemon rind and cinnamon stick, pour the sauce over the pears and leave them to marinate. Cover the dish and turn the pears once or twice in the next hour so that they colour evenly.
6. Refrigerate for at least 4 hours.
7. Serve each pear with a little of the sauce and a topping of cream or slivered almonds.

Blackberry Fool

900G (2LB) FRESH BLACKBERRIES

180ML (6 FL OZ) WHIPPING CREAM

Serves 4

🕐 1 hr, plus cooling and chilling time

1. Preheat the oven to 180°C/350°F/Gas Mark 4.
2. Pick over, wash and drain the blackberries and put them into a glass ovenproof dish. Cover and bake for 30 minutes. Push the berries through a fruit sieve and leave the mash to cool. If you like, you may chill the berry mash until ready to use.
3. Whip the cream to a stiff peak stage and fold carefully into the berry mash.
4. Turn into a pretty dish and serve immediately.

Spiced Quince

2 LARGE QUINCE

25G (1OZ) BUTTER OR MARGARINE

25G (1OZ) GRATED FRESH GINGER ROOT

1 TEASPOON CORIANDER, GROUND OR
CRUSHED

1 TABLESPOON BROWN SUGAR

2 TABLESPOONS RED WINE VINEGAR

1/4 TEASPOON FRESHLY GROUND BLACK PEPPER

A FEW LEAVES OF BATAVIA OR CURLY ENDIVE

55G (2OZ) FRESH WALNUTS, BROKEN OR
CHOPPED

2 TABLESPOONS SOURED CREAM

1. Peel the quince, cut them in half and core them.
2. Melt the butter in a saucepan over a medium flame and add the ginger root and coriander. Sauté for 1-2 minutes, stirring constantly, then add the quince. Continue to sauté for about 5 minutes, turning the quince two or three times so that they brown slightly on both sides.
3. Add the sugar, wine vinegar and seasoning and cook over a low heat, covered, for 10-12 minutes. Leave the quince to cool in the juice.
4. To serve, lay a few leaves of batavia or curly endive on the serving plates. Drain the quince halves and place them on top of the leaves. Fill the hollows in the centre of each quince half with the walnuts.
5. Mix the soured cream with the cool, spiced juice, pour over the walnuts and serve.

Serves 2-4

🕐 55 mins

Batavia is a leafy chicory — fancy that!

Baked Glazed Pineapple

2 RIPE PINEAPPLES

3 TABLESPOONS HONEY

1. Preheat the oven to 190°C/375°F/Gas Mark 5.
2. Quarter the pineapples along their length, leaving the skin on. Cut each quarter several times across its width without cutting through the skin: exactly as if you were preparing a melon. Place the quarters in an oven dish and drizzle a little honey over each piece.
3. Bake for 10 minutes and serve piping hot.

Serves 4

🕐 20 mins

Poached Pears

55G (2OZ) SUGAR

25G (1OZ) BUTTER OR MARGARINE

4 LARGE CONFERENCE PEARS, PEELED
AND CORED

2 TABLESPOONS LEMON JUICE

¼ TEASPOON GROUND GINGER

25G (1OZ) FLAKED ALMONDS

Serves 4

⏱ 25 mins

1.   Measure the sugar and butter into a frying pan and place over a low flame, stirring constantly until the sugar dissolves.

2.   Cut the pears into thick slices and add them to the frying pan; cook 2-3 minutes then turn and cook the other side. Pour in the lemon juice and add the ground ginger. Cook gently for 2-3 minutes longer, until the pears are soft.

3.   Serve at once into warmed bowls, spooning any remaining sauce over the pears.

4.   Sprinkle with a garnish of flaked almonds.

Dried Fruit Compote

85G (3OZ) PRUNES

85G (3OZ) DRIED APRICOTS

85G (3OZ) DRIED APPLE RINGS

85G (3OZ) SULTANAS

55G (2OZ) RAW CANE SUGAR

2 TEASPOONS ROSE WATER

1 TABLESPOON FINELY CHOPPED PRESERVED
GINGER

55G (2OZ) FLAKED ALMONDS

Serves 4

⏱ 30 mins, plus
soaking and
chilling time

1.   Mix the prunes, apricots and apple rings together in a mixing bowl and cover with cold water. Cover the bowl and leave the fruits to soak all day or overnight.

2.   Turn the soaked fruit into a saucepan with just enough of the soaking water to cover them. Add the sultanas and sugar and bring the mixture to the boil, stirring often. Lower the heat, cover the pan and simmer for 10-15 minutes, until all the fruit is just tender.

3.   Stir in the rose water and ginger and leave the mixture to cool in the pan. Turn it into a serving dish and chill in the fridge.

4.   Serve garnished with the flaked almonds.

Favourite Teatime Scones (page 204)

Iced Chocolate-lined Orange Bowl (page 255)

Frigid Fruit Pudding (page 253)

Cherry Glisten Flan (page 237)

PIES

Cherry Glisten Flan

180G (6OZ) SHORTCRUST PASTRY
900G (2LB) SWEET CHERRIES,
    PITTED AND HALVED
100G (4OZ) BUTTER OR MARGARINE
100G (4OZ) GROUND ALMONDS

100G (4OZ) SUGAR
2 EGGS, BEATEN
1 TABLESPOON ICING SUGAR OR VANILLA
    SUGAR

1. Preheat the oven to 200°C/400°F/Gas Mark 6.
2. Roll the pastry to a thickness of about 5cm (¼ inch) and line a 23cm (9 inch) pie dish. Spread the cherries in the flan case.
3. Blend the remaining ingredients together in a bowl and spread over the cherries.
4. Bake for 35 minutes. Leave to cool then sprinkle a little of the icing sugar over; slice and serve.

Serves 4-6

🕐 1 hr

Tip

Make vanilla sugar by placing a whole vanilla pod in a storage jar filled with castor sugar.

Banana Ginger Flan

225G (8OZ) GINGER BISCUITS,
    CRUSHED
85G (3OZ) BUTTER OR MARGARINE
2 TABLESPOONS STRAWBERRY OR RASPBERRY
    JAM

4 LARGE BANANAS, SLICED
JUICE OF ½ LEMON
1 TABLESPOON CUSTARD POWDER
140ML (¼ PINT) MILK
140ML (¼ PINT) WHIPPING CREAM

1. Preheat the oven to 200°C/400°F/Gas Mark 6.
2. Turn the crushed biscuits into a 30cm (12 inch) flan dish. Melt the butter in a saucepan and pour over the crushed biscuits. Stir well

Serves 4-6

🕐 45 mins, plus chilling time

then line the base and sides of the flan dish with the crumbs, pressing firmly.

3. Bake for 12 minutes, until crisp. Cool on a wire rack.

4. Spread the jam over the base of the flan and arrange the banana slices over that. Drizzle the lemon juice over the banana slices.

5. Mix the custard powder with 1 tablespoon of the milk in a cup. Bring the rest of the milk to a boil and pour over the custard mixture. Stir well over a medium flame while the custard returns to the boil. Remove from the heat and leave to cool, stirring occasionally.

6. Whisk the cream to a firm peak and fold it into the cooled custard. Spread this mixture carefully over the banana and chill for at least 1 hour.

7. Slice and serve.

Pecan Pumpkin Pie

For the pastry:
55G (2OZ) BUTTER OR MARGARINE
45G (1½ OZ) VEGETABLE SUET
200G (7OZ) PLAIN FLOUR

For the filling:
340G (¾ LB) PREPARED (TINNED) PUMPKIN

RAW CANE SUGAR
2 EGGS, BEATEN
½ TEASPOON GROUND GINGER
1 TEASPOON GROUND CINNAMON
¼ TEASPOON GROUND CLOVES
55G (2OZ) PECAN NUTS, COARSELY CHOPPED

Serves 4-6

🕐 1 hr 15 mins

1. Preheat the oven to 220°C/425°F/Gas Mark 7.

2. For the pastry, rub the two fats into the flour to make a crumb-like mixture. Add a few spoonfuls of cold water and mix well to make a soft dough. Wrap in plastic film and leave in the fridge for 30 minutes.

3. Roll out the pastry and line a 30cm (12 inch) flan dish; stand the dish on a baking tray.

4. Blend the pumpkin, 100g (4oz) sugar, eggs and spices in a mixing bowl. Pour the pumpkin mixture into the flan and bake for 15 minutes. Lower the oven temperature to 180°C/350°F/Gas Mark 4.

5. Sprinkle the flan with the nuts and 55g (2oz) sugar and bake for 25 minutes more.

6. Cool on a wire rack and serve warm or cold.

Roman Cheesecake

55G (2OZ) DRIED APRICOTS, FINELY CHOPPED

25G (1OZ) RAISINS

60ML (2 FL OZ) LIQUEUR (I.E. AMARETTO, COINTREAU, MARSALA)

1 TEASPOON BUTTER OR MARGARINE

15G (½ OZ) DRIED BREADCRUMBS OR BISCUIT CRUMBS

675G (1½ LB) RICOTTA CHEESE

100G (4OZ) HONEY

2 EGGS, SEPARATED

GRATED RIND OF 2 ORGANIC LEMONS

1. Soak the chopped apricots and raisins in the liqueur for at least 30 minutes.
2. Preheat the oven to 180°C/350°F/Gas Mark 4 and butter a 20cm (8 inch) springform or loose-bottomed cake tin. Dust with the breadcrumbs, covering the buttered tin as thoroughly as possible.
3. Beat together the ricotta, honey and egg yolks in a mixing bowl. Stir in the soaked fruit, liqueur and the lemon rind.
4. Beat the egg whites until stiff but not dry and fold into the ricotta mixture. Pour this into the prepared tin and bake for about 45 minutes, until a toothpick comes out clean.
5. Cool in the tin for 10 minutes, then release the sides of the tin and transfer the cheesecake – still on its base – to a wire rack to cool completely.
6. Serve cool.

Serves 8

🕐 1 hr 30 mins, plus cooling time

Peachy Butterscotch Pie

180G (6OZ) PUFF PASTRY

1350G (3LB) FRESH RIPE PEACHES

2-4 TABLESPOONS PLAIN FLOUR

4 TABLESPOONS BUTTER OR MARGARINE

4 TABLESPOONS DARK BROWN SUGAR

1 TEASPOON GROUND CINNAMON

½ TEASPOON GROUND GINGER

¼ TEASPOON GROUND NUTMEG

1 TABLESPOON WHITE SUGAR MIXED WITH

¼ TEASPOON GROUND CINNAMON

1. Divide the pastry into two portions, one slightly larger than the other and leave, covered, in a warm place for at least 1 hour.
2. Meanwhile, bring a pan of water to the boil and immerse each peach in it for about 30 seconds. Remove with a slotted spoon and immediately peel the skin from the peach.

Serves 4-8

🕐 2 hrs 15 mins

3. When all the peaches are peeled, slice them in half and remove the stones. Slice each half into approximately eight wedges and place on a deep, broad platter. Reserve any juice from the peaches and pour into a small jug. Sprinkle the flour over the peach slices, turning them gently so that they are well covered.

4. Preheat the oven to 180°C/350°F/Gas Mark 4.

5. Melt the butter and sugar together in a small pan over a low to medium heat. Stir often as the mixture caramelises slightly (it becomes slightly thickened and darker coloured). Stir in the cinnamon, ginger and nutmeg and any reserved peach juice and cook a further 3-5 minutes, stirring often.

6. Roll the larger portion of pastry into a round and line a large (at least 23cm/9 inch) deep pie dish.

7. Carefully spoon the peaches into the pastry, including any remaining juice or flour. Carefully pour the butter mixture over the peaches, aiming to fill the gaps between the peaches. The pie dish will be very full.

8. Roll out the remaining pastry and lay over the peaches. Seal the edges with a damp fork or by pinching the edges with your fingers. Prick the surface of the pastry.

9. Sprinkle the sugar and cinnamon over the pastry. Bake for about 45 minutes, until the pastry is crisp and golden and the juices bubble out from the edges slightly.

10. Leave to cool on a wire rack and serve warm or completely cool with your favourite ice cream or topping.

Pumpkin Chiffon Pie

500G (1LB 2OZ) DIGESTIVE BISCUITS

180G (6OZ) BUTTER OR MARGARINE

100G (4OZ) SUGAR

1 x 450G (1LB) TIN PREPARED PUMPKIN

285G (½ PINT) MILK

1 TEASPOON GROUND ALLSPICE

1 TEASPOON GROUND CINNAMON

½ TEASPOON GROUND CLOVES

½ TEASPOON GROUND GINGER

3 EGGS, SEPARATED

1. Preheat the oven to 180°C/350°F/Gas Mark 4.

2. Crush the digestives to a fine crumb, though not a powder, and turn into two deep 23cm (9 inch) flan dishes or pie tins. Melt the butter over a low heat and stir half the sugar into it. When the sugar is dissolved, remove from the heat and pour the mixture over the biscuit crumbs.

3. Stir with a wooden spoon and press the mixture to the base and sides of the dishes. Bake for 12-15 minutes, until the edges have darkened slightly. Cool on a wire rack.

4. Turn the tinned pumpkin into a saucepan with the remaining sugar, the milk, spices and egg yolks and bring to a simmer over a medium heat. Stir constantly while the mixture cooks, about 12 minutes, then remove from the heat and leave to cool to blood temperature.

5. Whisk the egg whites to a stiff peak and fold into the tepid pumpkin mixture. Do not over-mix. Turn the chiffon into the biscuit-lined dishes and chill in the refrigerator until set, about 1 hour.

6. Serve cold with whipped cream, ice cream or a section of fresh orange.

Makes 2 pies

1 hr, plus chilling time

Better in your mouth than on your body

Tip

Taste the pumpkin mixture several times as you cook it to get the spiciness just right.

PASTRIES

Nut and Honey Slices

100G (4OZ) ALMONDS, COARSELY
CHOPPED
4 TABLESPOONS HONEY
140ML (¼ PINT) ORANGE JUICE

½ TEASPOON GROUND ALLSPICE OR MIXED
SPICE
55G (2OZ) BREADCRUMBS
6 SHEETS FILO PASTRY
2 TABLESPOONS MELTED BUTTER OR OIL

Serves 6

⏱ 45 mins

Lovely and sweet... and oh so sticky

1.   Preheat the oven to 180°C/350°F/Gas Mark 4.
2.   Mix the almonds, honey, orange juice and spice together in a large bowl. When well blended, stir in the breadcrumbs.
3.   Lay one sheet of filo pastry on a board and brush with melted butter. Transfer to a shallow oblong oven dish and trim to fit. Repeat with another sheet of pastry, brushing the top generously with more butter.
4.   Spread half the nut and honey mixture evenly across the top of the pastry. Cover with a further two sheets of buttered pastry, then add the remaining filling. Finish with a double layer of pastry brushed with butter.
5.   Score the top of the pastry with a sharp knife, dividing it into six portions.
6.   Bake for 20-30 minutes, until lightly browned. Serve warm.

Tip

This is a quick version of the Greek pastry, baklava. For a special treat, substitute maple syrup for the honey.

Kadaifi

225G (8OZ) WALNUTS, CHOPPED

55G (2OZ) WHOLEMEAL BREADCRUMBS

55G (2OZ) SUGAR

140ML (¼ PINT) ORANGE JUICE

450G (1LB) KADAIFI PASTRY (SEE TIP)

225G (8OZ) BUTTER OR MARGARINE, MELTED

For the syrup:

225G (8OZ) SUGAR

180ML (6 FL OZ) WATER

1 TABLESPOON LEMON JUICE

1 TEASPOON GROUND CINNAMON

1.   Preheat the oven to 180°C/350°F/Gas Mark 4 and lightly oil a shallow 23 x 33cm (9 x 13 inch) baking dish.

2.   Stir the walnuts, breadcrumbs, sugar and orange juice together in a mixing bowl. Shred the kadaifi pastry and stir into the butter so that it is well coated.

3.   Line the baking dish with half the pastry. Spread the nut mixture evenly over the pastry and top with the remaining pastry. Press down and bake for 40 minutes. Leave the pastry in the tin.

4.   Meanwhile, make a syrup by combining the listed ingredients in a small saucepan and bring them to a boil, stirring continually. When the sugar has dissolved, lower the heat and continue simmering for 10 minutes: the syrup will become clear and slightly glossy. Pour the syrup over the hot pastry, spreading it as evenly as possible.

5.   Cover the baking dish with a clean tea towel. Set aside for at least 3 hours, though all day or overnight is ideal.

6.   Cut into squares or triangles and serve.

Serves 6-8

55 mins, plus standing overnight

Tip

Traditionally kadaifi is soaked in double this amount of syrup, so feel free to increase the syrup accordingly. Kadaifi pastry is available in specialty shops. It is made from flour and water and looks rather like Shredded Wheat.

*M*incemeat Vol-au-vents

180G (6OZ) PUFF PASTRY, AT
ROOM TEMPERATURE

For the mincemeat:
675G (1½ LB) MIXED DRIED FRUIT
JUICE AND ZEST OF 1 LARGE LEMON
2 APPLES, GRATED
180G (6OZ) SUGAR

180G (6OZ) ALMONDS, CHOPPED
1 TEASPOON ALLSPICE OR MIXED SPICE
½ TEASPOON GROUND CINNAMON
½ TEASPOON GROUND NUTMEG
60ML (2 FL OZ) BRANDY, SHERRY OR WHISKY
60ML (2 FL OZ) APPLE JUICE
180ML (6 FL OZ) OIL

Serves 4

 55 mins

1.   Mix all the mincemeat ingredients thoroughly, making sure they are well blended. Put to one side.
2.   Preheat the oven to 200°C/400°F/Gas Mark 6.
3.   Roll the pastry on a well-floured board to a thickness of 9mm (³⁄₈ inch) and cut into eight 7-10cm (3-4 inch) rounds. Cut a smaller round from the centre of four of the large rounds and place the resulting rings on top of the remaining four large rounds. Dampen the surfaces to help them adhere. These are your vol-au-vent cases.
4.   Bake them for 12-15 minutes then lift on to a wire rack to cool. Fill each case with mincemeat and serve with cream or ice cream.

Tip

This mincemeat mixture may be kept for one week provided it is stored in a sterilised jar and kept in a cool place.

Medlar Cream Flakes

180G (6OZ) PUFF PASTRY
2 TABLESPOONS FINE BROWN
    SUGAR
½ TEASPOON GROUND CLOVES

900-1350G (2-3LB) BLETTED MEDLARS
140-180ML (4-6 FL OZ) SINGLE OR DOUBLE
    CREAM
2 TABLESPOONS ICING SUGAR

1. Preheat the oven to 200°C/400°F/Gas Mark 6.
2. Leave the pastry at room temperature for at least 1 hour then roll to about 5mm (¼ inch) thickness and cut into rectangles or wedges. Mix the brown sugar and cloves together and sprinkle a little over each pastry.
3. Lift on to a baking tray, prick the pastries with a fork then bake for 15-20 minutes, until just crisp and golden. Lift on to a wire rack to cool.
4. Scoop the flesh from the medlars, discarding the rough skin. Blend the flesh with the cream and, when the pastries are cool, spread a little medlar cream over each.
5. Dust with a little icing sugar, to taste, and serve as soon as possible. These may be kept chilled for a couple of hours if necessary.

Makes approximately
24 small pastries

🕐 1 hr 40 mins,
plus cooling time

Tip

Bletted medlars are so ripe they appear rotten. The medlars are only exquisite after they have reached this stage. If you can't find a local tree, try a delicatessen for medlar jam instead.

Almond and Rose Bouquets

180G (6OZ) SHORTCRUST PASTRY
55G (2OZ) GROUND ALMONDS
100G (4OZ) DRIED APRICOTS, MINCED

55G (2OZ) FINE SUGAR
2 TABLESPOONS BUTTER
1 TABLESPOON ROSE WATER

1. Preheat the oven to 180°C/350°F/Gas Mark 4.
2. Roll the pastry into a thin rectangle and cut into eighteen equal-sized rounds.

Makes 18 bouquets

🕐 1 hr

3. Mix the remaining ingredients together in a bowl: first stir with a spoon then work the mixture with your hand to make a thick paste. Divide the paste into eighteen parts and roll each of these into a ball.

4. Flatten each ball on to half of each round of pastry, dampen the edges, fold over and seal.

5. Score the top of each pastry in a decorative leaf pattern (or cut pastry leaves, if you're that patient) and place the bouquets on a lightly buttered baking tray.

6. Bake for 20 minutes, cool on a wire rack for 5-10 minutes and serve hot or warm.

Quick Puff Cinnamon Croissants

340G (12OZ) PUFF PASTRY

2 TABLESPOONS FINELY GROUND ALMONDS

1½ TEASPOONS GROUND CINNAMON

2 TABLESPOONS HONEY OR BARLEY MALT SYRUP

ICING SUGAR

Makes 12 croissants

 1 hr 45 mins

1. Leave the pastry in a warm place for 1 hour. Preheat the oven to 200°C/400°F/Gas Mark 6.

2. Divide the pastry into six parts and roll each into a rough rectangle; cut each into two triangles to make twelve pieces of pastry.

3. Mix the almonds and cinnamon together and work in the honey. Spread a little of this mixture over the broad part of each triangle then roll up the pastry so that the narrow tip is uppermost and in the centre top. Pull each rolled pastry into a crescent shape and place on a lightly buttered baking tray.

4. Bake for 10-12 minutes, until the croissants are crisp and golden.

5. Lift on to a wire rack and serve warm or cool.

Glazed Citron Twists

340G (12OZ) SHORTCRUST PASTRY

GRATED RIND OF 3-4 ORANGES

1 TABLESPOON BUTTER

1 TEASPOON CORNFLOUR

JUICE OF 2 ORANGES

4-6 TABLESPOONS ICING SUGAR

1. Preheat the oven to 180°C/350°F/Gas Mark 4.
2. Divide the pastry into twelve parts and roll each to a thin rectangle. Sprinkle a little of the orange rind over each rectangle and fold the rectangle in half along its length. Lift the parcel and, holding on to each end, gently give it a complete twist or twist and one-half.
3. Place the twists on a lightly buttered baking tray and bake for about 15 minutes.
4. Meanwhile, melt the butter in a saucepan and stir in the cornflour to make a paste. Remove from the heat and add the orange juice and icing sugar, a little at a time, stirring after each addition to make a smooth, slightly runny sauce.
5. When the pastries come out of the oven, brush a little of this sauce over each and lift them on to a wire rack to cool.
6. Serve cool.

Makes 12 pastries

45 mins, plus cooling time

Variation

The orange zest and juice may be substituted, in whole or part, by lemon zest and juice.

PUDDINGS

Rhubarb Fool

285ML (½ PINT) MILK

25G (1OZ) CUSTARD POWDER

25G (1OZ) SUGAR

450G (1LB) RHUBARB, WASHED AND CHOPPED

4-5 TABLESPOONS GOLDEN OR MAPLE SYRUP

1 TEASPOON GROUND CINNAMON

PLAIN GRATED CHOCOLATE OR FLAKED

ALMONDS

Serves 4

⏱ 55 mins, plus chilling time

1. Whisk 2 tablespoons of the milk with the custard powder in a mixing bowl. Place the remaining milk in a saucepan over a low flame and bring to a low boil.

2. Pour the hot milk on to the custard mixture and stir briskly; add the sugar. When the custard begins to thicken, set aside to cool.

3. Turn the rhubarb into a saucepan with the syrup and cinnamon. Simmer gently until tender then push the rhubarb through a sieve to make a thick purée. Set this aside to cool also.

4. Stir the cooled custard and rhubarb together and spoon into serving dishes or glasses; chill for about 1 hour.

5. Sprinkle with grated chocolate or almonds before serving as a refreshing snack or dessert.

Apricot Mousse

225G (8OZ) DRIED (HUNZA) APRICOTS, WASHED

GENEROUS SQUEEZE OF LEMON JUICE

1½ TEASPOONS AGAR

285ML (½ PINT) ORANGE JUICE

2 TABLESPOONS CREAM OR SOYA CREEM

1 TABLESPOON MAPLE SYRUP

2 TABLESPOONS CHOPPED NUTS

Serves 4

⏱ 30 mins, plus soaking and chilling time

1. Turn the apricots into a mixing bowl and just cover them with boiling water (about 425ml/¾ pint); leave to soak overnight.

2. Turn the soaked apricots and their liquid into a saucepan, add the lemon juice and cook over a low flame for 12-15 minutes. Drain well, reserving the liquid, then mash or purée the apricots and leave to one side.

3. Return the reserved liquid to a boil and whisk in the agar; remove from the heat. Combine the apricot purée with the orange juice and agar mixture, then stir in the cream.

4. When it is very well mixed, divide among four attractive glasses and chill before serving.

5. Top with a drizzle of maple syrup and some chopped nuts.

Tip

The apricots described in this recipe are very hard and dull-looking when purchased. If you prefer to use the softer, bright orange apricots, you may omit the stage of soaking overnight. Simply cover the apricots in boiling water and cook, with the lemon juice, for 12-15 minutes. Proceed as above.

Cherry Almond Pudding

180G (6OZ) PLAIN FLOUR
100G (4OZ) SUGAR
2 TEASPOONS BAKING POWDER
25G (1OZ) BUTTER OR MARGARINE

450G (1LB) FRESH SWEET CHERRIES, PITTED
AND HALVED
100G (4OZ) FLAKED ALMONDS
140ML (¼ PINT) ALMOND MILK, SOYA MILK
OR FRUIT JUICE

1. Preheat the oven to 190°C/375°F/Gas Mark 5.

2. Mix the flour, sugar and baking powder together in a mixing bowl. Add the butter and work it into the dry ingredients to make a loose crumb texture. Stir in the cherries and almonds then blend in the milk until the mixture is just moist – don't spend too long stirring.

3. Turn the mixture into a lightly oiled 20cm (8 inch) cake tin and bake for 30 minutes. Cool in the tin for 10 minutes then serve hot, from the tin, or cool after turning it out on to a serving platter.

4. Serve with cream, ice cream or a sauce such as Caramel Crazy, page 256.

Serves 4-6

🕐 1 hr

This only needs a loving friend to help you eat it

Apple Cloud Pudding

1350G (3LB) COOKING APPLES
6 TABLESPOONS WATER
285ML (½ PINT) MILK
½ VANILLA POD
100G (4OZ) RAISINS

100G (4OZ) HONEY OR BARLEY MALT SYRUP
55G (2OZ) ROLLED OATS
55G (2OZ) FRESH BREADCRUMBS
25G (1OZ) FLAKED ALMONDS

Serves 4-6

🕐 1 hr

1. Wash and coarsely chop the apples and turn them, peel and cores included, into a large saucepan with the water. Cover and cook over a medium flame for about 30 minutes, until the apples are very tender.

2. Turn the apples through a sieve or hand mouli and discard the pips and peelings.

3. Meanwhile, heat the milk with the vanilla pod to nearly simmering. Remove from the heat, stir in the raisins and leave to steep while the apple cooks.

4. Blend the apple purée with the milk (remove the vanilla now), raisins, honey, oats and breadcrumbs. Stir over a low heat for 10 minutes then serve warm with a garnish of flaked almonds.

Rhubarb Cobbler

675G (1½ LB) FRESH RHUBARB,
    WASHED AND CHOPPED
55G (2OZ) BROWN SUGAR
½ TEASPOON GROUND CINNAMON
180G (6OZ) PLAIN FLOUR

2 TEASPOONS BAKING POWDER
55G (2OZ) SUGAR
55G (2OZ) BUTTER OR MARGARINE
1 EGG
60ML (2 FL OZ) MILK

Serves 4-6

🕐 1 hr

1. Preheat the oven to 180°C/350°F/Gas Mark 4 and lightly oil a 20cm (8 inch) cake tin.

2. Coarsely chop the rhubarb and mix with the brown sugar and cinnamon in the tin. Mix the flour, baking powder and sugar together in a mixing bowl and work in the butter to a loose crumb consistency.

3. Whisk the egg and milk together, stir into the flour mixture and spoon this batter over the rhubarb in the tin.

250

4. Bake at once for 35-40 minutes, until golden on top.
5. Cool for 10 minutes in the pan on a wire rack and serve warm, by itself or with cream.

Fruit Butter

2 TABLESPOONS BUTTER OR MARGARINE
1 TABLESPOON SWEET SPICE, GROUND OR
  BROKEN (SUCH AS CINNAMON, CLOVES,
  NUTMEG, ALLSPICE, STAR ANISE,
  CORIANDER, GINGER OR MIXTURE)

1350-2700G (3-6LB) FRUIT, WASHED AND
  COARSELY CHOPPED
UP TO 285ML (½ PINT) WATER, AS
  NECESSARY

1. Melt the butter in a small saucepan and sauté the spice over a low heat for 3 minutes, stirring often; put to one side.
2. Prepare the fruit, turn into a large saucepan or jam pan with a couple of tablespoons of water and place over a medium heat. Stir often as the fruit softens and looses its form, adding a little more water if necessary to prevent sticking or burning. You should expect it to cook for about 1 hour.
3. Press the mixture through a sieve, discard the pips, skin and coarse material, and turn the smooth fruit butter back into the pan. Add the sautéed spice and bring back to a simmer.
4. Ladle into sterilised jars and seal. Although this will keep for a week in well-sealed jars, I find that it goes so quickly that I often turn it straight into a pretty serving terrine.
5. We often eat it as a warming dessert with a dollop of plain yogurt. Or try spreading it on toast and in sandwiches, or douse some boring breakfast cereal with it to make a really scrumptious morning treat.

Makes 900-1800g
(2-4lb)

🕐 1 hr 30 mins

Tip

Just about any fruit or fruit mixture can be used to make up the weight of fruit necessary for this butter. And it needn't be whole, handsome fruit either: apple peelings and cores, badly bruised pears or berries and unhappy looking dried apricots, figs, dates and currants may all be thrown in the pot. Only ensure the fruit is clean, don't bother peeling it or removing blemishes. In fact, the pips and peels will make the final thickness of the butter more appealing.

Variation

To turn this into something more closely resembling a chutney, alter the spice combination along these lines:

1 TEASPOON SWEET SPICE (ANY COMBINATION)
$\frac{1}{2}$ TEASPOON EACH GROUND CUMIN, CARDAMOM AND TURMERIC
$\frac{1}{2}$ TEASPOON CHILLI POWDER

Sauté the spices then add the following:

5-7 CLOVES GARLIC, PEELED AND COARSELY CHOPPED
1 MEDIUM ONION, FINELY CHOPPED
100-250G (4-9OZ) DRIED FRUIT, CHOPPED IF NECESSARY
COARSE BASE OF 1 HEAD CELERY, FINELY CHOPPED
1 x 285G (10OZ) TIN SWEETCORN
1 GREEN PEPPER, FINELY CHOPPED

Add other ingredients which you might have waiting to be used up, such as grated carrot, finely chopped cabbage or diced courgette. Just ensure that they are softened in the sauté. Add the whole of the sauté to the butter after it has been sieved and returned to the pan. Bring back to a simmer and simmer a further 10 minutes before ladling into sterilised jars. Seal well and use within a week or so.

FROZEN DESSERTS

*F*rigid Fruit Pudding

180G (6OZ) PRUNES, CHOPPED

180G (6OZ) GLACÉ CHERRIES, CHOPPED

180G (6OZ) RAISINS

180G (6OZ) SULTANAS

180G (6OZ) CURRANTS

55G (2OZ) MIXED PEEL

285ML (½ PINT) RUM

2 LITRES (4 PINTS) VANILLA ICE CREAM

225ML (8 FL OZ) SINGLE CREAM

85G (3OZ) SLIVERED ALMONDS

55G (2OZ) PLAIN DARK CHOCOLATE, GRATED

55G (2OZ) CHOPPED WALNUTS

1. Mix the dried fruits and peel together in a bowl and pour the rum over. Leave to stand, covered, for 6-12 hours.
2. Turn the ice cream into a large mixing bowl and stir in the cream, almonds, chocolate and walnuts. Add the dried fruits and rum and stir well.
3. Turn the mixture into a very large (3 litre/5¼ pint) mould and press it well down. Freeze overnight or until required.
4. Serve garnished with more grated chocolate, chopped nuts or one of your favourite sweet sauces (see pages 256-59).

Serves 4-6

⏱ 24 hrs including freezing time

*R*ose Petal Sorbet

180G (6OZ) SUGAR

140ML (¼ PINT) WATER

450G (1LB) FRESH STRAWBERRIES, CLEANED

1 TABLESPOON ROSE WATER

25G (1OZ) FLAKED ALMONDS

FRESH OR DRIED ROSE PETALS

1. Dissolve the sugar in the water and place over a medium heat. Bring to the boil to make a syrup.
2. Leave to cool, then purée the syrup, strawberries and rose water together in a blender. Pour the mixture into a mould or individual ramekins and freeze.
3. To serve, scoop out of the mould or quickly run the outside of

Serves 2

⏱ approximately 4 hrs, including freezing time

the ramekins under hot water then turn out on to a serving dish.

4.   Garnish with flaked almonds and rose petals. A very romantic dish!

Tip

When you first cook sugar in water, it is very cloudy. It is a syrup once the liquid clears nicely and appears almost bright.

Exotic Sorbet

1350G (3LB) MIXED EXOTIC FRUITS, SUCH AS MANGO, BANANA, PAPAYA AND PINEAPPLE

340G (12OZ) SUGAR

285ML (½ PINT) WATER

1 TABLESPOON FRESH MINT LEAVES, CLEANED

140ML (¼ PINT) PLAIN YOGURT

Serves 4

approximately 4 hrs, including freezing time

1.   Prepare the fruit first by peeling and removing any pips or blemishes. Turn into a blender.

2.   Meanwhile, dissolve the sugar in the water and bring to a boil over a medium heat. Stir constantly while the mixture thickens slightly to a syrup (it will clear nicely, too). Let the syrup cool to no more than blood temperature then turn it into the blender with the fruit and fresh mint.

3.   Purée and turn into the sorbet dish.

4.   Freeze and, when serving, garnish with a tablespoon of plain yogurt.

Tip

Measure the weight of the fruit *after* it has been peeled and/or pitted.

Iced Yogurt Whirls

285ML (½ PINT) PLAIN YOGURT
GRATED RIND OF 1 ORANGE
180G (6OZ) SUGAR
140ML (¼ PINT) WATER

450G (1LB) BLACKCURRANTS, WASHED AND
DRAINED
85G (3OZ) GROUND HAZELNUTS

1. Blend the yogurt and orange rind and put in the fridge to chill.
2. Dissolve the sugar in the water and bring to a boil over a medium heat. Stir constantly until the mixture thickens into a syrup. Remove from the heat and cool to tepid.
3. Purée the syrup with the blackcurrants and turn into one large or four individual moulds. Place in the freezer for 1 hour: the mixture should be nearly frozen.
4. Spoon the yogurt and hazelnuts on to the sorbet and stir briskly but briefly with a knife or spatula to create a colourful whirled effect. Return the dessert to the freezer until the sorbet is well frozen.
5. You do not need to stir all of the yogurt and nuts into the blackcurrant; some may be reserved and used to garnish this dessert when it is served.

Serves 4

⏱ approximately
4 hrs

Iced Chocolate-lined Orange Bowl

4 LARGE SWEET ORANGES
100G (4OZ) SUGAR
140ML (¼ PINT) WATER

100G (4OZ) DARK, PLAIN CHOCOLATE
2 TABLESPOONS BUTTER OR MARGARINE

1. Wash the oranges and slice a 'lid' off the top of each one – about 2.5cm (1 inch) from the top. Scoop out the orange flesh and turn it into a blender along with any juice that might accompany it. Avoid scraping out the bitter pith until most of the sweet flesh has been removed, then scrape out the pith and discard.
2. Place at least two of the orange shells in the freezer (this makes enough for four, but it's more romantic for two!).
3. Dissolve the sugar in the water and bring to a boil over a medium heat. Stir constantly while the mixture thickens into a

Serves 2-4

⏱ approximately
4 hrs

syrup, then put to one side to cool to blood temperature.

4.   Meanwhile, melt the chocolate and butter together in the top of a double boiler. Stir until well blended and glossy. Pour half or one-quarter of the chocolate into each of two or four orange shells and tip the shell every which way to coat the inside with the chocolate.

5.   Purée the cool syrup and orange pulp together and turn into the chocolate-lined orange shells. Return to the freezer until the sorbet is well-frozen.

6.   Serve with the orange 'lid' and a garnish of fresh mint leaf, shredded coconut or a single chocolate shaving.

ICINGS, SAUCES AND GLAZES

Caramel Crazy

85G (3OZ) BUTTER OR MARGARINE	60ML (2 FL OZ) ORANGE JUICE OR MILK
55G (2OZ) DARK BROWN SUGAR	1 TEASPOON VANILLA EXTRACT

Makes approximately
200ml (7 fl oz)

 15 mins

1.   Melt the butter and sugar together over a medium heat then stir in the juice and vanilla.

2.   Pour hot or warm over your favourite dessert.

Perfect On Everything Sauce

225G (8OZ) FIRM HONEY

100G (4OZ) BUTTER OR MARGARINE

JUICE OF 1 ORANGE

1 TEASPOON GROUND CINNAMON

½ TEASPOON GROUND NUTMEG

100G (4OZ) GROUND WALNUTS OR
   HAZELNUTS

FINELY GRATED RIND OF 2 ORANGES

1. Place the honey and butter in a saucepan over a low heat. Stir often while the mixture melts, then add the orange juice, spices, nuts and orange rind.

2. Stir well and turn into a ramekin or pâté dish. Leave to cool and set in the refrigerator or use immediately, while still warm and runny.

3. This sauce is delicious spread on toast, or poured over pancakes, waffles, ice cream, cake . . . you get the idea.

Makes approximately 570ml (1 pint)

15 mins, plus chilling time

Dollop it over everything

Citrus Glaze

1 TABLESPOON BUTTER

1 TEASPOON CORNFLOUR

JUICE AND ZEST OF 2-3 ORANGES

4-6 TABLESPOONS ICING SUGAR

1. Melt the butter in a saucepan and stir in the cornflour to make a paste. Remove from the heat and add the orange juice, zest and icing sugar, a little at a time, stirring after each addition to make a smooth, slightly runny sauce.

2. This sauce will glaze a cake or pudding. Pour over the dessert while still hot, if possible.

Makes approximately 90ml (3 fl oz)

15 mins

Really Creamy Butter Icing

BUTTER OR MARGARINE
3 TABLESPOONS PLAIN FLOUR
180ML (6 FL OZ) MILK

½ TEASPOON VANILLA EXTRACT
180G (6OZ) SUGAR

Makes approximately
285ml (½ pint)

⏱ 30 mins

1. Melt 55g (2oz) butter in a saucepan or double boiler over a medium heat, then stir in the flour to make a thick paste, or roux. Add the milk, a little at a time, stirring after each addition as the sauce thickens.
2. Remove from the heat and cool to blood temperature. Add the vanilla. Cream 100g (4 oz) butter with the sugar and beat this mixture into the cooled sauce.
3. Beat until fluffy and then spread on your cake.

Cream Cheese Dressing

55G (2OZ) BUTTER OR MARGARINE
100G (4OZ) CREAM CHEESE

1 TEASPOON VANILLA EXTRACT
225G (8OZ) ICING SUGAR

Makes approximately
285ml (½ pint)

⏱ 10 mins

1. Cream the butter, cheese and vanilla together in a mixing bowl and gradually stir in the icing sugar. Use at once – especially delicious on carrot cake.

Variation

Add 100g (4oz) desiccated coconut to the finished icing.

Chocolate Butter Icing

3 TABLESPOONS BUTTER OR
MARGARINE
85G (3OZ) PLAIN CHOCOLATE

1 TEASPOON VANILLA EXTRACT
90ML (3 FL OZ) MILK
450G (1LB) ICING SUGAR

1. Melt the butter and chocolate together in a saucepan or double boiler over a low heat. Remove from the heat and stir in the vanilla, milk and icing sugar – in that order.
2. Leave to cool, stirring occasionally, before spreading.

Makes approximately
425ml (¾ pint)

🕐 10 mins

Cocoa Nut Brittle Icing

100G (4OZ) BUTTER OR MARGARINE
85G (3 OZ) PLAIN CHOCOLATE
90ML (3 FL OZ) MILK
1 TEASPOON VANILLA EXTRACT

100G (4OZ) CHOPPED NUTS (I.E. WALNUTS,
ALMONDS, HAZELNUTS OR PECANS)
450G (1LB) ICING SUGAR

1. Melt the butter and chocolate together in a saucepan or double boiler over a low heat. Stir in the milk and vanilla and remove from the heat. Add the nuts and stir in the icing sugar.
2. Pour, while still hot, over the cake and leave to cool.

Makes approximately
425ml (¾ pint)

🕐 10 mins

EDIBLE EXOTICA:
Fantasy Foods from the Four Corners of the Earth

One of the most exciting – and romantic – aspects of preparing good food is the eternal quest for exotic and enticing new ingredients to use in your recipes. Here, vegetarians are at a decided advantage over meat-eaters – after all, carnivores tend to eat just three or four species of animals, while vegetarians have hundreds of the world's plants at their disposal! Although the recipes in this book all use very commonly available ingredients, here I'd like to introduce you to a few of my favourite exotic foods – some of them from very distant shores, some of them from just round the corner. I've chosen them for several reasons. First, you can find them all quite easily in this country – although sometimes, you might have to search in a health-food shop or an ethnic grocer's (I love exploring!). Secondly, they are all, in their own way, rather spectacular . . . and easy to use, as well. So go ahead, fantasise a little . . . who knows where it might lead!

ACKEE Originating in Africa, ackees were taken to the West Indies on the first slave ships (the botanical name *Blighia sapida* refers to the infamous Captain Bligh, the first person to bring specimens to Britain). You can find them, tinned, in shops which cater for West Indian communities: in Jamaica, they virtually have the status of a national dish. Their taste and appearance is similar to scrambled eggs, and they are utterly sumptuous when cooked with grated coconut.

AMARANTH Slowly finding its way on to the shelves of health-food shops, amaranth seeds were grown by the Aztecs, whose women would grind them up, mix with honey or blood, and make shapes of snakes, birds, deer and gods as part of sacrificial rituals. Personally, I prefer to leave out the blood! Amaranth is especially valuable because of its tremendous nutritional profile, being high in phosphorus, iron, potassium, zinc, vitamin E, calcium and vitamin B complex. It also contains about 16 per cent protein, compared to the 10 per cent normally found in corn and other major cereals. The red variety is sometimes used to make a red, non-toxic food colouring. Try cooking it and sprinkling it on salads, vegetables and casseroles, or toast it and use as seasoning. It is possible to buy amaranth popcorn which is light and rather nutty, and even amaranth chocolate! Some ideas for you to experiment with:

♡ Boil amaranth seeds in two or three times their volume of water and chill. The seeds will then become gelatinous and can be used as a thickener in jams and preserves.

♡ To make an hypoallergenic wheat-flour substitute, sift 1 cup of cornstarch, 1 cup of rye, potato or rice flour and 1 cup of amaranth flour several times. The mixture can then be used for certain flat breads, pancakes and biscuits.

♡ For a tasty porridge, bring to the boil ½ cup of water or fruit juice and gradually add ¼ cup of amaranth seed grain. Lower the heat and parboil for about 30 minutes. Eat with nuts, fruit or honey. Or, for a savoury dish, add soy sauce, salt and ginger.

ARAME Try this exquisite food before you allow prejudices (yours or anyone else's) to interfere with your exploration and enjoyment of marine plants – that's right, seaweed! The fact is, this nutritious and bountiful group of plants has been eaten for centuries in all maritime regions of the world, and generations of cooks have devised many superb and subtle recipes. Most seaweeds contain remarkable quantities of the vitamins and minerals which are essential for good health and active libido, and are rich in a multitude of trace elements which are often lacking in today's fast-food diet. You can find arame in health-food shops, some supermarkets and macrobiotic or Japanese grocer's – it has an attractive, lacey texture, and is an excellent visual accompaniment to many other foods. Cooked arame has an extremely delicate and subtle flavour (however, the smell it gives off during cooking can be quite strong, but don't be misled by this!). Most packets give several easy recipes to try.

BAMBOO SHOOTS Several parts of the bamboo plant are eaten in Eastern countries, although the most common in the West is the bamboo shoot, available canned in most supermarkets and all Eastern grocery stores. In the wild, bamboo shoots can grow more than a foot in length every 24 hours, which puts many men to shame! They make an interesting and flavoursome ingredient in any stir-fry; they offer a unique texture and are used directly from the tin or sliced into matchstick-size strips.

COCONUT A tree of huge economic importance in many areas of the world, virtually all parts of this awe-inspiring palm are put to good use. Its root yields medicine; its durable leaves are woven into a wide variety of useful and aesthetically pleasing products, such as baskets, hats and floor covering. Wood from the tree is good for house-building, and the leaves once again provide excellent roofing material. Then, of course, there are the nuts themselves. Brought to the West by Marco Polo, we have barely begun to scratch the surface of the coconut's usefulness in the six hundred years since it arrived here. The coconut is an essential element in most African, Asian and South American cuisines but is used in cookery all over the globe. Its earthy-sweet flavour, slightly crunchy texture and creamy white colour all add a subtle depth and interest to the dishes in which it is used (see ackees, above). When using coconut cream or milk in a dish, avoid rapid boiling as this may cause the coconut to curdle. Instead, cook at simmering point and sprinkle a tiny bit of cornflour into the pot to help ensure the milk does not curdle. When using creamed coconut, cutting the block into shavings will help you avoid the need for high temperatures which could cause curdling. Coconut cream and milk are often added towards the end of the cooking process to avoid such problems. Desiccated coconut (simply shredded coconut, made fresh or purchased dried) does not present this challenge; its flavour and texture within the dish may be enhanced if you soak the shreds in liquid (milk, water, stock or fruit juice, for example) for a few moments before including it in the dish. Once you start to use this versatile nut, you'll find it lends an exotic touch to many, many dishes.

DULSE This seaweed, also called Irish moss, has a coarse, purple appearance and has for centuries been used as a foodstuff by the traditional maritime populations of the northern hemisphere. In common with many other seaweeds, you can use dulse to thicken soups and stews, and it is a wonderfully nutritious and tasty addition to stocks and broths. It should be chopped into quite small pieces before cooking to allow it to soften, although it always retains a degree of chewiness. Nutritionally, it is a very good source of iodine.

ELDERBERRY Though rarely if ever sold in shops, elderberries are nevertheless plentiful, come September, in the British countryside – and almost invariably neglected. The berries themselves yield a deep passionate purple and piquancy to any number of cooked autumnal dishes (they contain small amounts of a poisonous alkalide when raw, and for this reason should always be cooked before they are eaten). The flowers which precede the berries have one of the most exquisite aromas you'll ever experience, like muscatel grapes, only more intense, and more feminine than the most expensive perfumes. Just a few elderflower heads will give a light sweetness to any dessert, and, of course, they make celebrated white wines and a superb 'champagne'-type summer drink (ready in just two weeks). When picking elderberries or elderflowers, bear in mind that those by the roadside or close to agricultural land cannot be trusted to be pollution-free.

GUAVA In Western countries, these pink fruits are most usually encountered canned, and their use is therefore restricted to fruit salads and garnishes. However, fresh ones are sometimes found in ethnic grocer's, and if you're lucky enough to find them, try making guava jelly as follows. Take approximately 2000g (4½lb) of fresh guavas, wash them and slice into a large pan. Add water to cover, and optionally a couple of cardamom seeds, and bring to the boil for 15 minutes. Turn the pulp into a fine muslin jelly bag and leave to drain, carefully collecting the juice in a bowl. For each 570ml (1 pint) of resulting juice, add 450g (1lb) of sugar, then boil together for about 15 minutes until the jelly is ready to set. Pour into sterilised jars, seal and allow to cool. Alternatively, guava 'cheese' can be made by pushing the cooked guavas through a sieve and boiling the pulp until it is reduced to the consistency of jelly. Pour this pulp into a dish. When cool, it is firm enough to be sliced, and is a highly prized delicacy in Brazil.

KOHLRABI Literally meaning 'cabbage turnip' in the German, kohlrabi is the aristocrat of the cabbage family, often available in the autumn and used in a broadly similar way to turnips, or celeriac. Buy them small and young, preferably organically grown so that the skin need not be removed, for this is where most of the delicate and sweet flavour lies. The leaves can be lightly steamed, like collards, as can the root, which may also be diced and sautéed in oil and garlic. Alternatively, it can be shredded and added to a savoury winter salad.

KOMBU This dried seaweed deserves to have a permanent place in your larder. It serves three extremely useful functions. First, the addition of a 15cm (6 inch) strip of kombu to sautés, soups, stews, simmering rice or cooking beans will help the foods to soften evenly and quickly (remove it before serving – dogs love it!). Second, kombu has a magical, flavour-enhancing effect similar to that of monosodium glutamate (MSG) – but without the awful chemical side-effects. And thirdly, kombu adds important nutrients to whatever you cook it with. Among these are calcium, iron and iodine, in which, like most seaweeds, it is especially rich. Quickly rinse the kombu before you drop it in the pot but don't worry about a fine white deposit you might detect on the dried kombu, this is a natural salty residue. Keep it in a dry and airtight container until you are ready to use it.

KUMQUAT A mysterious miniature citrus fruit which originated in China but is now grown in many warm countries, the kumquat is paradoxical in as much as its rind is usually sweeter than its flesh. Consequently, they should not be peeled, but carefully washed before serving fresh. Some of them can taste very sour indeed, and for this reason are perhaps best stewed whole in sugar syrup, turned into a preserve, or simply used as a rather enchanting table decoration. Alternatively, they can be thinly sliced and seeded, and used as an ingredient in fruit salads.

LYCHEES Principally known in the West for being a compulsory ingredient on the menu of Indian and Chinese restaurants, lychees are at their most uninviting when served from the tin. Increasingly, you can find them sold fresh, mainly from November to January. They have an attractively dimpled appearance with a hard, dusky red skin which is easy to peel and protects their juice and exquisite flavour very effectively. Inside, you will find luscious flesh the colour of moonstones (could anything be more romantic?). Piled high on the dinner table, or incorporated into table dressings and decorations, the lychee makes a feature in its own right. Fresh lychees have an exquisite, sweetly perfumed aroma reminiscent of elderflowers. The *rambutan*, a close cousin of the lychee, has a similar, although rather more acidic, flavour and is distinguished from the lychee by its extraordinarily hairy appearance – a truly exotic-looking fruit.

MACADAMIA NUT This hazelnut-sized nut has a gorgeously expensive flavour – very rich and smooth, with none of the dryness or harshness often found in lesser nuts! For this reason, it is very appropriate to serve as a cocktail nibble on a special occasion, and it also makes an interesting addition to a tropical-style mixed salad, or – grated – can be sprinkled on desserts or other dishes. It has a flavour about half-way between a hazelnut and a coconut.

MILLET Hardly an exotic food, you might think? In fact, millet is an exquisitely flavoured grain frequently used in African and Asian cuisine (it is a major source of dietary protein and iron). Millet has been so completely overlooked in the West that most people probably couldn't even identify it in a dish. Millet features in one of the earliest recipes ever recorded: 'Take thou also unto thee wheat, and barley, and beans, and lentiles, and millet, and fitches, and put them in one vessel, and make thee bread thereof' (*Ezekiel*, Old Testament – 'fitches' are similar to broad beans). There are many varieties of millet, some of which are available in health-food shops primarily in the form of grains, flakes, and flour. Millet fell from grace in the West mainly because it contains no gluten, and is therefore not suitable for turning into leavened bread. Ironically, this very quality now makes it a popular food for those who are allergic to gluten. It is a highly adaptable grain, and is well worth including as a nutritious and healthy supplement in your diet every few days. It is extremely easy to prepare: simply cook it for about 20 minutes in twice its volume of boiling water. A nuttier flavour can be obtained by toasting the millet, prior to boiling, in a saucepan (with no oil) over a moderate flame for 3 minutes or so, until some of the grains begin to pop. Simply prepared like this, it makes an excellent base for a variety of accompanying vegetables. Millet flakes can be quickly cooked to produce a creamy and highly nutritious breakfast porridge – especially when combined with sunflower seeds, dried fruits, etc. One variety of millet which is increasingly available in health-food shops is the Ethiopian grain *teff* (the word literally means 'lost' because the seeds are so very tiny that they are impossible to recover if dropped or spilled).

MISO If you like the delicacy of soy sauce, you'll love miso. Paste-like in appearance and texture, miso is a fermented mixture of soya beans, salt and usually another cereal grain, such as rice or barley. It has subtle, aromatic flavours and comes in many different colours including orange, brown and yellow. It is one of the staples of every Japanese and Chinese kitchen, and is made by inoculating the basic ingredients with a mould (*koji*) and is then aged in cedarwood kegs for at least one year. A simple miso soup can be made by lightly sautéeing a selection of sliced vegetables (onions, leeks, turnips, potatoes) in a small amount of oil. Water is then added, and the soup slowly simmered, with a strip of kombu or wakame seaweed, for about half an hour. Finally, turn off the heat, and add a good dollop of miso to flavour. On no account should the soup be boiled with the miso in it, because this will destroy many of the beneficial, health-giving substances which the miso contains.

NATTO Though less readily available than tempeh at the moment, natto can be found in Chinese or Japanese grocery stores. Like tempeh, it is made by fermenting soya beans, but in this case, for less than 24 hours. The fermentation process makes the high-quality protein of the soya beans particularly easy to digest. Serve natto in a small bowl beside freshly steamed rice, stir-fried vegetables and your favourite dipping sauce – natto *must* be eaten with chopsticks to fully appreciate its dream-like texture. It has an ethereal, gossamer-like quality, and is truly one of the world's most unusual foods – like eating angel hair!

OKRA Native to Africa, and also found in the indigenous cuisines of India, the Middle East, Spain and the Balkans, okra was brought to Western attention with the transportation of slaves to the southern United States and the West Indies. There are three principal varieties; tall green, dwarf green, and lady finger. One of the original names for this plant was 'gumbo', although this has now been transferred to the thick stew made from it. It is a particularly interesting vegetable, partly for its unique shape, which lends immediate interest to any dish in which it is included; but mainly for the thickening quality it imparts to all dishes. Okra has a very delicate, slightly musty flavour by itself, and so combines with almost any other foodstuff or flavouring; the thick, juicy sauce it naturally produces greatly enhances the sensory allure of any dish. Although tinned okra is available, it should really be bought fresh for maximum thickening quality. Don't buy okra which seems thick, woody or stringy. Avoid cooking okra in iron, copper or brass because this will discolour the okra and make it look black; use glass or enamel pots instead.

PAPAYA An exotic fruit which is increasingly available in supermarkets, papaya looks like a pear-shaped melon, and has pink flesh when ripe, with the melting texture of an avocado and the delicate aroma of freesias. According to Christopher Columbus, the original Carib name for this fruit, *ababai*, meant 'the fruit of the angels', which gives you some idea of its sensual taste. However, some of the fruit reaching the West seems to have a watery, sometimes even musty, flavour which needs to be enlivened by sprinklings of lime juice or even a drizzling of rum. Less ripe fruits can be used as an ingredient in fruit salads, completely ripe ones may be sliced in half and their cavities filled with a dressing.

POMEGRANATES One of the most visually stunning of all fruits, the pomegranate's splendour and unsurpassed flavour has been celebrated for thousands of years. In the *Song of Solomon*, the Bible's most erotic book, the sensuous quality of pomegranates is well expressed: 'Thy lips are like a thread of scarlet, and thy speech is comely: thy temples are like a piece of a pomegranate within thy locks.' The prophet Mohammed enjoined his followers to 'eat the pomegranate, for it purges the system of envy and hatred'. It is referred to in ancient Sanskrit writings, in Homer's *Odyssey*, and in the *Arabian Nights*. King Solomon kept an orchard exclusively consisting of pomegranate trees, and the ancient Egyptians revered the fruit as a fertility symbol, and also made an extremely alcoholic brew from it. According to Greek mythology, the pomegranate's overwhelming allure is responsible for plunging the world into winter for six months; Persephone was kidnapped by Pluto, Lord of the Underworld, and carried off to that subterranean kingdom. Although vowing not to eat until her freedom had been regained, the pomegranate proved altogether too enticing, and Persephone consumed six luscious seeds. Her mother, Demeter, finally negotiated her release with Pluto, but only on the condition that Persephone should spend six months of the year – one for each seed consumed – in the Underworld. It is lucky for us that Persephone, Goddess of Spring, restricted herself to no more than six seeds! The fruits themselves vary considerably in taste. Some varieties are extremely sweet, with a slightly acidic undertone, whereas others can be so astringent as to leave the mouth quite dry. Preparing pomegranates is easy; they are simply cut in half and the seeds can be scraped out with a teaspoon, taking care to separate them from the very bitter white pulp. They can then be used to adorn any number of dishes, or alternatively, may be pressed through a sieve to extract the juice.

QUINOA Pronounced 'keen-wah', this seed has been cultivated since 3000 BC. The Incas called it 'The Mother Grain' and it is now grown by the Indians of the Andes. It contains an extraordinarily high 20 per cent protein, twice the amount normally found in wheat grains. It is a tiny golden-coloured grain with a delicate, slightly nutty flavour, and looks very attractive as part of a meal because, during cooking, the germ separates, giving a spiral effect. Quinoa is cooked just like rice, but does not stick! Eat it instead of rice or potatoes or with warm milk as a cereal or rice pudding. Try adding quinoa to soups and cook for a further 15 minutes for a thick, nourishing food. Alternatively, use cooked, cooled quinoa tossed with other vegetables into a salad. See Special Quinoa on page 190.

TEMPEH Pronounced 'tem-pay', this is a fermented soya bean product, made in the traditional manner for centuries throughout Indonesia where it is a basic food for millions of people. Like cheese, yogurt and ginger beer, it is made with a cultured 'starter'. It is highly digestible, has the highly carnal smell of fresh mushrooms and tastes remarkably similar to chicken or veal cutlets. You can find it in the freezer cabinet of health-food shops. Since the protein in tempeh is partially broken down during fermentation (the mould is called *rhizopusoligosporus*), it is a particularly suitable food for young children and older people. Tempeh is typically sold in 15cm (6 inch) squares which are approximately 2.5cm (1 inch) thick. The easiest way to serve it is to cut the square into half diagonally, and then cut each half into three thinner, wedge-shaped slices. These should then be pan-fried until crisp and golden brown on both sides, and then served with rice and a selection of vegetables. Shoyu or tamari sprinkled over the top will give it a little extra flavouring. Alternatively, it makes a sensational marinade (see page 158).

Peachy Butterscotch Pie (page 239)

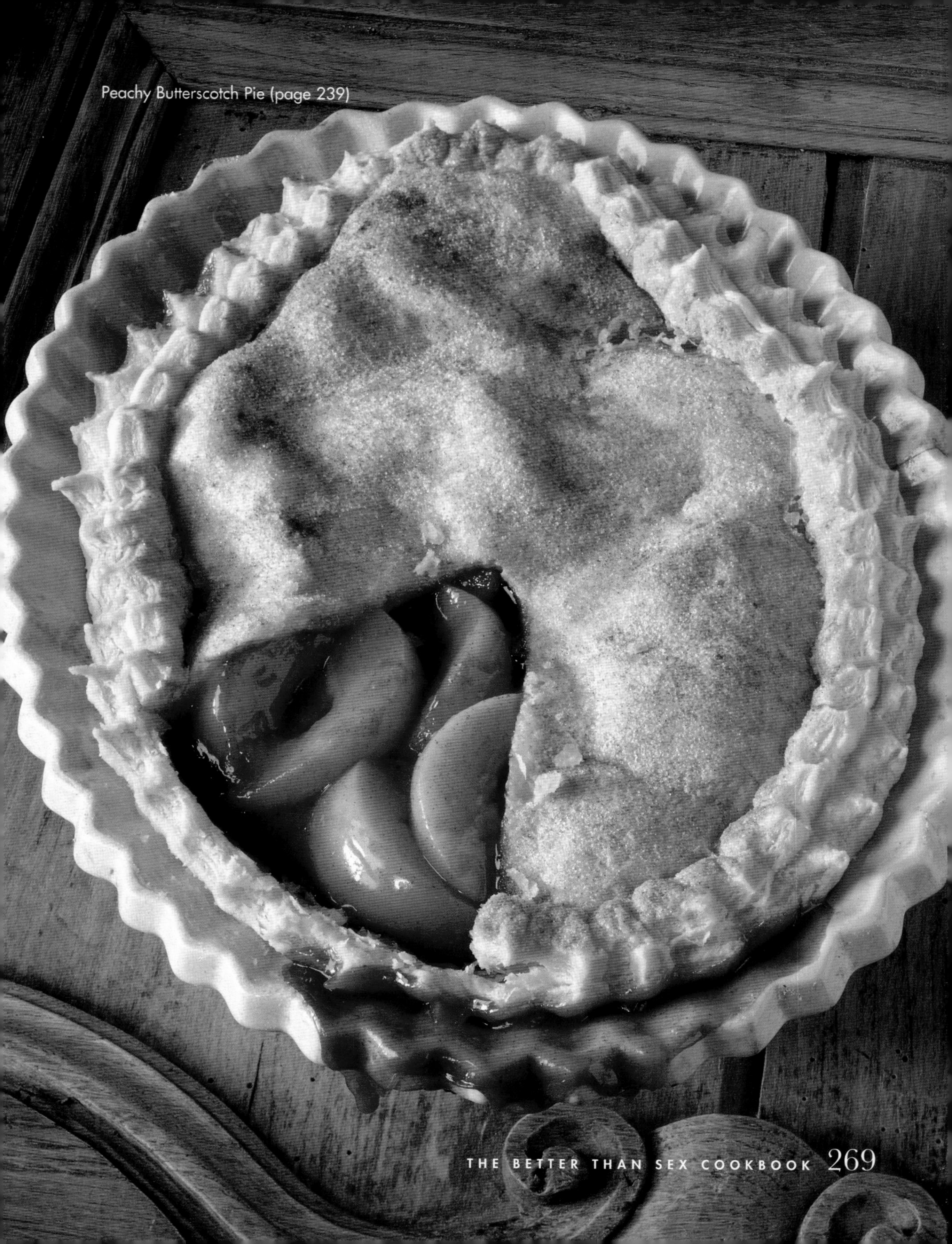

PART EIGHT
Drinks

Chilled Citrus Glory (page 277)

HOT DRINKS

Spiced Tea

285ML (½ PINT) MILK
285ML (½ PINT) WATER
2 TEASPOONS STRONG TEA LEAVES
½ TEASPOON GROUND GINGER

½ TEASPOON GROUND CINNAMON
3-4 CARDAMOM PODS, SLIGHTLY BROKEN
SUGAR, TO TASTE

1. Mix the milk and water together in a saucepan and bring to a low boil. Add the tea and spices, stir well and reduce the heat. Simmer gently for 3-4 minutes.

2. Strain into hot cups, add sugar if desired, and serve immediately.

Serves 4

🕐 10 mins

Turkish Cereal Brew

2 TABLESPOONS GROUND (NOT INSTANT) YANNOH (CEREAL COFFEE)
3 CARDAMOM PODS, SLIGHTLY CRUSHED

3 WHOLE PEPPERCORNS
1 x 2.5CM (1 INCH) PIECE CINNAMON STICK
2-3 WHOLE CLOVES

1. Mix the ingredients together in a bowl and turn into a deep saucepan. Cover with 1 litre (2 pints) cold water and place over a medium heat. Stir often as this mixture comes to a boil. Bring it to a rolling boil, where it wants to come right out of the pan, then reduce the heat and just simmer for 3-5 minutes longer, stirring constantly.

2. Pour or ladle into a cafétière and leave to steep for about 5 minutes.

3. Strain and pour into small, hot cups for a distinctive drink, reminiscent of Turkish coffee.

Makes approximately 570ml (1 pint)

🕐 30 mins

ot Apple Punch

1 LITRE (2 PINTS) APPLE JUICE
2 x 7.5CM (3 INCH) CINNAMON
STICKS

25G (1OZ) RAISINS
4 TWISTS OF LEMON

Serves 4

🕐 15 mins

1.   Simmer the apple juice, cinnamon and raisins together for 5 minutes in a saucepan over a medium heat.
2.   Strain the hot juice into four large cups in which a twist of lemon has been placed. You may garnish each cup with a piece of cinnamon floating on the surface, if you wish.
3.   Serve hot.

Variation

Add 4 very thin slices of fresh ginger to the simmering apple juice – equal to about 1 teaspoon grated ginger. These slices may be transferred to the cups, if you like, for added tang.

hocolate Espresso

2 TABLESPOONS STRONG GROUND
COFFEE
1 TABLESPOON BROWN SUGAR

285ML (½ PINT) BOILING WATER
2 SQUARES PLAIN, DARK CHOCOLATE

Serves 2

🕐 15 mins

1.   Measure the coffee grounds into a paper filter and place the filter over a pre-warmed pot (this drink is at its best when you can manage to keep its temperature up).
2.   Sprinkle the brown sugar over the coffee grounds and slowly pour the boiling water over. Let the coffee filter through then pour immediately into pre-warmed cups in which a tiny square of strong chocolate has been placed.
3.   Stir if you must, though the hot coffee will melt the chocolate for you.

Variation

Add the grated zest of 1 orange to the brown sugar in the top of the filter. The effect is subtle but wonderful.

Hops and Ginger Nightcap

1 SMALL HANDFUL DRIED HOPS

2 TABLESPOONS GRATED FRESH GINGER

570ML (1 PINT) BOILING WATER

JUICE AND ZEST OF 1 ORGANIC LEMON

SUGAR, TO TASTE

1. Turn the hops, ginger and boiling water into a deep saucepan and bring to a low boil. Simmer gently for 5-7 minutes then strain the hot liquid into hot cups in which the lemon juice and zest have been placed.

2. Stir in sugar to taste and leave to cool slightly before drinking.

3. A good night's sleep is very likely!

Serves 2-4

20 mins

Cosy and warm from head to toe. Blow us a kiss before you go!

COLD DRINKS

*F*ruit and Nut Breakfast Drink

180G (6OZ) DRIED APRICOT PIECES

100G (4OZ) ALMONDS

60ML (2 FL OZ) LEMON JUICE

140ML (¼ PINT) FROZEN ORANGE JUICE
CONCENTRATE (DEFROSTED)

½ TEASPOON ALMOND EXTRACT

CRUSHED ICE-CUBES (OPTIONAL)

COLD WATER

Serves 4

⏱ 10 mins,
plus soaking
overnight

1.   Wash the apricots, cover with boiling water and leave to soak overnight. Blend the drained apricot pieces, almonds, lemon juice, orange juice, almond extract and ice-cubes in a blender.

2.   Dilute the mixture with water, to taste. Pour into four tall glasses and serve at once.

Variation

Fill an ice-cube tray with fresh lemon or orange juice and freeze. Add 1 or 2 of these fruit cubes to the drink just before serving.

*I*ced Coffee

1 LITRE (2 PINTS) STRONG, BREWED COFFEE

2 TABLESPOONS SUGAR, OR TO TASTE

570ML (1 PINT) COLD MILK

ZEST OF 1 ORANGE

140ML (¼ PINT) SINGLE CREAM

Serves 4

⏱ 45 mins, plus
freezing time

1.   Leave the coffee to cool to blood temperature then use some of it to fill an ice-cube tray. Place in the freezer.

2.   Mix the remaining coffee with the sugar, if desired, milk and orange zest. Pour into a jug and keep in the fridge until ready to serve.

3.   Place a few coffee ice-cubes in tall glasses, pour in the iced coffee and top with a tablespoon of cream.

4.   Serve immediately.

Mango Soya Smoothie

2 RIPE MANGOES

1 RIPE BANANA

285ML (½ PINT) ICE-CUBES

285ML (½ PINT) SOYA MILK

1. Turn the flesh of the mangoes and banana into a blender with the ice-cubes. Purée to an even consistency then turn into a jug with the soya milk.
2. Stir well and serve immediately, with a straw.

Serves 2-4

🕐 15 mins

Chilled Citrus Glory

JUICE AND ZEST OF 2 ORANGES

JUICE AND ZEST OF 2 LEMONS

JUICE AND ZEST OF 2 LIMES

1.75 LITRES (3 PINTS) SPARKLING WATER

1 GRAPEFRUIT, PEELED

8-12 DESSERT CHERRIES, PIPS REMOVED

100G (4OZ) PINEAPPLE CHUNKS

1. Combine the juice and zest from the oranges, lemons and limes and turn into a jug along with the sparkling water. Chill in the fridge for 1 hour.
2. Remove the pith from the grapefruit and divide into segments. Chop each of these in half and remove any pips you see. Tip any escaped grapefruit juice into the jug with the water.
3. Use a long cocktail stick or bamboo skewer to make four brochettes of grapefruit, cherries and pineapple chunks. Stand these in tall glasses and pour the chilled citrus drink over.
4. Chill a further 30 minutes, if possible, before serving.

Serves 4

🕐 45 mins, plus extra chilling time

Variations

1. Fill an ice-cube tray with orange juice and freeze. Turn the orange cubes into the drink just before serving.
2. Add liberal amounts of fresh cleaned mint to the drink before chilling it.

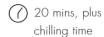ced Peppered Tea

1 LITRE (2 PINTS) BREWED TEA
¼ TEASPOON CHILLI POWDER OR GROUND
WHITE PEPPER

2 ORGANIC LEMONS

Serves 2-4

🕐 20 mins, plus
chilling time

1.   Prepare your brew as usual, but stir the chilli powder in with the tea leaves. Leave to cool to tepid, then strain into a large jug with the lemon rind – as twists – and the lemon juice.
2.   Chill in the fridge for about 1 hour then serve over ice with a twist of lemon showing in each glass.

Variations

1.   Add ½ tablespoon grated or thinly sliced fresh ginger to the brew at the same time as you add the pepper.
2.   Add a slightly bruised leaf of fresh sage to each glass. Of course, fresh mint is the usual leafy addition, if you prefer.
3.   Honey or barley malt syrup is a delicious sweetener: stir it well. You could also add some orange juice ice-cubes – see page 277.

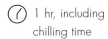oman Cup

1 LITRE (2 PINTS) DRY WHITE WINE
½ -1 TABLESPOON THINLY SLICED
FRESH GINGER

½ CUCUMBER, SLICED
1 ORANGE
FRESH BORAGE FLOWERS

Serves 4

🕐 1 hr, including
chilling time

1.   Measure the wine into a large jug with the fresh ginger and sliced cucumber.
2.   Grate the orange zest into the jug, stir well, then put the wine to chill. Slice the orange into thin rounds. Fold the orange slices, push them on to long cocktail sticks and stand in the wine glasses.
3.   Pour the chilled wine over the orange slices and serve with one or two borage flowers floating on each glass of wine.

Melon Cocktail

2 RIPE HONEYDEW OR OGEN MELONS

60ML (2 FL OZ) DRY VERMOUTH

2 TABLESPOONS BOURBON

¼ TEASPOON ANGOSTURA BITTERS

4 SWEET COCKTAIL CHERRIES

1. Slice a 5cm (2 inch) 'lid' off one end of each melon. Scoop the seed pulp out of the melons; discard this. Somehow stand the melons on their uncut end: for instance, twist a cloth napkin into a ring and place in a bowl then nest the melon in the napkin.

2. Blend the vermouth, bourbon and bitters together in a jug and add half to each melon. Place the melon lids in place and chill the melons for at least 4 hours.

3. Serve chilled, with the cherries thrown in, a straw and a spoon. Don't forget to eat the melon!

Serves 2

30 mins, plus chilling time

The Ingredient Finder

Although this part of the book is right at the back, I'll bet you'll find it the most useful, and return here again and again. One of the most irritating things about so many cookbooks is how hard they make it to easily find a recipe whose ingredients you already have in the larder! I mean, who's really going to go on a two hour shopping expedition just because some recipe book tells you to? Well, The Ingredient Finder is really easy to use. Just check your pantry or fridge to see what you've got, then look down the left-hand column to find which recipes have them as their main ingredients. Then you can look up the recipe, and see if you fancy it! Simple, eh? Yet another way to use it (as I do!) is like this: when I go shopping, I often buy food which looks new and interesting, or in season, or maybe just on special offer . . . and then when I get home, I wonder what to do with it. Well, here's what to do with it!

WHAT'S IN YOUR LARDER	TRY THIS RECIPE	page
BUCKWHEAT	Bean and Buckwheat Burger on a Bed of	
	Roses Salad	41
	Mixed Grain Pilaf	190
BULGHUR WHEAT	Mint and Parsley Salad (Tabbouleh)	105
BUTTER BEANS	Five-Bean Salad	99
CABBAGE	Almond Vegetable Chop Suey	150
	Autumn Soup in Baked Pumpkin	
	Tureen	86
	Choux Dolmades	60
	Pickled Cabbage	182
	Vegetable Chartreuse	153
CANNELLONI	Cannelloni Florentine	134
CARROTS	Arame and Carrot Stir-Fry with	
	Ginger	121
	Bean and Nut Salad	97
	Carrot and Fruit Salad	93
	Carrot and Turnip Flan	143
	Carrot Cake	211
	Carrot Muffins	201
	Haricot Bean Soup	79
	Mulligatawny Soup	80
	Rich Vegetable Stew	140
	Sesame Glazed Carrots	179
	Sobronade Serenade	139
	Vegetable Chartreuse	153
CASHEW NUTS	Cashew Stir-Fried Rice	119
	Mushroom and Cashew Nut Pâté	68
CAULIFLOWER	Cassoulet	139
	Coconut Vegetable Rice	152
	Kidney Bean Salad	98
	Red Pepper Soup	84
	Rigatoni in Pine Nut and Gorgonzola	
	Sauce	130
	Spiced Cauliflower	177
CELERIAC	Bean and Nut Salad	97
	Steamed Celeriac Salad	103
	Stir-Fried Spring Vegetables with Smoked	
	Tofu	120
CELERY	Celery and Stilton Soup	82
	Creole Jambalaya	149
	Haricot Bean Soup	79
	Sobronade Serenade	139
	Sweet and Sour Celery	180
CHEESE, BLUE	Celery and Stilton Soup	82
	Roulade of Spinach	78
CHEESE, CREAM	Nori Ring Mould	155
	St Malo Herb Cheese and Olive Roll	32
CHEESE, CURD	Dolmades of Lettuce	59
CHEESE, CURD OR RICOTA	Asparagus Filo Pie	74
CHEESE, DOLCE LATTE	Radicchio alla Trevigiono (Radicchio	
	Lasagne)	131
CHEESE, EDAM	Apple and Cheese Bundles	72
CHEESE, FROMAGE FRAIS	Garlic Mushroom Strudel	73
CHEESE, GORGONZOLA	Rigatoni in Pine Nut and Gorgonzola	
	Sauce	130
CHEESE, GRUYÈRE	Asparagus Soufflé	156
CHEESE, HARD	Glamorgan Sausages	27

WHAT'S IN YOUR LARDER	TRY THIS RECIPE	page
CHEESE, HARD	Grand Slam Slayers	30
	Rich and Famous Pâté	68
	Hero Pancakes	36
CHEESE, RICOTTA	Roman Cheesecake	239
	Rotolo Ripieno	132
CHEESE, STRONG	Scouse Rarebit	23
CHEESE, CREAM	Cream Cheese Dressing	258
CHEESE, FETA	Greek Salad	106
CHERRIES	Cherry Almond Pudding	249
	Cherry Glisten Flan	237
	Melon Fruit Salad with Nut Cream	95
CHERRIES, GLACÉ	Frigid Fruit Pudding	253
CHESTNUTS	Candied Chestnuts	65
CHESTNUTS, DRIED	Wild And Carefree Rice with	
	Chestnuts	192
CHICKPEAS	Bean and Broccoli Marinade	159
	Chickpea and Onion Ambrosia	186
	Coconut Aubergine	180
	Falafel	59
	Five-Bean Salad	99
	Mixed Bean Salad	97
	Rich and Famous Pâté	66
CHICORY	Chicory au Brézier	174
CHINESE LEAVES	Chinese Leaf Salad	102
CHINESE NOODLES	Sesame Noodles	191
CHIPS	Cuba Tubes	30
CHOCOLATE	Chocolate Butter Icing	259
	Chocolate Nut Clusters	215
	Iced Chocolate-Lined Orange Bowl	255
	Plain Chocolate Digestive Biscuits	215
	You're Kidding! Aubergine and Chocolate	
	Cake	212
COCONUT, CREAMED	Coconut Aubergine	180
	Spiced Lentil Soup	82
COCONUT MILK	Thai Tofu Curry	148
CONCHIGLIE	Conchiglie with Roasted Fennel and	
	Tomato Sauce	124
CORIANDER	Virgin's Tears	168
CORNMEAL	Irish Soda Bread	203
	Tortillas	188
COURGETTES	Crêpes Provençal	75
	Vegetable Chartreuse	153
CREAM, SOUR	Avocado Sour Cream Sauce	108
	Spiced Cauliflower	177
CUCUMBER	Bed of Roses Salad	42
	Bread Salad (Farroush)	105
	Greek Cucumber Salad (Tzatziki)	107
	Red Pepper Soup	84
CURRANTS	Favourite Teatime Scones	204
	Frigid Fruit Pudding	253
	Orange Oat Bread	203
DATES	Carrot and Fruit Salad	93
	Date and Almond Nougat	63
	Date and Walnut Loaf	202
	Melon Fruit Salad with Nut Cream	95
DIGESTIVE BISCUITS	Pumpkin Chiffon Pie	241
DRIED FRUIT, MIXED	Mincemeat Vol-au-Vents	244

Index